THE
RIGHTS OF
WOMEN

THE AMERICAN CIVIL LIBERTIES UNION HANDBOOK SERIES

AN AMERICAN
CIVIL LIBERTIES
UNION HANDBOOK

THE
RIGHTS OF
WOMEN
THE BASIC ACLU
GUIDE TO A
WOMAN'S RIGHTS

Susan C. Ross

General Editors of this series:
Norman Dorsen, *General Counsel*
Aryeh Neier, *Executive Director*
Special Editor:
Ruth Bader Ginsburg, *Coordinator,*
  ACLU Women's Rights Project

A Richard Baron Book
Sunrise Books, Inc. / E. P. Dutton & Co., Inc.

For V.V.L., H.A.R., D.K.R., and N.E.S.

346.73
R73r
89217
June 1974

Published simultaneously in Canada by Clarke, Irwin & Company
Limited, Toronto and Vancouver

ISBN: 0-87690-136-4
Library of Congress Catalog Card Number: 73-84702

Table of Contents

Preface

This guide sets forth your rights under present law and offers suggestions on how you can protect your rights. It is one of a series of guidebooks published in cooperation with the American Civil Liberties Union on the rights of teachers, servicemen, mental patients, prisoners, students, criminal suspects, women, and the very poor.

The hope surrounding these publications is that Americans informed of their rights will be encouraged to exercise them. Through their exercise, rights are given life. If they are rarely used, they may be forgotten and violations may become routine.

This guide offers no assurances that your rights will be respected. The laws may change and, in some of the subjects covered in these pages, they change quite rapidly. An effort has been made to note those parts of the law where movement is taking place but it is not always possible to predict accurately when the law *will* change.

Even if the laws remain the same, interpretations of them by courts and administrative officials often vary. In a federal system such as ours, there is a built-in problem of the differences between state and federal law, not to speak of the confusion of the differences from state to state. In addition, there are wide variations in the ways in which particular courts and administrative officials will interpret the same law at any given moment.

If you encounter what you consider to be a specific abuse of your rights you should seek legal assistance. There are a number of agencies that may help you, among them ACLU affiliate offices, but bear in mind that the ACLU is a limited-purpose organization. In many communities, there are federally funded legal service offices which pro-

—

vide assistance to poor persons who cannot afford the costs of legal representation. In general, the rights that the ACLU defends are freedom of inquiry and expression; due process of law; equal protection of the laws; and privacy. The authors in this series have discussed other rights in these books (even though they sometimes fall outside the ACLU's usual concern) in order to provide as much guidance as possible.

These books have been planned as guides for the people directly affected: therefore the question and answer format. In some of these areas there are more detailed works available for "experts." These guides seek to raise the largest issues and inform the non-specialist of the basic law on the subject. The authors of the books are themselves specialists who understand the need for information at "street level."

No attorney can be an expert in every part of the law. If you encounter a specific legal problem in an area discussed in one of these guidebooks, show the book to your attorney. Of course, he will not be able to rely *exclusively* on the guidebook to provide you with adequate representation. But if he hasn't had a great deal of experience in the specific area, the guidebook can provide some helpful suggestions on how to proceed.

Norman Dorsen, General Counsel
American Civil Liberties Union

Aryeh Neier, Executive Director
American Civil Liberties Union

Introduction

Most books about women's rights accept the fact that women do not have a great many rights. So they counsel that women have a right to support, that they must follow the husband when he moves, that they must take his name when they marry, and so on. In fact, most such books assume that the only rights women will want to learn about will have some relationship to the fact that they are married.

This book is different: it assumes that, in reality, women work for pay, that they work for free, that they are students, that they bear children, that they practice birth control and have abortions, that they watch television, that they visit bars, that they break the law, that they would like to start a business or buy a house—that they are, in short, members of the general community with interests similar to men's and are not limited by marital status. This book also assumes that women will have problems stemming solely from the fact that they are women, and that meaningful rights are those which will help women to cope with those problems.

So this book will not tell you that you have to take your husband's name, or even your father's name, or that you must follow your husband. Instead, it will tell you how to cope with discrimination—on the job, at school, in the courtroom, in hospitals, on television, at the bank, and in the local bar. That is the true meaning of women's rights.

Acknowledgments

I would like especially to thank Barbara Babcock, Ann Freedman, Judy Potter, and Nancy E. Stanley for their valuable suggestions and ideas for various chapters and for comments on the manuscript. The chapter on "Names and Name Change" could not have been written without the research of several Georgetown University law students: Dayle Berke, Betty Branda, Lois Frankel, Sandy McCandless, Max Richtman, Faye Stank, and Grey Wilson. Similarly, Bruce Green and Ruth Rowse did the painstaking research for Charts A and B. The following also were generous in reviewing the manuscript or offering suggestions: Alexandra Buek, Eleanor Lewis, Jeffrey Orleans, Eve Paul, Harriet Pilpel, Nancy Stearns, and David Zugschwerdt.

I

Constitutional Rights— The Concept of Equal Protection and The Equal Rights Amendment*

Much of the discrimination women face is caused or supported by the legal system itself and by various governmental decision-makers. Laws persisting into the 1970s mandate that a woman's right to a name is different from a man's, that a woman can be jailed when a man would not be, that a woman may not work extra hours to earn overtime pay when a man may, that a wife cannot control property she owns jointly with her husband because he has sole control. Government officials decide that girl highschool students must take homemaking and cannot play

*Readers who are not familiar with the legal system and legal terminology should turn to Chapter X, "The Legal System." Although this book was written for laypersons, use of legal terms is sometimes unavoidable. The explanations in Chapter X should help alleviate any confusion.

on the tennis team, that a girl who runs away from home is a juvenile delinquent but the boy who does so is a normal, high-spirited kid, that a woman who wants a passport must take it in the name of her husband and not in her own name, that a poor woman who wants to enter a government training program must wait until all poor men have had the chance to do so.

Both the laws and the actions of government officials are open to attack under the United States Constitution. Women must understand the relevant constitutional doctrines because the laws and practices to which these principles can be applied are pervasive, affecting or causing almost every type of sex discrimination discussed in this book. Thus there will often be many ways to attack a particular problem, but women should always consider an additional attack based on the Constitution. And sometimes this will be the only route possible.

What are the pertinent constitutional doctrines?

The first doctrine is generally referred to as "Equal Protection," and is derived from the Fourteenth Amendment to the Constitution. The key language in the amendment provides that:

> No State shall . . . deny to any person within its jurisdiction the equal protection of the laws.

The second doctrine is embodied in a proposed amendment to the Constitution, the "Equal Rights" Amendment. Congress finally passed this amendment in early 1972—forty-three years after it was first proposed. It has now been sent to the states for ratification. If accepted by thirty-eight states, it will become the law. The proposed amendment provides:

> Equality of rights under the law shall not be denied or abridged by the United States or by any State on account of sex.

What does the Equal Protection clause mean?

The Equal Protection clause is generally used to combat discriminatory laws and practices. Historically, the principal concern has been with discrimination directed against blacks: segregated public schools, denial of voting rights, segregated public accommodations. But the concept of equal protection has also been used to protect the rights of other groups: aliens, ethnic minorities, voters, poor persons, even—of late—women.

Technically, the Equal Protection clause prohibits discrimination because the courts have interpreted the phrase "no State shall deny any person the equal protection of the laws" to mean "no State shall deny any person the protection of equal laws." In other words, a state legislature may not treat its citizens differently. The state must pass laws that apply equally to blacks and whites, to Chicanos and Anglos, and that do not single out any one group for favored treatment over another group. If a state legislature does pass a law favoring one group, the courts will declare that law invalid because it violates the precept of equal treatment compelled by the Equal Protection clause of the Fourteenth Amendment.

This summary explanation of the meaning of Equal Protection bears qualification. In a variety of contexts, state laws do single out different classes of citizens for different treatment. Residents of a state for more than thirty days can vote; those who have resided in the state for less than thirty days cannot vote. People over sixteen who have passed a state driver's test may drive; people under sixteen and those who have not passed the test may not drive. Such distinctions are valid under the Equal Protection clause. How, then, can you tell whether a law that provides different treatment for different classes of people is legal or illegal?

What tests has the Supreme Court used to determine whether a state law violates the Equal Protection clause?

The Court has used two distinct tests. The first, which it has used in the majority of cases, is basically a test of reasonableness. Did the state have a reasonable purpose in passing the law? Is there some difference between the two classes of people that makes it reasonable to treat them differently? If the answer to both questions is yes, the law is valid.

While this approach sounds fair, it has proven virtually meaningless because of the Court's refusal to apply the test to the facts in any real sense. The Court will even make up or accept a spurious purpose for the law in order to justify differential treatment. A classic example of manipulating "state purpose" to uphold a state law as reasonable occurred in a famous sex-discrimination case. The Supreme Court said that Michigan could prohibit all women from holding bartender jobs without violating the Equal Protection clause because the state's purpose was to prevent moral and social problems, and prohibiting women from bartending was a reasonable way to prevent those problems. Both steps in this reasoning were fallacious. The

Court assumed without proof that Michigan had this purpose, and it cavalierly ignored the more obvious state purpose, saying that ". . . we cannot give ear to the suggestion that the real impulse behind this legislation was an unchivalrous desire of male bartenders to try to monopolize the calling."[1] Since the real purpose of the Michigan law was undoubtedly to discriminate against women, it should have been invalidated—for the desire to treat equals unequally cannot be a reasonable purpose under the Equal Protection clause.

The Court's second step was to assume—again without supporting facts—that women bartenders cause "moral and social problems," which men bartenders do not cause and which will be prevented if the state keeps women from holding these jobs. At first blush, this reasoning may have a certain logical appeal. Women cause problems; if you remove the women, you remove the problems. The logic falls apart when one realizes that the Court is indulging in pure fiction. How do we know there really were any problems? Even if problems existed, is it likely that women were the sole cause? The phrase "moral and social problems" was probably a euphemism for illicit sex. If this is the problem, why not exclude men from bars rather than exclude women from bartending? Better yet, why not simply demand that bar owners take measures, directed equally against both the male and female participants, to prevent illicit sex in bars and any attendant disruption? The Court's intellectual dishonesty in examining this law lay in its willingness to make up nonexistent "facts" to support its assumptions and in its refusal to examine alternatives. In short, when the Court "applies" the reasonableness test, it generally mentions the test as a cover for the fact that it is ducking the real issues, thus giving states free reign to discriminate.

The second test used by the Supreme Court to decide whether a state law violates the Equal Protection clause is much more stringent. It is a test that the Court has generally applied to racially discriminatory laws or to laws affecting certain fundamental rights, such as the right to vote. Consequently, experts say that use of the test is triggered by a law that sets up a "suspect classification" (e.g., treating blacks and whites differently) or that affects fundamental rights. The test itself is called "strict scrutiny" because the Court scrutinizes the law very closely. The questions are: (1) Does the state have a purpose of over-riding public importance in passing the law? (2) Is the classification established by the law necessary to accom-plishing that purpose? That is, both the law's purpose and the differences between the two classes of people affected by the law are looked at very closely.

An example of this approach is found in the Supreme Court's analysis of a Florida law that made sexual conduct between a black person and a white illegal, although the same conduct was not illegal if the two persons were either both black or both white. The State of Florida argued that its purpose in passing the law was to maintain sexual decency. But the Supreme Court could not find any dif-ferences between persons engaging in interracial sex and those engaging in intraracial sex that made it necessary to single out the first group for criminal punishment.[2] In other words, the classification—treating the two groups differently—was not necessary in order for the state to achieve its claimed purpose of maintaining sexual decency. Therefore, the law was invalid because it denied, without a valid reason, the protection of equal laws to persons who engaged in interracial sex.

What relevance do the two Equal Protection tests have to women's rights?

In the past, the Supreme Court's decision about which test to apply has almost invariably determined the outcome of the case. If it used the reasonableness test, the state law was valid. If it used the strict scrutiny test, the law was invalid. Since the Court has always used the reasonableness test when examining sex-discriminatory laws, it has almost always upheld these laws—such as the Michigan bartender statute. Even though in 1971 the Court finally struck down a law that discriminated against women,[3] this does not mean that it will now invalidate every sex-discriminatory law. Far from it. Earlier the same year, the Court casually upheld the validity of sex-segregated public colleges, without even bothering to write an opinion explaining its reasons.[4] (Atypically, in this case men sought access to an all-female institution.) In 1972, the Court told states with equal casualness that they could force women to use their husbands' names on drivers' licenses, unless the women used a name-change procedure to keep their maiden names; men, of course, were not subjected to such a requirement.[5] And when the Court, again in 1972, found unconstitutional a law denying unwed fathers parental status, not all the members of the Court believed that this was an Equal Protection violation.[6] However by May, 1973, four out of nine Supreme Court members finally declared sex a suspect classification and applied the strict scrutiny test to a discriminatory military-benefits law (see the discussion of this case, note 9, page 30). Thus, while there is still no guarantee that the Court will invalidate all or most sex-discriminatory laws, it is one tantalizing vote away from that stern position.

Why is it important to ratify the Equal Rights Amendment?

Ratification of the Equal Rights Amendment would increase dramatically the chances of winning sex-discrimination cases because it would be tantamount to telling the courts that they were wrong to refuse to deal with sex discrimination. It would also offer a long-awaited opportunity for feminists to force the United States Congress and the state legislatures to rewrite all Federal and state laws that discriminate on the basis of sex. The Equal Rights Amendment would insure for the first time that no one's rights and responsibilities under the law will be determined solely on the basis of a person's sex.

How will the Equal Rights Amendment be interpreted by the courts?

No one can ever be sure how courts will interpret any new law or amendment. The Fourteenth Amendment, ratified just after the Civil War, was originally intended to guarantee that blacks would be treated equally with whites. Yet the Supreme Court completely changed the meaning of this amendment by interpreting it to allow "separate but equal" treatment. Courts could distort the meaning of the Equal Rights Amendment in much the same way.

But if the courts do not deliberately destroy the plain meaning which the proponents of the Equal Rights Amendment intend it to have, the result will be clear: with rare exceptions intimately related to personal privacy, laws and official action establishing or supporting sex-based distinctions will be prohibited. Thus, the kind of laws and practices mentioned at the beginning of the chapter would be illegal and would have to be changed. A woman would not be jailed for a crime for which men are not punished; public high schools would not be able to exclude girls from athletic programs; the Federal government would not be allowed to exclude women from, or establish quotas to limit their enrollment in, job training programs.

Are there any articles which explain the Equal Rights Amendment in more detail?

Yes. Anyone interested in exploring this subject in greater depth should consult:

1. Brown, Emerson, Falk, and Freedman, "The Equal Rights Amendment: A Constitutional Basis for Equal Rights for Women," 80 *Yale Law Journal* 871 (1971).
2. Citizen's Advisory Council on the Status of Women, *The Proposed Equal Rights Amendment to the United States Constitution* (1970). (Available from the Woman's Bureau; see Chart D.)
3. Dorsen and Ross, "The Necessity of a Constitutional Amendment," 6 *Harvard Civil Rights—Civil Liberties Law Review* 216 (1971).
4. Eastwood, "The Double Standard of Justice: Women's Rights Under The Constitution," 5 *Valparaiso Law Review* 281 (1971).
5. Note, "Sex Discrimination and Equal Protection: Do

We Need a Constitutional Amendment?" 84 *Harvard Law Review* 1499 (1971).

Does either the Equal Protection Clause of the Fourteenth Amendment or the Equal Rights Amendment prohibit discrimination by private individuals or institutions?

No. Both amendments are limited by the concept of "state action," which is derived from similar language in each. The Fourteenth Amendment provides that *"no State shall deny . . . equal protection . . ."* and the Equal Rights Amendment commands that *". . . rights . . . shall not be denied . . . by the United States or by any State. . . ."* The courts have interpreted those words to mean that only Federal, state, and local governments are forbidden to discriminate. The prohibition covers a broad range of governmental activities—from passing discriminatory laws to engaging in discriminatory practices—but it is still limited to action in which the government is implicated. Thus, if a public school official decides to bar women from a physics class, even though there is no law requiring him or her to do so, this would be a prohibited *state practice*. But if a private school official made the same decision, it would not violate the Equal Protection clause.[7]

State action sometimes reaches more activities than the above discussion indicates because courts have found "state action" present when a government involved itself with or supported the activities of a private institution. And a private institution fulfilling functions normally considered governmental may be deemed to engage in state action. Thus, if the government provides most of the funds for building a private hospital or if a private company owns a town where all of its employees live, the courts would say that both the hospital and the town are embued with "state action," even though they are nominally private institutions. The hospital and the company town will have to measure up to the standards of Equal Protection or Equal Rights.

Understanding the state-action concept is important for several reasons. First, where there is no state action, women will need other laws to protect them against discrimination. Many banks, for instance, discriminate against women in their lending policies without breaking the law. No court has yet found state action in a bank's activities, so the bank is not subject to attack under the Equal Protection Clause and would not be under the Equal Rights Amendment. Few legislatures have passed laws prohibiting this form of discrimination. Thus, even with the Equal Rights Amendment, we will need new laws to reach this practice. Second, where there is state action, women will be able to attack discriminatory practices, although no law prohibits the specific practices. The women students who succeeded in integrating the University of Virginia at Charlottesville were able to do so because it was a state school. Finally, courts have used the state-action doctrine to expand the coverage of the Fourteenth Amendment by finding state action where previously none had been found. It is possible, then, that a private institution appearing not to be subject to the amendment will become so if further expansion of the state-action concept develops. Consequently, women should always consider using a constitutional attack based on Equal Protection, or on Equal Rights when that amendment is ratified.

What action must be taken for the Equal Rights Amendment to become part of the Constitution?

In early 1972, the United States Congress finally passed the Equal Rights Amendment. Several states, led by Hawaii, ratified the amendment immediately. Thirty-eight states in all must ratify it by 1979, and it will become effective two years after ratification by the thirty-eighth state. As of January 1, 1973, twenty-two states have ratified.

What can women's groups do to help obtain ratification?

They can engage in speaking and publicity efforts to obtain support for ratification throughout the state, lobby other state organizations and state legislators, and coordinate the overall campaign. State and local branches of several national organizations are working for ratification or have prepared background materials for use in publicity and lobbying efforts. To find out where your state stands, what you can do to help, or to get these materials, contact:

Catherine East, Executive Secretary
Citizens' Advisory Council on the Status of Women
Room 1336, Department of Labor
14th and Constitution Avenue, N.W.
Washington, D.C. 20210
  (202) 961-3791

Lucille Shriver, Executive Director
National Federation of Business and Professional
   Women's Clubs
2012 Massachusetts Avenue, N.W.
Washington, D.C. 20036
   (202) 293-1100

Flora Crater
The Woman Activist
2310 Barbour Road
Falls Church, Virginia 22043
   (703) 573-8716
   (Send $2.00 for a lobbying kit on the Equal Rights
   Amendment and $5.00 for a subscription to *The
   Woman Activist,* a newsletter on legislation affect-
   ing women's rights.)

Carol Burris, Equal Rights Amendment Coordinator
Women's Lobby, Inc.
1345 G Street, S.E.
Washington, D.C. 20003
   (202) 547-0082

Ann Scott, Legislative Vice-Chairperson
National Organization for Women
1522 West Mount Royal
Baltimore, Maryland 21201
   (Send $1.00 for a lobbying kit on the Equal Rights
   Amendment.)

Doris Meissner, Executive Director
National Women's Political Caucus
Suite 603
1302 18th Street, N.W.

Washington, D.C. 20036
(202) 785-2911

Dr. Alice Beeman
American Association of University Women
2401 Virginia Avenue, N.W.
Washington, D.C. 20037
(202) FE8-4300

Pat Keefer
Common Cause
2100 M Street, N.W.
Washington, D.C. 20037
(202) 833-1200

Will anything more need to be done once the amendment is ratified?

Yes. In a sense, the job will just have been started. Someone must search through all the state and Federal laws for those making sex distinctions, and propose new laws to eliminate all such distinctions, for the Amendment to have maximum effectiveness. Where the states don't change their laws and practices, women can bring lawsuits to force the necessary changes. But lawsuits are time-consuming, cost money, and carry no guarantee that judges will obey the mandate of the Equal Rights Amendment. Nor will women whose rights are still being denied under unchanged discriminatory laws always be willing or able to bring lawsuits to assert their rights.

Committees should be formed in each state to work on this project. Ideally the members would include the key feminist lobbyists for the Amendment, its legislative sponsors, law-school professors, important legislators needed to pass the new laws, and feminist lawyers from feminist law firms or legal groups. Feminist groups should command a majority on these committees in order to assume the lead role in decision-making about the kinds of new laws needed. The committee's work will have important policy implications, and there will be temptations to avoid difficult decisions and preserve sex distinctions. For instance, if the present law states that girls can marry at age eighteen without parental consent but that boys must be twenty-one, should that difference be resolved by lowering the age for boys to eighteen, raising the age for girls to twenty-one or perhaps selecting a middle ground of nineteen for each? The answer will depend on whether people wish to encourage marriage at an early age or encourage more education or job training for everyone before marriage.

Another reason feminists should play a key role on these committees is to insure that certain laws are rewritten to protect both men and women, rather than eliminated entirely. Some people have opposed the Equal Rights Amendment on the ground that it would invalidate such laws as these providing for alimony or for lunch and rest breaks for women workers. This opposition is not justified because valid protection for women can always be extended to men;[8] but the subject does warrant special attention when state laws are rewritten.

Is there any way women can assert their constitutional right to equal treatment before the Equal Rights Amendment becomes effective?

Definitely. Women should continue to bring lawsuits challenging unequal treatment under the Equal Protection clause of the Fourteenth Amendment. No lawsuit is guaranteed to win, but the chances of doing so are much better than they were ten years ago. Nor are all courts the same. Some Federal and state court judges are much more likely than others to give women relief.[9] California, for example, has adopted the "strict scrutiny" test of Equal Protection for laws discriminating against women, so it should be easier to win lawsuits based on Equal Protection in that state.

Must any steps be taken before bringing a lawsuit based on the Equal Protection clause or the Equal Rights Amendment?

No. All you need to do is find a lawyer. There is no need to file charges with a state or Federal agency first, as is true in the area of employment discrimination.

If you are having trouble locating a lawyer, try the local ACLU chapter. Other groups that provide legal assistance to women are listed in Chart D in the Appendix. Should you find a local lawyer who will help you but who is inexperienced in this field, the listed groups can offer assistance and possibly even participate in the case by writing "friend of the court" briefs to raise feminist issues.

Is it possible to assert the right to equal treatment without bringing a lawsuit?

Legal rights can be asserted in informal discussions and negotiations with officials or even in demonstrations and publicity-engendering events. Merely raising a question of the legality of the actions of public officials will often have a commendable effect on those actions: public officials do not like to be accused of lawlessness. And an indication of a readiness to pursue lawsuits may convince officials that you are serious about your claim for fair treatment.

Are there any other constitutional rights that women can use?

Many other sections of the Constitution will be useful in fighting important women's issues. For example, the right to privacy is derived from several amendments and has been used to establish the right to practice birth control and abortion, and thus the right for women to control their own bodies. The "Due Process" clause of the Fourteenth Amendment may be invoked in a number of situations. But this chapter has focused on the concept of equal treatment because that problem pervades most of the issues women are now raising. It is thus essential to understand Equal Protection and Equal Rights in order to recognize their application to different problems—and to apply them vigorously when needed.

NOTES

1. *Goesaert* v. *Cleary*, 335 U.S. 464, 467 (1949).
2. *McLaughlin* v. *Florida*, 379 U.S. 184 (1964).
3. *Reed* v. *Reed*, 404 U.S. 71 (1971).
4. *Williams* v. *McNair*, 316 F.Supp. 134 (D. S.C. 1970), *aff'd.*, 401 U.S. 951 (1971).
5. *Forbush* v. *Wallace*, 341 F.Supp. 217 (M.D. Ala. 1971), *aff'd.*, 405 U.S. 970 (1972).

6. *Stanley* v. *Illinois,* 405 U.S. 645 (1972).
7. The decision might, of course, violate other laws. See Chapter III, "Education," for a discussion of Title IX of The Education Amendments of 1972 Act.

Other methods can be used to attack the discriminatory practices of private schools and institutions. One court recently found—based on an interpretation of the Internal Revenue Code—that the Federal government cannot give racially discriminatory private schools tax-exempt status or allow gifts to the schools to be tax deductible: *Green* v. *Connally,* 330 F.Supp. 1150 (D. D.C. 1971), *aff'd. sub nom. Coit* v. *Green,* 404 U.S. 997 (1971). If the courts deny tax benefits to private schools that discriminate against women, this would be a potent weapon, even if women could not force changes in discriminatory practices under the Equal Protection clause because of a lack of state action.

In a case subsequent to *Green,* the court ruled that the government cannot give racially discriminatory fraternal orders tax-exempt status or allow gifts to such fraternal orders and nonprofit clubs to be tax deductible: *McGlotten* v. *Connally,* 338 F.Supp. 448 (D. D.C. 1972). This ruling went further than the first because it was based both on an interpretation of the Internal Revenue Code and on a finding that a governmental grant of these tax benefits would constitute state action, thus bringing Equal Protection concepts into play. If the Supreme Court accepts this concept of state action, the Equal Protection clause would have a new, broad scope and could be used against many private institutions.
8. For an extended discussion of this subject, see the articles cited on page 21, particularly the *Yale Law Journal* article. See also the discussion of state labor laws in the next chapter, "Employment Discrimination."
9. *Frontiero* v. *Richardson,* 36 L.Ed. 583 (1973). The Court invalidated the requirement that women in the military prove their husband's dependency in order to get medical and housing benefits, while men received them automatically for their wives. The decision's sweeping language —women's legal status was once like that of slaves; "romantic paternalism" has "put women not on a pedestal, but in a cage"—will add to its impact.

II

Employment
Discrimination

Every company in the United States discriminates against its women workers on a daily basis. This costs women a lot of money and is illegal as well, but it saves the companies even more money. Because of that harsh fact, no company is going to stop discriminating if it can avoid doing so.

Women have begun to fight against this reality, but the attack is still sporadic. Most women do not fully understand the mechanisms used to discriminate or the legal weapons available to attack them. Laws already on the books enable women to mount a major and systematic attack on discriminatory employment patterns throughout the United States with the aim of opening up more meaningful and better-paid jobs for all women. This chapter seeks to give women the basic information necessary to start or carry on that campaign by explaining the laws that make discrimination illegal, advising how to enforce them, and suggesting some strategy for the effective utilization of those laws.

31

What is job discrimination?

The answer to this question may appear obvious—but it isn't. Discrimination of the most conspicuous kind is the boss who openly brags that he pays female sales clerks less than male clerks, or who tells his talented secretary that she'll never be promoted to a managerial position because he can't stand bossy women. But such blatant examples do not begin to tell the full story. Only recently have people begun to realize how sex discrimination in employment operates. A 1970 Senate Committee, while discussing a major employment discrimination law, described the new realization:

> In 1964, employment discrimination tended to be viewed as a series of isolated and distinguishable events, for the most part due to ill-will on the part of some identifiable individual or organization. It was thought that a scheme that stressed conciliation rather than compulsory process would be most appropriate for the resolution of this essentially "human" problem, and that litigation would be necessary only on an occasional basis in the event of determined recalcitrance. This view has not been borne out by experience.
>
> Employment discrimination, as viewed today, is a far more complex and pervasive phenomenon. Experts familiar with the subject generally describe the problem in terms of "systems" and "effects" rather than simply intentional wrongs, and the literature on the subject is replete with discussions of, for example, the mechanics of seniority and lines of progression,

perpetuation of the present effects of pre-act discriminatory practices through various institutional
devices, and testing and validation requirements. In
short, the problem is one whose resolution in many
instances requires not only expert assistance, but
also the technical perception that a problem exists
in the first place, and that the system complained
of is unlawful.[1]

Women, too, must adopt this new, broader perspective.
In the past, they have often complained about symptoms,
not root causes. The emphasis has been on the individual:
a specific woman who doesn't get a particular job or promotion. Or they have stressed the importance of equal pay
for equal work. But attacking these forms of discrimination will do little to change women's basic lot in the
employment world. If feminists are serious about improv-
ing the situation, their major efforts must be directed
toward something broader.

6
What major concepts define job discrimination?
Before analyzing specific employment practices that
discriminate against women, three basic factors operative
in sex-discrimination cases should be made clear.

First, any effort devoted exclusively toward solving the
problem of an individual woman is likely to have minimal
impact. By definition, discrimination is a class problem
necessarily affecting large numbers of women—whether
they be fifty women in a small company, five hundred
thousand women in the AT&T system, or the millions of
women workers nationwide. To illustrate, if a company
refuses to promote Susie Smith because she is a woman,

that company is really saying that all women in Susie's position are ineligible for the promotion. Susie should not just attack the particular decision not to promote her. She should also fight the general policy not to promote women. Unfortunately, women often fail to fight the general policy. When a woman complains about discrimination, she understandably focuses on her own job opportunities. Those in a position to help her often adopt the same focus rather than translating her complaint into its broader framework: a policy of discrimination against a class (women). This means that women who are afraid to risk their jobs by complaining or who fail to perceive the discrimination go unhelped. When another woman complains, the whole process must be repeated. Moreover, it is far more difficult to prove discrimination against a particular woman than discrimination against many women. Companies can always find specific reasons for not promoting Susie Smith —she was late to work three days in a row or she refused to sharpen her boss's pencils. When the employer must give reasons for a failure to promote all women, the excuses are harder to manufacture.

Thus, cardinal rule number one should be to look for the way any sex-discrimination problem affects other women. In legal terms, this generally means litigating on behalf of classes of women—"class action" lawsuits. Even before litigation, the problem must be visualized as one encountered by a class of women. It is not enough to help the individual while leaving the job-market situation unchanged for her sisters.

A second basic point in examining employment bias is to set sex segregation of jobs as the prime target rather than simply equal pay for equal work. Equal pay has been a rallying cry for women. The first major Federal legislation against sex discrimination, the Equal Pay Act, embodied this concept. According to the public-opinion polls, most people now believe in equal pay. But equal pay is not the real problem.

Women are paid less than men for doing the same work, of course. But most women don't do the work men do. Look at the statistics.

In 1960, women were:

- —99 percent of all private housekeepers;
- —98 percent of all professional nurses, babysitters, chambermaids and maids, and receptionists;
- —97 percent of all secretaries, nonfactory dressmakers, and seamstresses;
- —96 percent of all private household workers, telephone operators, stenographers, practical nurses;
- —95 percent of all typists.[2]

These job categories alone accounted for almost one quarter of all women workers. And salaries in these jobs won't be raised by equal-pay laws because there are virtually no male housekeepers, nurses, or typists. Legally, if there are no men who get paid more than women, there is no way for the women to claim they are getting "unequal pay."

The statistics above show that some jobs are almost totally female. The converse is that women are almost totally excluded from such lucrative skilled jobs as electrician, plumber, auto mechanic, construction worker, and long-distance truck driver. They are also excluded from the upper-level, white-collar jobs in administration and business management. We must learn to recognize this situation for what it is: sex segregation of the job market. Certain jobs are typed female—generally, the low-paying, repetitive jobs. Other jobs are male—they pay more and in many cases offer a chance to be creative as well. Sometimes the sex-typing of the job changes: cornhuskers are female in the Midwest, but male in the Far West. But jobs are almost always sex-typed, one way or the other; and whenever the job turns out to be female, it also turns out to be low-paying.

To summarize, the legal standard of "equal pay for equal work" requires that you have men workers to compare with women workers, that both do work that is substantially the same, and that both work in the same place. Only if all conditions are present does the employer have to increase female wages to the level of male wages. If women and men are segregated into very different, or unequal, kinds of work, a demand for equal pay will be futile. Since workers *are* segregated by sex in this country, women must switch their focus from equal pay, as it is now defined, and concentrate instead on the integration of jobs and on increasing the wage level of the "female" jobs.

Integrating jobs will open up more interesting work to women, who will then command the higher pay that goes with such work. Real integration will also help change the wage structure because as men enter traditionally female jobs the pay level of these jobs should rise. The classic example is the rise in pay and status of secondary-school teachers and social workers as men entered these fields.

It is not enough, however, to hope for a better wage structure as a side effect of integration. The wage structure itself must also be attacked in order to help, right now, the women who have already been shunted into the low pay of "women's work." Traditionally female jobs do not pay less because the work is inherently worth less; they pay less because women do this work. It is the wage structure itself that is discriminatory, and women must seek court decisions that will end wage segregation by forcing employers to raise the pay scale for traditionally female jobs.[3] Of course, this will also have the effect of attracting more men to these jobs, thus promoting job integration. The cycle goes full circle.

A third fundamental concept is that many employment policies are illegal, even though they appear to be fair on the surface and even though the company never *intended* to discriminate. A good example of such a policy is the decision of a large company to upgrade the educational level of its labor force by hiring only college graduates. That looks like a fair policy—it seems to apply equally to everyone, female and male, black and white—and no one in the company has any intention of discriminating. But is it a fair policy? First of all, more men receive college educations than do women. And the percentage of whites with college educations far exceeds the percentage of blacks. Thus the effect of the policy is to exclude a disproportionate number—relative to the population as a whole—of women and of blacks from jobs with the company. The *effect*, not the intention, of the policy is discriminatory. Furthermore, the company does not have a bona fide reason for discriminating in this way. It has never conducted a study to see whether a college education is really necessary to do these jobs. In fact, many current employees, persons hired before the new policy was established, do not have college degrees, which in itself is proof that a college degree is not necessary. These two factors— the discriminatory effect of the policy and the lack of any real business need for it—render the policy as unlawful as the practice of the boss who refuses to promote his secretary because he can't tolerate women in positions of authority. The Supreme Court has even ruled, in a case involving discrimination against blacks, that a policy of the kind just described is illegal: *Griggs* v. *Duke Power Company*.[4]

Lawyers often refer to this concept as the "neutral-rule" doctrine, by which they mean that any employment policy appearing to be facially neutral but which in fact adversely affects employment opportunities of women or of a minority group is discriminatory. And if the employer has no provable business justification (which lawyers refer to as business necessity) for his policy, then it is illegal discrimination. This legal concept is at the very core of antidiscrimination law, and has been used over and over in different situations against different employment policies. It is important that women understand the concept, apply it to their own work situations, and be prepared to fight for a nondiscriminatory alternative policy.

Another example of such a policy is a company's refusal to hire unwed parents. Again, the policy appears at first blush to be even-handed. But it affects more women than men because it is easier for men to hide the fact that they are unwed parents and because women more often have the custody and care of children born out of wedlock. Since an employer would be hard-pressed to show that the legitimacy of one's children affects work performance, the policy is illegal.

In conclusion, three key concepts should be kept in mind when attacking discriminatory employment practices. Always look for the way discrimination affects a large *class* of women, not just an individual. Go after sex *segregation* of jobs and wages. Don't just attack obviously discriminatory policies; carefully examine apparently neutral policies for discriminatory effects. With these basic concepts in mind, we can turn to the specifics of job discrimination.

Under what laws is it illegal to discriminate against women workers?

Five major Federal laws and a myriad of state laws forbid such discrimination. The Federal laws are Title VII of the 1964 Civil Rights Act (generally referred to as Title VII); the Equal Pay Act; two Executive Orders, issued by Presidents Johnson and Nixon, Executive Order 11246 (as amended by E.O. 11375) and Executive Order 11478; and the Age Discrimination Act of 1967.

What is the most important law prohibiting sex discrimination?

Title VII of the 1964 Civil Rights Act is the furthest-reaching law and has the greatest potential for forcing change in employment practices. In fact, the three key concepts of job discrimination—its class effects, the necessity to challenge sex segregation, and the "neutral-rule doctrine"—are all concepts that developed under Title VII.

This chapter will cover each of the five major Federal laws, in turn, but will go into more detail on Title VII because of its importance.

A. Title VII of the 1964 Civil Rights Act

Is it ever legal to segregate jobs by sex?

Almost never. This question arises because of a particular provision in Title VII that allows a company to hire people of one sex only if the company can prove that being a person of that sex is a "bona fide occupational qualification." In legal jargon, this provision is referred to as the BFOQ, and companies use it as their chief justification for job segregation. Whenever a woman tries to get a "man's job," a company fighting her claim will contend that being a man is a BFOQ—a qualification—for that job.

Actually the BFOQ does not have much practical significance despite frequent references to it. After an initial period of uncertainty about whether Title VII protected women in a meaningful way, no judge has found that a contested job could be done only by women or only by men. One Federal court has even declared that only when a sexual characteristic itself is necessary to do the job can the employer refuse to hire people of the opposite sex. It used the example of a wet nurse. Someone who employs wet nurses can refuse to hire men in general, without considering their individual characteristics, since having breasts is necessary to do the job. Female sex is in this rare instance a BFOQ. Similarly for the job of sperm donor, male sex is a BFOQ. The case limiting the BFOQ to these untroublesome situations is *Rosenfeld* v. *Southern Pacific Railroad Company*;[5] and it should be mentioned whenever a company tries to claim that being a man is a BFOQ for a job.

Only one other kind of job has been mentioned frequently as a suitable candidate for requiring one sex as a BFOQ. That is acting or modeling, on the ground that one sex may be necessary to make a role seem authentic or genuine. This example has never been tested, however, and if we remember Shakespeare's day, when boys were commonly used to portray women in plays, even this example may not be accepted by the courts.

In practical terms, then, courts will not use the BFOQ provision to let companies hire women for some jobs and men for others. That is, jobs may not be segregated by sex.

May a company give "light work" to women and "heavy work" to men?

No. Companies have historically indulged in this practice; and since "light" work is generally paid less than "heavy" work, it obviously discriminates against women. The practice was one of the first that women workers attacked under Title VII. One famous case involved the Colgate-Palmolive Company. Before Title VII was passed, Colgate-Palmolive completely segregated its women workers into light work and its men workers into heavy work, with the highest pay for light work less than the lowest pay for heavy work. After the new law passed, the company decided to allow men to do light work (giving them an advantage in times of layoff), but did not let women do the more highly paid heavy work. A Federal court found this to be illegal and ordered that the women be paid all the money they had lost by their segregation into light work.[6]

A similar practice is to divide work into an A-B-C system—"A" (light) work being primarily of interest to women; "C" (heavy) work of interest to men; and "B" (moderate) work of interest to both. This system is also illegal because it continues to segregate jobs by sex. Title VII requires that companies analyze the individual qualifications of each worker—male and female—and assign jobs on the basis of those individual qualifications. The company can never prejudge the weight-lifting ability, or any other ability, of female or male workers as a class, and then assign jobs on the basis of this prejudgment.

May a company deny jobs, promotions, or overtime work to women because of state "protective" labor laws?

No. The so-called "protective" labor laws are a series of state laws passed since the beginning of the twentieth century to regulate women's—but not men's—work. It has become increasingly evident that these laws now restrict women more than they protect them. Some forbid women to hold certain jobs, such as bartender or mine worker. Others assume that a woman never wants to work long hours or at night, and consequently forbid her to do so. Still others, based on the assumption that all women are physically weak, declare that no woman may lift moderate or heavy weights or work before and after childbirth. Of course, none of these laws prohibits the unpaid housewife from working under such conditions; only the paid worker is "protected." And many of the "protections" are inapplicable to the least desirable "female" jobs—night work is seldom closed to charwomen. These facts provide a clue to the real effect of such "protective" laws. Companies use them to deny women jobs, and women workers have used Title VII to attack this practice. The most famous case involved Lorena Weeks, a worker at Southern Bell Telephone, who bid for the more lucrative switchman job. The company denied her bid, claiming she would have to lift a thirty-one-pound fire extinguisher, which the Georgia law on weight lifting for women forbade. (The company conveniently forgot that she already had to lift a thirty-five-pound typewriter.) After several years of litigation,

Lorena eventually won the job and thirty thousand dollars as well to compensate her for lost wages.

Other women have challenged laws forbidding overtime work (at overtime pay rates) and closing certain jobs to women, and they have all won their lawsuits even though the companies argued that the male sex was a BFOQ for the work or jobs which the women were trying to get. The Federal courts have flatly rejected this claim and have ordered the companies to stop using these laws to discriminate against women workers. The courts have been joined by the Federal agency that administers Title VII— the Equal Employment Opportunity Commission (known as the EEOC).

To convince employers or unions of the illegality of such laws, the best legal precedents to show them are the EEOC regulations,[7] and the case of *Rosenfeld* v. *Southern Pacific Railroad Company*.[8]

May a company refuse to hire women because it must provide them with seats or lunch breaks under other state labor laws, if it would be expensive to provide these benefits?

No. A recent EEOC ruling said that not only must the company hire women in these circumstances, but it must also start giving these benefits to men.[9]

Other items provided for by state laws of this kind are ten-minute rest periods, restrooms, a minimum wage, and premium pay for overtime work. The last two provisions are generally available for men workers; in fact, the Federal minimum-wage and overtime-pay law covers both men and women, and at a higher rate than all but one state law. But some men workers are not covered by the Federal law and could benefit from the few state laws making a minimum wage or overtime pay available to women only—an obvious category is male agricultural workers. In Wisconsin, a group of such workers brought suit to extend the state female minimum wage to men.[10] California male employees sued—unsuccessfully—to get the same rest periods provided for women under a California law;[11] the state legislature later provided the benefits, even though the men had lost their lawsuit.

The courts may greet favorably the attempts of men in other states to change such women-only laws, as indicated by a Federal appellate case in Arkansas. A company called Potlatch Forest thought it saw a good opportunity in Title VII to stop paying women overtime, as required by the state law. It sued the state to have the law declared invalid. The court refused to do so, pointing out that Potlatch Forest could easily comply with both the state law and Title VII by paying men the premium overtime rates, too.[12]

Women in states with labor laws applicable to women should keep in mind the distinction between laws that protect workers and laws that protect men's jobs from female competition. Laws that hinder women workers should be attacked; laws that benefit them should be extended to cover men as well.

How valid is the opposition of some labor unions to the Equal Rights Amendment on the ground that it would be used to get rid of "protective" state labor laws for women?[13]

This labor-union argument is totally worthless. The union leaders who make it are either operating to preserve discrimination in favor of their male members or they are incapable of analyzing present-day realities. First, some of these labor laws—maximum-hour and weight limitations, for example—are so restrictive that they have been attacked over and over again by blue-collar women workers across the country. Both the courts and the EEOC have found the laws illegal because they are used to discriminate against women. There is no longer any question that these laws are already invalid under Title VII, and it is only a matter of time before every such law will be invalidated by a Federal court or declared inoperative by a state authority—whether or not the Equal Rights Amendment passes. Nor do women workers want to save these laws as some labor unions contend.

Second, laws that women workers are not attacking, like the overtime-pay or rest-period laws, can be preserved by giving the same benefits to men workers. This has already been done under Title VII, and it can certainly be done under the Equal Rights Amendment. In fact, the ERA would provide the golden opportunity to lobby for worker-protective laws applying equally to men and women. Such laws would answer classic labor-union complaints—for example, that women need and want maximum-hour laws so they can get home to their children. The best solution to this problem would be new laws providing that overtime work must be voluntary for all workers.[14] A voluntary overtime law would penalize neither the man who wanted to get home to his children nor the woman who wanted double-time pay to put her son through college. That the labor unions have not seized on this obvious solution does cast some doubt on their good intentions. Could it be, after all, that they really want to preserve all the double-time pay rates for men?

May a company hire men and women only for separate departments in a plant?

No. This is just another form of illegal sex segregation.

Is it legal for a company to forbid transfers between departments when it once segregated those departments by sex in initial hiring but no longer does so?

No. Usually the "men's" department will have higher pay scales than the "women's" department. The no-transfer policy appears to be even-handed because it applies equally to all workers, but very few men will want to transfer to a department where the pay is less; conversely, many women will want to transfer to more highly paid work. This is a classic example of the illegal "neutral rule": more women than men will be adversely affected by the policy which, in effect, locks women into low-paying jobs.

Are seniority rules also illegal if they operate to lock women workers into low-paid jobs?

Yes. Seniority is a fairly complex subject, but it is an essential component of many industries and must be understood because seniority arrangements often have highly discriminatory effects.

Seniority, or length of time with the company or the job, often determines a worker's right to bid for better jobs that open up and to keep a job when there is not enough work to go around. That is, the company gives the person who has been working for the longest time the first chance to bid for a new, better-paying job. It will also lay off the person who has been there the shortest time first and keep the person who has been there longest. Other fringe benefits, such as first choice on vacation time or pension pay, may also depend on work seniority, and wage scales often are set by seniority.

Many employers measure seniority in a particular department rather than in the whole company. Under departmental seniority, every time a worker starts in a new department he or she loses all the seniority built up in the former department. Even if, for instance, a woman employee has worked for a company for twenty years, she will be at the bottom of her new department in terms of her chance to bid for better jobs, the probability of her being laid off, and even her wages. In these circumstances, most workers hesitate to move into a new department, even one that will pay better in the long run, because of the short-term wage cut and the possibility of being laid off. Since past hiring practices have given men the choice of better-paying departments, the workers locked in by this system are women. Once again, a neutral employment policy—departmental seniority—operates to discriminate against women.

Given this situation, the courts may order the company to use a seniority system based on time with the company rather than with a department within the company. Then when a woman worker moves to a new department, she will not have to sacrifice her seniority in competition with the men who have worked for a longer time in that department but for less time with the company. Taking her company seniority with her will insure that she is not laid off when the first work shortage occurs and that she will be able to compete for better-paying jobs. The courts might also order the company to allow her to transfer at her current wage rate rather than suffering a short-term cut and starting at the bottom of the wage scale in the new department, a technique referred to as "red-circling" the old wage.

Courts may devise, and have done so in the past, other solutions to the discrimination caused by departmental-seniority rules, but the basic concept remains the same. Women who have been discriminatorily assigned to lower-paying departments have a legal right to new seniority rules that will not penalize them for attempting to move into better-paying branches of the company.

Can a company give seniority rights to men only?
No. This is just an offshoot of the problem of job segregation. In one case, only men had been assigned to "unionized" jobs, although some men were not union members; women were all assigned to nonunionized jobs. Since only unionized jobs had seniority rights, only men had seniority rights—in this case, the right of a more senior person to avoid layoff by "bumping" a junior person out of his job (that is, taking his job). A woman who had worked twenty years for the Phillips Petroleum Company lost her job in a layoff to a man who had worked for a far shorter time with the company because she had no bumping rights. The court ordered the company to hire her back, saying that the company could not hide behind the policy of giving bumping rights only to people in unionized jobs when those people were all of the male sex.[15]

The potential behind this theory is enormous. Unions

have frequently ignored women workers in their organizing campaigns, but this case could eventually lead to giving women all the benefits the unions have obtained for their male workers.

Can a company force women employees to quit by assigning them to heavy jobs that they cannot manage?

No. This practice is the other side of the coin of excluding women from better-paying jobs requiring lifting. Both practices point up the need for treating women on an individual basis, since some women can lift heavy weights and some cannot. For those who cannot, a job assignment to lift weights discriminates just as effectively as a refusal to let women lift weights discriminates against strong women. If a company merges formerly segregated departments and fires anyone who cannot do heavy work, more women than men will lose their jobs. Similarly, during a layoff in departments that were once segregated, where women will have to bump men, the formerly men's jobs may sometimes be too heavy for some women. If the company lays off people who can't perform the first job they're allowed to bump into, more women than men will be affected by the practice. Some companies have even been known to take one heavy job and distribute its heavy task components among several men to insure that women will be forced out when they have to bump men from these heavy jobs.

All of these practices are illegal under the "neutral-rule" doctrine since more women than men are unable to do heavy lifting. The EEOC has said that companies must use alternate ways of distributing the heavy work in order to avoid this discriminatory effect. The heavy work might be assigned to one or two strong workers (male or female) who can handle it all, rather than spreading it among all workers. The company might get machines to do the lifting. Or it might institute a bumping policy under which employees would be moved only into jobs they are capable of handling. In short, heavy work cannot be used as a device to force women off the job.

May a company or employment agency place help-wanted ads in sex-segregated newspaper columns?

No. This practice is blatantly illegal.

Is it legal for newspapers to segregate help-wanted advertising columns by sex?

Strangely enough, this is sometimes legal even though it's illegal for any company to *use* the columns. Title VII applies only to labor unions, employers, and employment agencies. Only if a newspaper acts as an employment agency when it publishes want ads can a court say that the newspaper violates Title VII. So far, two Federal judges have decided that newspapers are not employment agencies for this purpose and that they can segregate columns without violating the Federal law. These decisions may not be the last word on the subject, but in any case there are other ways to force the newspapers to change.

First, many states have laws similar to Title VII that do cover newspapers. Women have used these laws successfully to force the *New York Times* and the *Pittsburgh*

Press to stop their discriminatory practices.[16] They can be so used in other localities.

The second method is a roundabout but effective way of using Title VII. Women should sue, in one lawsuit, all the companies and employment agencies that place ads in segregated columns. This class-action lawsuit would pit the class of all women job applicants against the class of all companies and agencies using one paper's sex-segregated want ads. Because women are suing a class, the judge can order everyone in that class to stop using the columns. And if no one may use the columns, the newspaper will be forced to stop the practice. This project would be fairly easy and exciting to undertake in any city with newspapers that so discriminate. A suit against the defendants as a class is a new theory, which no one has yet tried as a way to solve this problem. Most people, including lawyers, would tend to think first of suing the newspaper rather than the class of employers and agencies that advertise with the newspaper.

Once the want-ad columns are integrated, may an ad itself specify or suggest that only men or only women need apply for a particular position?

No. This practice is just as discriminatory—and just as common—as sex-segregated columns. Theoretically, under the BFOQ provision of Title VII, there might be some jobs for which the company could advertise in this way. But as already explained, the BFOQ provision is virtually meaningless, so as a practical matter no ad can use discriminatory language, such as "boy," "girl," "man," or "woman."

May a company or employment agency give job applicants employment tests if it gives the same tests to all applicants and grades them all in the same way?

It depends. If the proportion of women who pass the test is the same as the proportion of men who pass, the test is perfectly legal. However, if fewer women than men pass, the test may well be illegal under the "neutral-rule" doctrine. In that case, a court will order the company to stop using the test unless it can prove that the test validly predicts who will perform the job better. Proving this is called validating the test and is required by the EEOC guidelines.[17] Readers interested in testing should also read *Griggs* v. *Duke Power Co.*,[18] which set forth this theory.

The EEOC definition of tests is extremely broad and basically includes any formal, scored technique to assess job suitability. Women have not yet launched major challenges to the use of any of these tests because testing is usually viewed solely as a problem for minorities. However, women test less well than men in areas such as mathematics, science, weight lifting, and mechanical aptitude—areas that women have systematically been taught to ignore as unfeminine. A barbell-lifting test has, in fact, been challenged in a recent New York State case.[19] Studies have shown also that students will devalue an article if they think it is written by a woman;[20] thus any test involving evaluation of written essays by a grader who knows the sex of the test-taker should be examined for sex bias. The same is true for evaluations of face-to-face interviews. Other studies have shown boys perform-

ing better than girls on mathematical-aptitude tests.[21]
Thus women need to be aware of and ready to challenge
sex bias in testing.

Can a company maintain sex-segregated restrooms?
Of course.

**Can a company refuse to hire women because it doesn't
want to build a women's restroom?**
No. Absurd as it seems, companies that have never hired
women really do use the argument that they can't hire
women now because it would cost too much money to
install a toilet for women. So far, cost has never deterred
any court from ordering a company to stop discriminating,
and the EEOC doesn't give credence to this "restroom"
argument, either. This should be a sufficient response to
any company's questions on this subject, but it would be
wise to be ready with some common-sense answers as
well, since many men become emotional when discussing
this topic. Point out, for example, that instead of building
a whole new bathroom, an employer could construct a
new wall in the middle of an existing bathroom and build
separate entrances for men and for women. Or the employer could install a Porta-Can in the corner of an unused
room, or place a lock on a small bathroom so that only
one person (of either sex) could use it at a time.

May a company refuse to hire or promote mothers because of their child-care responsibilities if it hires or promotes fathers?

No. This answer comes from one of the most famous cases under Title VII, *Phillips* v. *Martin Marietta Corporation*.[22] The company told Ms. Phillips that it wouldn't hire her to be an assembly trainee because she had preschool-age children, even though it would hire fathers who had such young children. All the lower Federal courts agreed with the company that this policy was permissible, but the Supreme Court disagreed, saying that it's illegal to have "one hiring policy for women and another for men—each having pre school-age children." Ms. Phillips thus won a big battle and helped make it clear that Title VII means what it says: women and men must be treated equally on the job.

May a company fire women when they get married if it doesn't fire men who get married?

No. Notice that this is just a variation on the above question. Men and women in the same position must be treated in the same way, whether that position relates to children, to marriage, to age, or to anything else. Airlines that used to fire stewardesses when they married or when they turned thirty-two years old found to their surprise that they were breaking the law. (The airlines were also startled to find that they could not exclude men from employment as cabin attendants.)

Are different retirement ages or benefits for men and women legal?

No. There have been two court decisions on this issue, both unambiguous.[23] The EEOC guidelines take the same position.[24]

Companies sometimes force women to retire earlier than men, to the disadvantage of any woman who wants to keep on working, and they sometimes give women an *option* to retire earlier, to the disadvantage of men who would like to leave earlier. Sometimes men will be allowed to retire at the same age as women but with a lower pension than the women are allowed. Another variation is to give women lower monthly pension benefits than men on the theory that the average woman lives longer than the average man. Because this prejudges and penalizes any individual who does not fit the average, it too is illegal. In fact whatever the variation, the different retirement plan is illegal under EEOC guidelines. Many employers and insurers do not yet agree, of course, but a few more lawsuits will probably change that situation.

Does a company have time to change an illegal retirement plan gradually so that some women (or men) will get a more favorable benefit formula than the opposite sex for a few years?

Again, the answer is no. Any policy that openly treats men and women differently will almost surely be held illegal.

May a woman be fired or forced to take unpaid mater-nity leave just because she is pregnant?

No, according to the EEOC. Most courts have given the same answer. The reason is fairly simple. Pregnancy is like other medical conditions; if the woman is physically incapable of working, just as a man with a broken leg may be incapable of working, she does not have to be kept on the job. But if she can work, the employer has no right to get rid of her, whether his motivation is Victorian paternalistic concern for her welfare or prudish embarrassment because she is pregnant.

Is a woman who is physically disabled by pregnancy, abortion, childbirth, or related conditions entitled to the same fringe benefits given to other disabled employees?

Yes. Recent EEOC guidelines state:

> Disabilities caused or contributed to by pregnancy, miscarriage, abortion, childbirth, and recovery therefrom are, for all job-related purposes, temporary disabilities and should be treated as such under any health or temporary disability insurance or sick leave plan available in connection with employment. Written and unwritten employment policies and practices involving matters such as the commencement and duration of leave, the availability of extensions, the accrual of seniority and other benefits and privileges, reinstatement, and payment under any health or temporary disability insurance or sick leave plan,

formal or informal, shall be applied to disability due to pregnancy or childbirth on the same terms and conditions as they are applied to other temporary disabilities.[25]

This means that pregnant women are entitled to the same sick-leave pay that a man might get for his broken leg, to the same health-insurance payments, to the same amount of time off. In short, pregnant women must be treated just like all other sick or disabled employees in every employment policy relating to sickness or disability.

On the other hand, a pregnant women who is *not* disabled from working is not entitled to sick benefits. The distinction is important because most people fail to realize that, depending on the job and the woman, there will be various periods of physical disability in any pregnancy. Some women will not be disabled until labor starts; others will hemorrhage and be sent to bed for several months. The EEOC guidelines apply only to "disabilities *caused or contributed to by*" pregnancy and childbirth—not to the entire period of pregnancy (unless the woman is disabled from doing her job during the entire pregnancy).

Most employers now treat pregnancy and childbirth less favorably than all other medical conditions. Many do not give pregnant women any sick-leave pay; others exempt childbirth from health-insurance plans; still others require a woman to pay a large deductible for pregnancy, but not for other disabilities, under the health-insurance plan. There are hundreds of other variations on the basic scheme of treating women disabled by pregnancy and childbirth differently from employees disabled by other conditions. All these variations are illegal.

Women workers will have to push this issue, though, because both the insurance companies and the employers have resisted it so far. Companies are saving a lot of money now by offering limited, if any, sickness and disability benefits for pregnancy.

How long a period of sick leave is a pregnant woman entitled to?

She is entitled to the same length of time as are employees on sick leave for other physical conditions.

Is a pregnant woman entitled to extensions of time if the sick leave period is too short?

If employees can get extensions for other physical conditions, she can, too. Even if extensions are not available, the EEOC· has said that she may be able to get a longer leave if she can show that more women than men lose their jobs because leave periods are too short. If that is true, the company may have to allow longer leave time for everyone.

Are workers entitled to voluntary time off under Title VII for rearing infants or for family emergencies?

Not yet; although if the company gives time to women for this purpose, it must also give the same time to men. A preliminary decision in a New York State case presenting this issue is *Danielson* v. *Board of Higher Education.*[26] Some lawyers would argue, under the "neutral-rule" doctrine, that companies should extend the two-year leave they give men who are drafted to women (and men) who want to rear their babies. So far, no legal authority has ruled on this argument.

Is it legal to provide health-insurance coverage only to employees who are "head of household"?
No. This practice would exclude more women than men from health benefits.

If a company can prove that it costs more to provide some kinds of insurance to women than to men, may it give women smaller benefits than men?
Absolutely not, under EEOC guidelines.[27] Title VII forbids averaging costs by sex, just as it would forbid averaging costs by race. Averaging is a way of attributing to the individual the experience of the group even when the individual does not conform to average group behavior. Title VII says women are to be judged as individuals, and the cost for the group is therefore irrelevant. Employers and insurance companies can be expected to contest this concept, but the EEOC guidelines should win out.

May a company recruit for jobs by encouraging its present employees to bring in their friends as applicants?
Not if the jobs are segregated by sex, for men will then tend to recruit male friends for the jobs they hold and women will recruit other women. The company has an obligation to correct sex segregation, so it must take

affirmative steps to insure an integrated pool of applicants for every job.

What steps must a company take to insure an integrated pool of applicants?

There are no hard and fast rules. Basically, the company must do what it takes to accomplish the result. This means changing advertising, recruiting methods, and educating company personnel. For example, if the company's advertising and brochures show men and women segregated by sex in different jobs, the company will have to change the materials. The Bell Telephone companies have historically maintained rigid sex segregation in all telephone-company jobs, and their advertising reflected this. After the EEOC launched a major investigation into their practices, the telephone companies changed their ads, and pictures of a young woman perched high up on a telephone pole appeared in major magazines along with pictures of a young male operator. This is just one example of the kind of action that needs to be taken to achieve the ultimate goal of attracting both men and women applicants for all jobs.

Can training programs—whether for management or for blue-collar skilled craftwork—exclude women?

Under the law, no, although in practice this is done over and over again. Training programs are often a good place to start the attack on segregated jobs, because management's claim of not finding qualified women applicants has no validity when it refers to a program designed to give people those qualifications.

Is it illegal for a company to promote a higher percentage of male employees than female employees?

Tested under the "neutral-rule" doctrine, this practice would probably fail unless the company could prove valid business reasons for the differential. In technical or professional fields where more men than women have the necessary qualifications, the practice would probably survive; but it would not in jobs or fields that require only the generalist background equally available to men and women in our society.

Can an employment agency deal with persons of one sex only?

No. This would be legal if there were any jobs for which one sex is a BFOQ, but there are practically no such jobs.

If a company requests an employment agency to send a man to fill a certain job, is it legal for the agency to comply with this request?

No. The fact that someone else urges the agency to discriminate does not give it a license to do so. The agency must consider and refer women applicants for the job as well as male applicants.[28]

May a labor union limit its membership to males or refer only the male members for most jobs?

Theoretically, the answer should be no. Actually, women have not yet challenged these widespread practices. The notion that blue-collar, skilled craft jobs are male jobs, and should be so forever, is so deeply engrained that even the government agencies that are supposed to eradicate sex discrimination disregard the obvious fact that these highly paid jobs are the most male-monopolized jobs in our society. The government has allocated major resources to eradicating racial discrimination in this area, but it allows the even more pervasive sex discrimination to go unchallenged. Women, too, are deeply trained to believe that only men should hold these jobs, but they must re-educate themselves and challenge the barriers. For one thing, women might more than double their incomes if they do so, an incentive particularly important for women with little formal education who are now trapped in low-paying, dead-end jobs.

May a labor union use its bargaining power to negotiate contracts that discriminate against women?

No, under the law, although unions do it all the time. Besides suing such labor unions, women members will undoubtedly find that an excellent remedy against this practice is to seize some power for themselves in the unions so that women do the negotiating, too.

Are there any other illegal employment practices that have not been mentioned?

Hundreds. The practices detailed here are designed to give the reader some sense of the kind and degree of discriminatory employment practices, but the list could go on and on. The best guide is simply to trust one's own judgment as to what is discriminatory. Under Title VII, discrimination can be classified under one of two headings: practices discriminatory on their face, which are judged by the standards of the BFOQ; and apparently neutral practices, discriminatory in effect, which are judged by the standards of business necessity. Each kind is almost always illegal since the courts have rarely found a company's BFOQ or business-necessity claim to be genuine. So whenever a woman senses that she has been discriminated against, she should do something about it, whether or not she has the information needed to prove it and whether or not some court has already declared the practice illegal. Proving the facts and changing the law are up to those charged with responsibility for investigation and presentation of her claim. Her responsibility is to identify the practice and to demand strict adherence to, and vigorous enforcement of, antidiscrimination policy.

What Federal agency administers Title VII?

The Equal Employment Opportunity Commission, often called the EEOC.

How does a woman enforce her rights under Title VII?
The initial steps are easy. You visit an EEOC office and fill out a simple form, called a "charge" form because you are "charging" the company with discrimination. The main question on the charge form is to "explain what unfair thing was done to you" and "how were other persons treated differently." The EEOC will then investigate your charge. If it believes you, the commission will try to get the company to stop discriminating; and if that doesn't succeed, you have the right to go to court to enforce your rights.

What process does the EEOC go through to enforce your rights?
If you live in a state or city that has passed a law against sex discrimination in employment (see Chart A for the state laws), usually called a fair-employment practice law (FEP law), the commission's first step will be to send a copy of your charge to the state or city agency. This is called deferring your charge to the other agency. It is done because Title VII requires that any person filing a charge with the commission must first file the charge with such a state agency; to insure that this is done, the commission files your charge for you. After this, the commission usually must wait sixty days before it has any power to act on your charge. Then it sends a notice of your charge to the person you charged with discrimination and starts its investigation. Someone will either be sent to the place where you work to look at company

records and talk to people, or a list of questions will be sent to the company to fill out. After the investigation, the EEOC may either try to settle the case at once—by getting the company to agree to take steps to end the discrimination and reimburse you for any losses—or it may wait until a later stage. If no satisfactory settlement is reached, the EEOC writes a final decision on whether "reasonable cause exists to believe there is discrimination." Where the commission finds "reasonable cause," EEOC personnel make a final effort to settle the case, technically referred to as conciliation efforts. If conciliation fails, either because you cannot accept what the company offers or because the company will not offer anything, the commission will give you a "notice of right to sue," and you may then take the company to court. You may also sue even if the commission finds "no cause," although it will be more difficult to find a lawyer in this instance. Other possibilities—both currently somewhat remote—are that the EEOC will itself bring a lawsuit on your behalf or that the Justice Department will in certain even more remote instances.

How long will this procedure take?
Unfortunately, the EEOC has a very large backlog of cases, and it will probably take two to three years for EEOC personnel to take all these steps.

Is there any way to shorten the process?
Yes. You have an automatic right to bring your lawsuit one hundred eighty days after EEOC acquires the

power to act on your charge (*i.e.*, one hundred eighty days from the time you go to the EEOC in a state without an FEP law and one hundred eighty days after the deferral period is over in a state with an FEP law). If you want faster action than the EEOC can give you, and you can find a lawyer to take your case, request the EEOC letter giving you the right to sue (the "notice of right to sue"). Don't ask for this notice until you have a lawyer, though, because she or he must start the lawsuit within ninety days of your receipt of the notice and will need time to prepare the case.

Are there any timing problems to watch out for?

Definitely, and they are extremely important. You can even lose your lawsuit if you don't comply with certain time requirements under Title VII, even though you were really discriminated against.

The first timing problem involves the date you file your charge with the commission. Title VII says you must do so within one hundred eighty days of the date you were discriminated against in a state with no FEP law, and within three hundred days in a state with an FEP law. Even if you think you have missed the time deadlines, you may still be able to comply with this requirement. Several courts have said that if the discrimination is of a continuing nature, such as a policy the company has never countermanded, then a charge is always filed within the time limits because the discrimination is still going on. You should, therefore, always write on the charge form that the discrimination is continuing, instead of limiting your charge to a particular date. When you think about it, almost every form of discrimination can be viewed in this manner. Thus, if the company refuses to promote you on August 11, 1972, because you are a woman, you can visualize the situation in two ways. You can either say you were personally discriminated against on August 11, 1972, or you can say that the company has a continuing policy of refusing to promote women into certain jobs, which you became aware of on August 11! The second way is always better, not only because it avoids this timing problem but also because it makes the point that other women besides yourself are affected by the policy.

Another reason to file your charge as soon as possible is to increase the amount of money you can win in a lawsuit. Under Title VII, you can win back wages, that is, the amount of money you would have earned if you had not been discriminated against. But you can collect back wages only for a period of time dating from two years prior to filing the charge up to the end of your lawsuit. The later you file your charge, the later the date from which the judge will compute the back pay due you. For instance, if you file on January 1, 1972, and ultimately win your lawsuit, you will collect back wages from January 1, 1970, up to the date you win the lawsuit, and the company will be ordered to increase your future wages to what you should be earning. If you wait to file until September 1, 1972, the back wages will be computed from September 1, 1970, and you will lose eight months of back wages that you are really entitled to.

The second timing problem posed by Title VII involves going to court. You have only ninety days after the day you receive your EEOC "notice of right to sue" to file the court complaint that starts the lawsuit. Never ask for the notice until you have a lawyer and make sure that your lawyer understands that the complaint must be filed within that time period, or you will lose your case. (If by some chance this happens to you, your lawyer has been extremely negligent, and you should go to another lawyer to sue the first one for malpractice.)

Who can file the charge of discrimination with the EEOC?

Anyone who believes she has been discriminated against can file the charge, or an organization can file on her behalf. Women workers who are afraid the company will find out and fire them if they file charges should ask an organization to file for them. However, the organization filing the charge must get the women's authorization, and the EEOC will check to see that it did so. If an organization files, the EEOC will ask for the workers' names and addresses, but will keep this information confidential.

Whom can the charges accuse of discrimination?

Four kinds of entities can be charged: an employer, a labor union, an employment agency, and, in some cases, a joint labor-management committee controlling apprenticeship or training. The employer must have at least fifteen employees to be covered by Title VII, and the labor union must have at least fifteen members. (Until March 24, 1973, each had to have twenty-five employees or members to be covered.) The only important exception to the fifteen-employee rule is the United States Government, which is not covered by Title VII in the same way that other employers are covered. (Questions on Federal employees are discussed a little later.)

Are school teachers and employees of state and local governments protected by Title VII?

Yes, as long as the school boards and governments have at least fifteen employees. However, these two groups were only recently added to the coverage of Title VII so many of their employees may not be aware of their rights. Their rights are the same as those of other employees covered by Title VII, with one difference: only the Justice Department can sue on their behalf, and not the EEOC. These employees can still bring their own lawsuits, though, and will almost surely have to do so to protect their rights because the Justice Department is almost totally uninterested in contributing to the effort to eradicate sex discrimination.

Will your employer or union find out if you file a charge?

Yes. Ten days after someone files a charge with the EEOC, it sends a notice of the charge to the employer or union, and the notice includes the name of the person filing the charge. To avoid this, women could have an organization file on their behalf (see page 68), but the company will usually find out the names of the women at some stage, because the EEOC will have to discuss remedies for specific people with the company.

If your company fires you when it finds out about a charge, or if some other retaliatory action is taken against you, is there anything you can do about it?

Yes. Retaliation for filing a charge of discrimination is just as illegal as the discrimination itself. If your company retaliates, file another charge with the EEOC and sue the company for damages. If you need to get your job back or end any other retaliation immediately, request the EEOC to bring a lawsuit to accomplish this. Under recent amendments to Title VII, the commission has the authority to bring lawsuits for what is called "temporary or preliminary relief"—i.e., relief for you pending final disposition of your initial charge. If the EEOC won't help you, ask your lawyer about bringing a suit to force the company to reinstate you.[29]

Will women be able to afford the court costs and attorney's fees for a Title VII lawsuit?

Title VII provides that the court may award court costs and attorney's fees to the successful party. Although courts have frequently awarded both items to successful plaintiffs, they almost never require an unsuccessful plaintiff to pay the company's fees. The awards of attorney's fees have sometimes been very large—substantial awards have ranged from twenty thousand to two hundred twenty-five thousand dollars. These facts should encourage attorneys to take your case—and to take them on the basis that if you win, they'll get their fee; if you lose, they won't. You should not accept a contingent-fee basis, which means that lawyers will take their fee from a portion of *your* earnings, because the statute clearly allows the court to make a separate award for the attorney, based on the value of the lawyer's work. Another approach is to make it clear that the lawyer should first attempt to get a separate award for attorney's fees; and if that does not cover the value of the work, the lawyer can then make up the difference between the award and the value on a contingent-fee basis. (Careful time records should be kept by the attorney in order to support the claim for a substantial attorney's fee award.) If the attorney is adamant about a contingent-fee basis, try to get another lawyer. As for court costs, you probably will have to reimburse the lawyer for these as the case progresses, even though ultimately you can expect to win them back.

How should women go about finding a Title VII lawyer?

The best source of information is your local EEOC office, which maintains a list of Title VII lawyers. If that doesn't work, try the sources suggested under the same question in the chapter, "Divorce," and also check Chart D in the Appendix.

What can women read in order to understand more of the legal technicalities about Title VII?

It cannot be overemphasized that laywomen are capable of reading and understanding the statute and regulations, which set forth in more detail all the procedures described above. Women should also read the cases cited in the "Notes" at the end of this chapter and any pertinent

law-review articles. The statute (Title VII) is found in 42
U.S.C. §2000e *et seq.* The regulations are found in 29
C.F.R. Part 1601 (the sections dealing with procedures)
and Part 1604 (the sections dealing with sex discrimination). A convenient place to find all Federal laws and regulations dealing with sex discrimination in employment is a
book produced by the Commerce Clearing House, Inc.
(CCH), *Employment Practices Guide,* Volume 1. Another
publisher, the Bureau of National Affairs (BNA), has a
similar book, *Fair Employment Practice Manual.* Ask a
law librarian to help you locate these works and then turn
to the section on Federal laws. A good law-review article
to read is "Developments in The Law—Employment Discrimination and Title VII of the Civil Rights Act of 1964,"
84 *Harvard Law Review* 1109 (1971), although it is somewhat technical and was written before the recent amendments to Title VII.

**What can you do if the EEOC refuses to accept your
charge?**

Sad to say, this sometimes happens even though it is
illegal under the commission's own regulations. Commission personnel are often not sensitive to sex discrimination or are misinformed on the law; so if you are faced
with this situation, write a letter to the Chairman of the
EEOC, William H. Brown, 1800 G St., N.W., Washington,
D.C. 20506. Explain what has happened and also set
forth your charge of discrimination. This should constitute
filing for the purposes of bringing a lawsuit, and the chairman will probably put pressure on the local office to act
on your charge.

It would also be a good idea to get a local feminist

group, with the aid of a lawyer, to put pressure on the local EEOC director. Use publicity, if necessary. The problem of nonacceptance of charges is symptomatic of a larger problem at EEOC—general blindness to the problems of sex discrimination. The more pressure women bring to bear on EEOC, the more it will become an organization that can help them.

Are Federal employees covered by Title VII?

Yes, but to enforce their rights they must follow different procedures than do other employees, and the EEOC has no power to help them.

What agency enforces the Title VII rights of Federal employees?

The Civil Service Commission does, under recent amendments to Title VII. Even before these amendments, the Civil Service Commission played this role, but its power to do so derived from an Executive Order issued by President Johnson and not from Title VII. Now Civil Service has the power under both sources.

Does Title VII define discrimination against Federal employees differently from discrimination against other employees?

This question arises because there are two different sections of Title VII that outlaw employment discrimination—one for Federal employees and one for all other

employees. Federal employees must also follow different
procedures from other employees. Given this separation of
employees into two groups, it becomes important to know
whether the definition of what constitutes discrimination
for other employees is the same for Federal employees.
Since the section of Title VII dealing with Federal employees is still relatively new, no one knows the answer to
the question, but courts undoubtedly will be strongly in-
fluenced by existing Title VII law. For the purpose of
challenging sex discrimination in Federal employment,
then, women should use the standards of what constitutes
employment discrimination under Title VII that have already been set forth and should look for the same remedies.

**Do Federal agencies have any obligation under Title
VII to develop affirmative-action programs?**

Yes. This is another separate requirement imposed only
on the Federal government. Thus the government has two
duties under this law: (1) it must not discriminate; and (2)
it must develop affirmative-action programs to increase
opportunities for minorities and women. Both duties also
arise under Executive Order 11478, which has been in
effect for a longer time. (See pages 88–101 for a discussion of the Executive Orders and more detail on the
meaning of affirmative action.)

Each Federal department or agency must draw up national and regional Equal Employment Opportunity plans
(EEO plans), which are reviewed annually by the Civil
Service Commission. The agency must also prepare semi-
annual progress reports on its program, again with review
by the commission. A special requirement to set up train-

ing and educational programs to encourage maximum advancement by every employee has also been imposed by Title VII.

In general, women employees of the Federal government should begin demanding a meaningful input into these EEO plans, for they might be able to convert them into a real instrument for change. The provision of Title VII requiring the Civil Service Commission to consult with interested individuals should aid women in this effort.

What procedures should be followed by a Federal employee to assert her Title VII right not to be discriminated against?

In rough outline, she must first consult with an Equal Employment Opportunity Counselor (EEO counselor) in her agency or department, who will try to resolve her complaint informally. If the counselor cannot do so, the employee should file a formal, written complaint of discrimination with the agency, which will be followed by an agency investigation and, if the employee so requests, a hearing. The agency then reaches a decision, which the employee may appeal to the Civil Service Commission if she is unhappy with the result. The commission can order the agency to pay lost wages and correct the discrimination, including hiring or reinstating the injured employee. If the employee is still unhappy with the results, she can start a Title VII lawsuit against the agency, either at this stage or at several earlier stages.

May an organization file a complaint of discrimination with a Federal agency on behalf of an individual?

Yes, but it must be with the person's consent. In addition, Civil Service Commission regulations allow organizations and other third parties to file general complaints of class-wide discrimination, unrelated to individual complaints. This might be a potent weapon to develop.

May a woman be represented by another person during the procedures before the agency and the Civil Service Commission?

Yes. An employee may be represented by someone else at any stage of the proceedings. The representative does not have to be a lawyer, although this probably would be useful.

Are there any time problems of which Federal employees should be aware?

Yes. The original contact with the EEO counselor must be made within thirty days of the discriminatory act, although the counselor can make exceptions to this rule. Similarly, the employee has only fifteen days after her final interview with the EEO counselor to decide whether to give the agency a formal, written complaint. If she appeals to the Civil Service Commission, she must do so within fifteen days of the agency's final decision. These time limits may not be proper under Title VII and may thus be subject to attack in the courts, but for now women should follow them. The continuing-violation theory should also be used as a way to comply with the need to complain within thirty days of the discrimination.

Another set of time limits relates to the worker's right to go to court. Congress wrote some safeguards into the act so that if the agency or the Civil Service Commission stalls, the employee can get action by going to court. Thus if the agency has not issued a final decision by one hundred eighty days after the worker files her complaint, she can go to court. The Civil Service Commission, likewise, has only one hundred eighty days to take action on an appeal before she can go to court. When the agency does reach a final decision, the employee has thirty days from that time to sue, and the same amount of time after a final decision of the Civil Service Commission. The courts are apt to enforce these limits strictly by throwing women out of court who do not abide by them, so it is very important to get a lawyer and move fast when you want to sue.

Can a court award attorney's fees and court costs in a successful suit against the Federal government?

Yes. Again, this is an important feature because it should encourage attorneys to take such cases.

Can each Federal agency discipline agency personnel responsible for discriminatory practices?

Yes, and this remedy should be pressed, as it is likely

to have a salutory effect on other agency personnel inclined to discriminate.

Is the Civil Service Commission apt to do much to help women?

No. The commission has been notoriously unwilling to
take any effective action against the rampant sex and
race discrimination in the Federal government. Its regulations reflect a bias toward a single-event and single-person
concept of discrimination, which disables the commission
from dealing with the far more important class aspects of
discrimination. Much of the discrimination in Federal government, moreover, is caused by the commission's own
rigid personnel rules, which it will presumably be unwilling
to eliminate. For instance, the commission's practice of
tying a secretary's pay to the pay level of her boss, no
matter how good the secretary is, helps keep many
women's salaries at too low a level. Given all these factors, women should look at the Civil Service Commission
procedure merely as a necessary prelude to going to court,
and they should start their lawsuits as soon as possible.
They will find agencies much more responsive to court
litigation than to meanderings through other parts of the
Federal bureaucracy.

Is there anything women can read to understand Civil Service Commission procedures better?

Yes. For a more complete description of the procedures,
read the regulations of the Civil Service Commission, set
forth at 5 C.F.R. §§713.201-713.282, and the portion of

Title VII dealing with Federal employees, 42 U.S.C. §2000e-16.

A recent Nader report, *Behind the Promises: Equal Employment Opportunity in the Federal Government* (1972), written by Weldon Brewer, details the abysmal record of the Civil Service Commission in attacking employment discrimination. To obtain the report, send twelve dollars for each copy, or to find out about the 1974 paperback version, write to:

> Public Interest Research Group
> 2000 P Street, N.W. (Room 511)
> Washington, D.C. 20036
> (202) 833-9700

Do other laws besides Title VII make it illegal to discriminate against women workers?

Yes. They all cover some of the ground covered by Title VII, so the rest of the chapter will not discuss them in as much detail as Title VII. They include the Equal Pay Act, two Executive Orders, the Age Discrimination Act, and many state fair-employment practice laws.

B. The Equal Pay Act

What does the Equal Pay Act forbid?

The name of this law suggests the answer: companies may not pay women who are doing the same work as men less than they pay those men. However, "equal pay for equal work" is not as simple as it first appears. The law is surrounded with a lot of technical distinctions. The work of the men and women must be compared to see whether it meets certain standards before there can be a decision that it is "equal work" so as to require "equal pay."

First, both the men and the women must work in the same "establishment"—that is, a distinct physical place of business or location (such as a complex of buildings). The jobs of each must require equal skill, equal effort, and equal responsibility—each factor to be examined separately. The work must be performed under similar working conditions. Finally, the work itself must be "equal"—which means that the tasks involved in a woman's job are substantially similar, even if not identical, to those in the man's job. If any one of these standards is not fulfilled, a company does not violate the Equal Pay Act when it pays women less than men—which leaves companies with a lot of loopholes.

Can an employment practice be legal under the Equal Pay Act but illegal under Title VII?

Definitely. As the previous question indicated, the Equal Pay Act covers one very narrowly defined form of wage discrimination. In contrast, Title VII covers a panoply of discriminatory practices and can be used to force change in employment patterns where the Equal Pay Act cannot. For instance, a company that assigns all its assembly-line work to men and all its clerical work to women, with the men receiving a salary double that of the women, does not violate the Equal Pay Act since the jobs are in no way equal. This practice would violate Title VII because the company has assigned jobs on the basis of sex and denied women the chance to double their incomes. The women could sue under Title VII to force the company to integrate the two jobs and to recover the income lost in the past. Integration would be a major change in employment patterns, and it would probably lead to other changes as well. The men workers in the clerical jobs might well force the wage scale up—which would also benefit the women clerical workers. Viewed in this light, Title VII offers a far greater chance for meaningful change in employment practices than the Equal Pay Act.

It is important to grasp the differences between the two laws because of a provision in Title VII that says if wage discrimination is legal under the Equal Pay Act, it is also legal under Title VII. Notice that the example just discussed involved discrimination in *job assignment*, not in *wages*, and therefore it did violate Title VII. Some lawyers and EEOC officials have not understood this distinction, and women have reported that EEOC officials have refused to accept charges of sex discrimination out of a belief that the practice involved did not violate the Equal Pay Act and was, therefore, legal under Title VII. As we have seen, this is not true and women must learn not to accept this answer. They should pursue Title VII charges against the company and, in the process, challenge and publicize miscomprehension by EEOC officials of the law they are supposed to enforce! The cardinal rule remains: even if a practice does not violate the Equal Pay Act, it may still violate Title VII.

May a company avoid complying with the Equal Pay Act by transferring all the men who receive higher wages into another job so that only women are left doing the first job at the lower rate?

No. Once the company establishes a higher rate for
men, it must pay women that rate even after the men are
transferred out. Be aware, also, that it would violate Title
VII to transfer workers out of a job on the basis of sex.

**May a company comply with the Equal Pay Act by
lowering the wages of the more highly paid men?**

No. One of the provisions in the act says that companies must always *raise* the wages of the more lowly
paid sex (women) and not lower the wages of the other
sex.

**May a company avoid the Equal Pay Act by giving
men extra weight-lifting tasks?**

No, although several companies have tried to do this.
When the Wheaton Glass Company was sued, it listed
seventeen extra tasks its male selector-packers had to perform to try to justify higher wages for men, but the court
found that the work of both men and women workers was
"substantially equal" and warranted equal pay.[80] The
amount of back wages the women won shows the importance of this concept. The women were underpaid by only
twenty-one cents an hour—but this added up to almost a
million dollars under the final court order.

**May a company avoid responsibility for unequal wages
when a union threatens to strike if the company pays
equal wages?**

No. It is just as illegal for the union to try—by any

method—to force unequal wages on the company, as it is for the company to pay them. In such a situation, both would be found guilty of violating the act.[81]

What kinds of jobs have been found to be equal under the Equal Pay Act so that companies must raise the wages of women workers?

Jobs found to be equal include: nurse's aides and orderlies in hospitals; assembly-line workers in factories, where some of the men do a little heavy lifting; janitors and maids in colleges; and salesclerks in department stores, no matter what kind of merchandise they sell. Other jobs where women gained back wages were bank teller, laboratory technician, inspector, press operator, machine operator, and packer. The list could, of course, continue; so women who suspect they are being paid less than men for doing the same work should be sure to challenge the practice.

Which Federal agency enforces the Equal Pay Act?

A section of the Department of Labor, the Wage and Hour Division, administers this law. It has offices both in Washington, D.C., and in cities around the country. If there is a local office, it will be listed in the telephone directory under United States Government, Labor Department, Wage and Hour Division.

How should women enforce their rights under the Equal Pay Act?

Contact a local office of the Wage and Hour Division, or write to the national office at: Wage and Hour Division, United States Department of Labor, Constitution Avenue and 14th Street, N.W., Washington, D.C. Explain that you believe you or other women are being paid less than men; give the name and address of the company and your own name and addess so you can be contacted for further information. If you have a lawyer, you can bring a lawsuit against the company immediately without going to the Labor Department at all.

Will the Labor Department keep women's names confidential on request?

Yes. The Labor Department will go to great lengths to protect the anonymity of anyone who fears exposure.

May an organization report unequal wages to the Labor Department?

Yes, and there is no requirement that the organization obtain the permission of any of the affected women.

What steps will the Labor Department take to enforce your rights?

The Labor Department will send investigators to your

company to find out whether there is a violation of the
Equal Pay Act. It often does this even without receiving
any complaints. If a violation is found, the investigator will
try to collect the wages that are due to the underpaid
women and will ask for a formal agreement by the company to increase the wages of women workers to the
level of the men. Failing that, the Labor Department will
bring a lawsuit on behalf of the underpaid workers, both
to obtain the past wages due and to force the company to
change its future pay rates. You can always bring your
own lawsuit without going to the Labor Department, of
course.

**Will it take the Labor Department as long to act on
your complaints as it does the EEOC?**

No, because the Labor Department does not have a big
backlog of unresolved cases. Don't forget, though, that
the Labor Department can help you only on wage discrimination, so you should contact both Labor and EEOC if
you suspect discrimination. The Labor Department may resolve the wage discrimination fairly rapidly, and then you
will still be able to enforce your other rights under Title
VII.

What companies are covered by the Equal Pay Act?

The official definition is that the company must be
"engaged in commerce" or "engaged in the production of
goods for commerce." This definition is not very helpful,
but the courts have interpreted it broadly to reach many
companies and even some public institutions like schools

and hospitals. If in doubt, act as though your employer is covered, until you find out differently. One test is whether your employer must comply with the Federal minimum wage and overtime pay law, called the Fair Labor Standards Act. If so, he must also obey the Equal Pay Act. If you can't find out, contact a local Wage and Hour Division office of the Labor Department or the national office.

In companies covered by the Equal Pay Act, are executive, administrative, and professional workers protected against wage discrimination?

Yes. Until recently, executive, administrative, and professional workers were not covered, but the law was amended to cover them in July 1972.

Are there any timing problems under the Equal Pay Act?

Only one. You must bring the lawsuit within two years of the discrimination, or within three years if the company discriminated "willfully." Obviously, if the company is still underpaying its women workers, there is no problem. But if the company recently decided to comply with the law, you must start the lawsuit within two years from the time the company stopped discriminating.

The two-year limit also affects the amount of back pay. You can collect only for the two years prior to starting the *lawsuit*; hence, the sooner you sue, the more money you'll collect. (Compare this to Title VII, where the time you file your charge with the EEOC is the relevant date for computing back wages. Unlike that situation, inform-

ing the Labor Department of your problem will not
increase your back wages; here the relevant date is starting the lawsuit, so it is important not to waste time in
doing so.)

What may women win in a successful lawsuit under the Equal Pay Act?

They can win the wages they should have earned, up
to two years worth ("back wages"), plus the same amount
as punishment for the company,[32] plus attorney's fees
and court costs. Since Title VII does not provide for
the recovery of "double" back wages, an Equal Pay Act
charge should be added to every Title VII lawsuit. The
provision for attorney's fees will help women locate a
lawyer, just as the Title VII provision does. A court may
also award back wages for three years, doubled as punishment for the company, if the lawyer can prove that the
company discriminated "willfully." However, in a suit
brought by a worker or workers, the judge cannot order
the company to raise the salaries of the women to the legal
level for the future (as he can in lawsuits brought by the
Labor Department).[33]

What can women read to understand better the Equal Pay Act?

The statute is found in 29 U.S.C. §206(d), and the
regulations of the Wage and Hour Division are published
in 29 C.F.R. §§800.0-800.166. Both are also found in
the CCH and BNA books previously referred to under
Title VII (see page 72). An article worth reading is

Berger, "Equal Pay, Equal Employment Opportunity and Equal Enforcement of the Law for Women," 5 *Valparaiso Law Review* 326, 338-350 (1971), which will also refer readers to some of the more important cases. Another article is Murphy, "Female Wage Discrimination, A Study of the Equal Pay Act 1963-1970," 39 *University of Cincinnati Law Review* 615 (1970).

C. The Executive Orders

What are executive orders?

Executive orders are directives issued by the President, telling the executive branch of the government to take certain action as set forth in the order. In most respects, an executive order has the force and effect of law.

What executive orders forbid employment discrimination against women workers?

There are two such executive orders currently in effect. President Johnson issued E.O. 11246, which requires any employer that has a contract with the Federal government not to discriminate. Initially, E.O. 11246 forbade race discrimination only, but the President later issued E.O. 11375, which amended the former order by adding sex discrimination to its prohibitions. President Nixon issued E.O. 11478, which modifies the earlier Johnson executive order and forbids discrimination by the Federal government.

Which employers are covered by E.O. 11246 (as amended by E.O. 11375)?

The executive order applies to any company or institution that has a contract with the Federal government, whether it be to sell typewriters to the government, to do scientific research, or to produce missiles. The order also applies to subcontractors of the contractor (both are referred to in this chapter as contractors), although the order is seldom enforced as to subcontractors. Finally, anyone applying for Federal construction money (referred to here as "applicant") is also covered, and must obtain promises of nondiscrimination from the contractors who will perform the construction work for the applicant.

The executive order applies to all branches of a company that has a contract with the government, even though only one branch may have the contract. It does not apply directly to any unions involved with the company, although strong pressure is exerted on the unions indirectly.

What action must the executive branch take under the executive order?

Every agency or department in the executive branch must obtain a promise from any contractor with whom it has a contract that the company will not discriminate against its workers. The agency must also demand that applicants for Federal construction money agree to put the same promise in their contract with the construction company doing the actual work. Pertinent portions of the promise, generally called the Equal Employment Opportunity clause (EEO clause), read as follows:

> During the performance of this contract, the contractor agrees as follows:
>
> (1) The contractor will not discriminate against any employee or applicant for employment because of race, color, religion, sex, or national origin. The contractor will take affirmative action to insure that applicants are employed, and that employees are treated during employment without regard to their race, color, religion, sex, or national origin. Such action shall include, but not be limited to the following: Employment, upgrading, demotion, or transfer, recruitment or recruitment advertising; layoff or termination; rates of pay or other forms of compensation; and selection for training, including apprenticeship.

Unless the contractor or applicant for Federal money agrees to this clause, he cannot get the contract or the Federal money. For example, if Columbia University wants a Federal contract to do research on guinea pigs, it will have to agree to these conditions before the government will give it the contract. And if New York City wants Federal money for a construction project, it will have to put this clause in its contract with the Big Bull Construction Company, which will actually do the work.

What practices by a contractor constitute discrimination against women workers in violation of the EEO contract clause?

Discrimination under the executive order is generally

measured by the same standards as discrimination under Title VII; therefore, if something is illegal under Title VII, it is almost always a violation of the contract, too. (There are some variations, but they are not very important.) Given this fact, women workers should consider and use all the legal standards of what constitutes discrimination set forth for Title VII when they want to bring charges against a contractor, including the charge of retaliation, which is illegal under both laws.

Must the contractor do anything besides refraining from discriminating?

Yes. Under the EEO clause, he must also take "affirmative action" to insure fair treatment to women workers. All contractors have this obligation if they want the Federal contract, and therein lies the chief difference with Title VII. Whether or not anyone ever files a charge against a particular contractor, he will have to undertake "affirmative action" under the executive order. Under Title VII, a company almost always has the same theoretical obligation, because affirmative action is necessary to correct the effects of past discrimination, and most companies have discriminated in the past. But as a practical matter, any company can gamble that no woman will sue it under Title VII, and thereby avoid the trouble and expense of affirmative action. Of course, if women *do* sue under Title VII, the company will have to take action and recompense the women for its failure to do so earlier, but that is a gamble many companies are willing to take.

What exactly is an affirmative-action plan?

This is the formal plan the contractor must draw up to meet its affirmative-action requirements. Generally the contractor must analyze those jobs in which it underutilizes women, set numerical goals and a specific timetable for increasing the utilization of women, and describe in detail the methods it will use to do so, including which company personnel will be responsible for the program. Setting goals and timetables constitutes the heart of the program. An example would be an agreement by the company to increase women blue-collar workers to 10-15 percent of its work force during the first year of the contract and to 12-17 percent during the second year.

The requirements for the affirmative-action plan are too elaborate to discuss in detail, and readers interested in learning more should read the applicable government regulations. They are found at 41 C.F.R. Part 60-2 (as amended on December 4, 1971) and are commonly referred to as Revised Order No. 4.

If the contractor fails to meet the numerical goals it sets on the specified time schedule, will the government penalize it?

Not necessarily. All the government requires is that the contractor make an effort in good faith to meet the goals. Even if the company fails but can demonstrate that it took action in good faith, it will be home free.

Does the government ever require applicants for Federal construction money to demand that their construction companies set goals and timetables for increased utilization of women workers?

No. That women might want to do highly paid and often challenging construction work is still unthinkable for most government bureaucrats, as it is for most people engaged in the construction industry. Even though the executive order forbids sex discrimination by both Federal contractors and contractors with applicants for Federal construction money, the government has demanded action only from the Federal contractors. This is a gross violation of what the order requires, for the virtually total exclusion of women from the construction industry is among the most blatant forms of sex discrimination practiced today. And construction jobs would offer poor women with little formal education a significant way to earn a decent living. For that reason, women should exert pressure on the government to conform its actions in the area of construction work to the requirements of the executive order. And the opportunities that open up should be well publicized so that women will take advantage of them.

What government agency enforces Executive Order 11246 (as amended by E.O. 11375)?

It is enforced by a special office in the Department of Labor, the Office of Federal Contract Compliance (OFCC). OFCC, in turn, plays a kind of monitoring role over other Federal agencies it has selected to do the more direct work of insuring compliance with the orders. These agencies are called compliance agencies, and there are fifteen in all:

Agency for International Development; Department of Agriculture; Atomic Energy Commission; Department of Commerce; Department of Defense; General Services Administration; Department of Health, Education and Welfare; Department of Housing and Urban Development; Department of the Interior; National Aeronautical and Space Administration; Post Office Department; Department of Transportation; Tennessee Valley Authority; Department of the Treasury; and Veterans Administration. For the list of the particular industries regulated by each compliance agency, write to: Director, OFCC, U.S. Department of Labor, 14th Street and Constitution Avenue, N.W., Washington, D.C. 20210; or you can check the two reference books on employment discrimination, *Fair Employment Practice Manual* and volume 1 of *Employment Practices Guide.*

How do OFCC and the compliance agencies enforce the executive order?

There are two basic methods: compliance reviews and complaint procedures. In theory, the appropriate compliance agency conducts periodic reviews of every contractor to see whether the contractor discriminates or has fulfilled his duty to take "affirmative action." Any company negotiating for a contract of one million dollars or more with the government must pass the compliance review before getting the contract. In actual practice, compliance reviews are not conducted regularly, even for contracts of more than one million dollars. The compliance agencies are so understaffed that it is impossible for them to do their job, and most companies have never been subjected to review.

OFCC has also established a complaint procedure, un-

der which any employee of or job applicant with a contractor can accuse the contractor of discrimination by
writing to OFCC or the compliance agency. This is the
second way of turning up evidence that a contractor is
violating the terms of its EEO contract clause.

**How should women file complaints of discrimination
with the OFCC or the compliance agency?**

Send a letter to the Director of OFCC, Department of
Labor, Washington, D.C. 20210, setting forth: (1) your
name, address, and phone number; (2) the name and address of the contractor; (3) a description of the discrimination (using the Title VII standards set forth in the first
half of this chapter); and (4) any other pertinent information. Or write to the appropriate compliance agency, if
you know the proper one, for faster results. Organizations
may file on behalf of the person who is discriminated
against, but the OFCC regulations require the person to
authorize this. The regulations also require that the complaint be filed within one hundred eighty days of the
discrimination. (Don't forget to use the concept of a
continuing policy of discrimination.)

**What will OFCC or the compliance agency do with
such a complaint?**

It will send the complaint to the EEOC, which will
treat the complaint as an EEOC charge, conduct an investigation, make findings of fact, and write a decision.
The file will then be referred back to OFCC, which has
the discretion to accept and act on these results or to make
different findings and reach a different decision.

What penalties can OFCC or a compliance agency impose when it finds that a contractor discriminates against women or has not carried out its affirmative action plan?

OFCC or the compliance agency may hold up funds on the contract until it gets compliance, cancel a contract or part of the contract, or order the contractor debarred from future contracts with the government. All of these penalties could have an enormous impact on companies that depend on government contracts for most of their business, for if they lose government work they will often go out of business. A final penalty (though this has never been done) is to refer the company's case to either the Justice Department or to the EEOC. Justice can sue the company to enforce the EEO contract clause provisions or for a violation of Title VII; it can also bring a criminal lawsuit. EEOC can sue for violations of Title VII.

Similar penalties may be imposed on an applicant for Federal construction money and on the construction company with whom the applicant has a contract, although sex discrimination provisions are not enforced in the second area.

Will OFCC or the compliance agencies usually impose any of these penalties?

Emphatically not. OFCC has often been criticized severely for its failure to use the very powerful sanctions it has available or to encourage compliance agencies to use them. To some extent, the inaction was probably due to gross understaffing; but it has clearly been a political decision as well. In any case, OFCC and the compliance agencies have rarely, if ever, imposed any of the penalties that the executive order requires, although some compliance agencies—such as HEW—are better than others.

Given the failure of OFCC and the compliance agencies to penalize significantly contractors who discriminate, should women bother to file complaints under the executive order?

It depends on what the women hope to accomplish. If their purpose is to force the company to stop discriminating, this is not the best way to do it because there is no way they can force OFCC or the compliance agency to take action against a company. On the other hand, the executive-order complaint is an excellent way to put some extra pressure on the company, especially when this method is used in conjunction with other laws. The courts do not have the political freedom to refuse to act on a Title VII or Equal Pay Act complaint the way OFCC and the compliance agencies refuse to act on an executive-order complaint. Courts may try to duck the issue, they may find the facts against you, but they cannot refuse to act at all; and you can always appeal to higher courts if you don't like the result. Moreover, many courts have reached excellent decisions, under Title VII and the Equal Pay Act, which have forced companies to take effective action to end discrimination. Given these factors, women should concentrate their main enforcement efforts on Title VII and use executive-order complaints and negotiations as a backstop to the main action.

Some women have failed to understand this point and have used the executive order as their main weapon. That way was once useful in the area of university discrimination against teachers, who were not protected by

Title VII until the March 1972 amendments and therefore had no other way to protest sex discrimination. But executive-order complaints should not be the prime route for women protected by Title VII, which now means most women workers. Any woman covered by Title VII should use a lawsuit under that statute as her main enforcement method. It can't hurt to file complaints with OFCC or the compliance agency in addition to such a lawsuit, because that will maximize the pressure on the company. Even if OFCC or the compliance agency does nothing in the short run, action may be taken during a compliance review if OFCC or the compliance agency finds that women have lodged many complaints against a company. And some compliance agencies have a better record than others. HEW, for instance, has shown some inclination to force universities to take affirmative action by holding up funds on university contracts at the University of Michigan, Harvard, and Columbia—much to the surprise of university officials, who then took initial steps in the direction of doing what they claimed they could never do. So if you are dealing with an agency willing to use its power, take full advantage of that fact. Negotiate, discuss what needs to be done, give evidence of discrimination. But, whatever your situation, do not forget to bring the Title VII lawsuit as well.

May women bring a lawsuit under the executive order against a Federal contractor if OFCC or the compliance agency refuses to take action?

No. Several persons have tried this, and to date the courts have always said that there is no right to sue under the executive order. Since suit can almost always be brought against the same company under Title VII to get the same results, this is not very important.

What can women read to understand the executive order better?

Read Executive Order 11246 (as amended by E.O. 11375) and the OFCC regulations. The first is found at 3 C.F.R. §339; the second at 41 C.F.R. Parts 60-1, 60-2, 60-3, and 60-20. Both are also found in the CCH and BNA books. Part 60-1 of the OFCC regulations deals with compliance reviews and complaint procedures. Part 60-2 discusses the affirmative-action program and is the part generally referred to as Revised Order No. 4.

The Commission on Civil Rights has published a readable account of the executive order as well as other Federal civil rights laws: *Federal Civil Rights Enforcement Effort, A Report of the U.S. Commission on Civil Rights* (1970). It is available for $8.50 from the Superintendent of Documents, United States Government Printing Office, Washington, D. C. 20402. One cautionary note: the book is now somewhat out of date as it was written before the recent amendments to Title VII and also before Order No. 4 was revised to include a requirement that companies establish detailed affirmative-action programs on behalf of women workers. In addition, the Civil Rights Commission was not at that time charged with responsibility for reporting on sex discrimination, as it now is. However, the report does provide good histories of the various laws, explanations of how they work, and criticisms of the laws in operation. There is also a supplement to the report, called *Federal Civil Rights Enforcement: One Year Later* (1971), for $1.75.

What steps can women take besides filing complaints to protect their rights under the executive order?

One possibility is to get involved in helping the company develop its affirmative-action plan. Women workers who hesitate to start a lawsuit might still make a significant impact on company policy by insisting on a voice in these plans. Women at all levels in the company should be involved—not just the professionals. Many women caught in dead-end, low-paying jobs, like that of telephone operator, clerk, salesperson, or assembly-line worker, will have strong ideas about how to improve their job situation.

Another step is to ask to see the company plan in order to monitor the company's compliance with it. In general, OFCC encourages companies to reveal these plans, although the regulations do not explicitly require this. The company could be pressured about its good faith if it is unwilling to let women employees see what it promised the government it would do. OFCC has recently published a *Standard Compliance Manual,* and women should seek copies of it. Comparing the program to the requirements of the manual is another way to monitor the company's progress.

Finally women's groups can and should start pressuring the compliance agencies and OFCC genuinely to enforce the executive order. Pressure from women has already forced OFCC to amend its regulations to require affirmative-action plans for women workers. Federal agencies are vulnerable to pressure, and much more needs to be applied to these agencies.

What does Executive Order 11478 require?

This executive order applies only to the Federal government. It requires all Federal agencies and departments not to discriminate and to set up affirmative-action programs. The order is found at 3 C.F.R. §133; Civil Service regulations appear in 5 C.F.R. Part 713.

How does Executive Order 11478 differ from the sections of Title VII that apply to employment by the Federal government?

Although covering much the same ground, the executive order was issued long before these sections of Title VII became law. Under the executive order, the Civil Service Commission monitors the government's efforts, and the new Title VII provisions have preserved this structure. The biggest difference from the executive order is that Title VII gives the Civil Service Commission more power. The commission can now order different branches of the government to take action to correct discrimination; for example, hiring someone or paying back wages. Because the two laws cover the same ground, readers should refer to the questions covering Federal employment under Title VII (pages 73–79) and should also review the questions on the meaning of affirmative action at pages 89–92.

D. State Anti-Discrimination Laws

What are state fair-employment practice laws?

Most states have passed one or more laws forbidding employment discrimination, often using language or concepts parallel or identical to the Federal laws discussed in this chapter. States have their own equal-pay acts, fair-employment practice acts modeled on Title VII, public-works laws modeled on Executive Order 11246, and public-employees laws modeled on Executive Order 11478. The Federal and state laws cover much the same practices, although state laws are often interpreted more conservatively. Chart A in the Appendix sets forth the type of laws each state has and several details about these laws.

E. Age Discrimination Laws

What laws forbid discrimination on the basis of age?
A Federal law, the Age Discrimination in Employment Act of 1967, forbids discrimination against workers aged forty to sixty-five. The act is found at 29 U.S.C. §621 *et seq.*; the regulations, at 29 C.F.R. Part 860. Several states have passed age-discrimination laws, some with different age limits; these laws are listed in Chart A. Both the Federal and the state laws provide another avenue of redress for older women, who often face virulent discrimination, especially if they are entering the labor market for the first time. Women should be aware of the potential of these laws, although this book will not discuss them in detail.

Which Federal agency enforces the Age Discrimination Act?
It is enforced by the Wage and Hour Division of the Labor Department, the same branch that enforces the Equal Pay Act. For more information, write to the Division.

F. General Considerations

Why is it important to understand the differences among all these laws?

Different laws prohibit different practices and help different workers. For instance, Title VII forbids segregating jobs by sex; the Equal Pay Act does not. On the other hand, Title VII does not protect workers in companies with fewer than fifteen employees, but many state fair-employment laws do.

If a woman turns to the wrong law, she will not succeed in changing her situation, even though another law may offer her protection; thus it is crucial that women know the range of laws available and the details of their application. Sometimes, too, there is overlap among the various laws. When more than one prohibits the same practice, women can maximize the pressure on their employer or union by resorting to *all* the applicable laws to stop the discrimination.

What are the chief differences between each of these laws?

First, each differs drastically in the number of discriminatory practices covered. Title VII is the broadest law of all, covering almost all forms of discrimination; the Equal Pay Act goes to the opposite extreme, prohibiting only a very narrowly defined kind of wage discrimination; Executive Order 11246 (as amended by E.O. 11375) lies somewhere in between, primarily because the agencies that enforce it are oriented more toward setting up affirmative-action plans than toward compensating particular women for past discrimination. The number of practices prohibited by state laws generally parallel these three Federal laws, but often with significant differences. For example, many state fair-employment practice laws forbid newspapers to carry segregated help-wanted advertising columns, while Title VII reaches only the advertiser.

A second difference is found in the kinds of entities covered by each law. Title VII covers employers, unions, and employment agencies; the Equal Pay Act is limited to employers and unions; Executive Order 11246 reaches only employers; and there are wide variations among the state laws. Within each covered group, there are other differences, with Title VII reaching employers of fifteen or more, the Equal Pay Act directed at producers of goods for interstate commerce, and the executive order limited to contractors with the Federal government. Many state fair-employment practice laws reach employers with fewer than fifteen employees.

Other important differences concern the nature and extent of the relief available under each law; whether there will be a practical necessity for getting a lawyer; how vigorously an agency will enforce your rights; and the number of procedural obstacles, such as strict time limits, to bringing successful lawsuits.

As emphasized throughout this chapter, women should try to use Title VII whenever possible. It reaches the most discrimination and holds out the best hope of getting an effective remedy. But if getting a lawyer is a problem or you want to preserve total anonymity, consider using the Equal Pay Act, even though it is much narrower than Title VII. The executive order may provide an effective organizing and negotiating tool in some instances, although it provides little or no guarantee of any effective relief. State laws could be useful where a small company

is not covered by any of the Federal laws, to get faster
action than might be available in a Federal forum, or to
get back pay for a longer period of time; generally, however, state agencies are too conservative to offer effective
relief.

The foregoing is not a comprehensive list of the relevant
factors to consider, and women will have to gain experience with all the laws in order to understand how best
to use them. In summation, however, the best advice is to
start with Title VII, supplement it with action under as
many other laws as possible, and turn to other laws where
Title VII is not available or is tactically disadvantageous.

**What concrete proof must someone have of discrimina-
tion before she can file a charge or complaint?**

Absolutely none. Women often believe that they must
have some conclusive evidence that their employer or
union discriminates before they can walk into a Federal
or state agency and ask for help. They hope to discover
the incriminating memorandum from the company president stating that he will never, in a thousand years, hire
a woman salesman. In fact, it is the agency's job to do the
investigation that uncovers evidence of discrimination, not
the woman's job.

Women who have nothing stronger than their own
suspicions can walk into the right agency and fill out a
generalized complaint. It might read, for instance, that
Company X deprives women of employment opportunities
and discriminates against them as to wages, terms, conditions, and privileges of employment, and that the union has
negotiated contracts that do the same thing. That will be
enough to require the agency to look into the matter.

There is a significant practical caveat to the statutory re-

quirement that an agency investigate any filed complaint.
Most agencies are overworked and understaffed and often
have little understanding of how sex discrimination
operates. The more specific information women can point
to, the better the job the agency will do for the women.
Therefore, they should analyze the work situation in light
of all the concepts in this chapter, as well as their own
gut feelings of fairness, in order to identify discriminatory
practices and point them out to the agency in charge. For
instance: Are all the secretaries women and all the man-
agers men? What are the comparative pay scales and
fringe benefits of "male" and "female" jobs? Analyze the
collective-bargaining agreement—are sex distinctions built
into it? Some companies and unions have so clearly con-
ceived of particular jobs as either male or female that the
contract will describe some jobs using female pronouns
and other jobs using male pronouns. What does the contract say about fringe benefits? Are pregnancy leaves excluded from the sick-pay and medical-insurance provisions?
Are women allowed to retire earlier than men or are they
forced to retire earlier? And so on. In considering these
questions, women should remember that they know their
own job situation better than anyone else, and their analysis of its discriminatory nature is therefore potentially
better than that of anyone else, no matter how expert
that other person may be.

**How do lawyers and agencies prove that someone has
been discriminated against on the basis of sex?**
There are many different ways. One of the most important is the use of statistics. Courts have said that if
statistics show a lopsided distribution of particular population groups into certain kinds of jobs, they will presume

that the company or union has discriminated. Unless the company can come back with some evidence showing that this effect is absolutely necessary to the conduct of its business, the people complaining of discrimination win their lawsuit. The ramifications of this point are enormous since the statistics in almost every company show discrimination. For instance, many companies hire a lot of women, but a closer look at the statistics will reveal that women hold only 0 to 1 percent of the managerial or highly paid blue-collar jobs and 95 percent of the low-paid secretarial jobs. Those statistics prove a "prima-facie" case of discrimination. Another example is a company that hires very few women overall compared to other companies; here the statistics show discrimination in the hiring process rather than in the assignment of particular jobs. Lawyers generally use statistics to show not only a disproportionate distribution of men and women, but also to find out at what point in the employment process the maldistribution takes place.

Another way to prove discrimination is through various company documents. Since very few companies have yet grasped the fact that sex discrimination is illegal, or that particular forms of sex differentiation constitute sex discrimination (after all, it's "natural"!), company documents will often set forth blatantly discriminatory practices. The pension-plan booklet, when read carefully, may reveal that men and women must or may retire at different ages, solely because of their sex. The health plan will show that pregnancy is not covered or is minimally covered, although full coverage is provided for all other medical conditions. The collective bargaining agreement may use female pronouns for certain jobs, male pronouns for others— clearly indicating that the company reserves some jobs for men, others for women. The company might place help-wanted ads in segregated newspaper columns or use sex-typed language in the ad copy. All these documents can be introduced at trial to prove discrimination.

Still another way to prove discrimination is through the testimony of various workers and officials. Co-workers may be willing to testify that the manager told them he would never hire a woman for a particular job because it's not suitable for women, or that they knew of the existence of a discriminatory job practice, or that the company's claim that women do different work from men is untrue.

What can women workers do to help their lawyer prove discrimination or to convince the EEOC or other agencies that they have been discriminated against?

The workers are the people who best know their job situation. They also have friends in the company or union who have access to important documents proving discrimination. If women will study the concepts of what constitutes job discrimination set forth in this chapter, and analyze their job situation in the light of those concepts, they can help their lawyers enormously. For, unfortunately, many lawyers and agencies do not understand all these concepts, nor do they have the time and energy to go after the necessary evidence, nor do they always care about sex discrimination. The more kinds of discrimination women workers analyze, therefore, and the more statistics, documents, and testimony or affidavits of friends and sympathizers they produce, the more likely they are to win their case. In other words, trying to end discrimination must be a joint venture between the women on the one side and the governmental agency personnel and lawyers on the other side.

If you win a lawsuit, what can the judge order the company to do?

First, he can order the company to pay you any wages you lost because of the discrimination. The amount of "back wages" available depends on the statute in question. (See the questions on pages 67 and 86–87 for a discussion of how the wages are computed under Title VII and the Equal Pay Act.) The judge can also award you money to cover the costs of bringing the lawsuit, the lawyer's fees, and interest for the company's use of your back wages.

Second, under Title VII the judge can order a company to change its employment practices in the future. This applies to any discrimination and is a way of forcing the company to recruit and hire more women, to transfer them to better jobs, to train them for different positions, to change the health plan, to increase their wages, and so on. (Under the Equal Pay Act, only the wages can be increased.) It is this power to change employment practices that makes Title VII such a powerful weapon.

Can women get back wages and changes in company practices through negotiations with the company?

Yes. Under both Title VII and many of the state fair-employment practice laws, the company will be asked by the appropriate agency to negotiate a settlement of the case. Women should be wary of accepting settlements, though, that do not effectively provide the relief they want. This is particularly so of settlements negotiated by state agencies, which are often more responsive to business interests than to women workers, and the settlements they propose are at times so vague as to be meaningless. Since a court may later refuse to award you the relief you are entitled to because you signed such a settlement, it is important not to enter into one lightly. Thus, if you believe the proposed settlement is inadequate, reject it and keep on pursuing your legal remedies—including suing the company, if necessary.

What role can women's paralegal groups play in the field of employment-discrimination law?

First, they might establish a counseling service to help women who call in with complaints of job discrimination. After studying employment-discrimination law and procedures, the paralegal groups can direct these women to the proper agency or agencies and make sure that they comply with all the necessary procedural steps. More important, these groups can help women analyze the discrimination at their company, question them to find forms of discrimination that the women may have overlooked, and make sure they fill out the charge or complaint forms with all the discriminatory practices that can be identified. The woman worker who calls or walks in the door may have seized on a single form of discrimination because it is particularly onerous at that point in time; the chances are she faces a myriad of other discriminatory practices in her job, all of which should be attacked at once in order to maximize resources.

Counseling can continue even after the charge is filed with the appropriate agency. Paralegal advisors can help women locate evidence of discrimination by telling them what to look for and can refer these women to lawyers. They can also try to convince other women workers to join in the lawsuit by alleviating fears and explaining what the lawsuit is about and the advantages of joining in.

Besides individual counseling, paralegal groups can also take on a very important educational function. Most women simply do not understand the full extent of their rights. Speeches should be made, radio and television programs developed, printed materials distributed—all with the aim of helping women understand their rights and how to assert them.

A third paralegal project would be to start organizing women workers. Women need to push their labor unions to help them with sex-discrimination problems, and new unions should be formed where the workers are unorganized. A labor-union lawyer, with the force of the union behind her, can accomplish broad institutional changes—often without having to bring a lawsuit. For instance, Ruth Weyand, one of the lawyers for the International Union of Electrical Workers, has taken action on a broad front to eliminate sex discrimination in IUE companies. Her program has included educating the workers to understand sex discrimination, asking locals to fill out questionnaires to find out what the discriminatory practices are, taking trips to inspire local union action, negotiating with the companies for institution-wide changes when new developments in the law occur, and bringing lawsuits on behalf of women workers when a company remains recalcitrant. Much more action of this kind is essential if women want to make real changes in the employment world.

The workers themselves can also do much by organizing other women in the process of bringing employment-discrimination lawsuits. One excellent example of this technique involved a woman named Suann Hecht, who worked for CARE and wanted to challenge CARE's discriminatory practices. When she started her campaign, she was alone, and her major complaint was that CARE refused to send women overseas and paid women less than men. Instead of proceeding solely on her own behalf, she studied the CARE operation and thought of all the ways CARE discriminated against its women workers, which she listed when she filed her charges with EEOC. As EEOC proceeded with the case, Ms. Hecht gradually enlisted the support of other women in CARE; and when she started her lawsuit, other women were ready to join her. She finally even found male employees who were willing to testify about the discriminatory effect of CARE policies. When Suann has finished, it's safe to say that she will have forced CARE to make some major changes in its policies; just as important, she will have heightened the consciousness of many women workers who were too frightened even to discuss the subject of discrimination when she started. This is the kind of action women must take to achieve real change.

NOTES

1. S. Rep. No. 91-1137, 91st Cong., 2d Sess. 15 (1970).
2. U.S. Department of Labor, *Handbook on Women Workers* 96 (1969).
3. Women have not yet attacked this practice, and there are no decisions to date. However, the wage structure should be vulnerable to attack through careful analysis by professional job evaluators of the skills, training, and experience required for "male" pay rates and for "female" pay rates within a company. The company's methods for setting pay rates for different jobs should be examined to make sure that the criteria for determining pay rates are the same for men as for women.

Historical treatment may buttress this analysis: for instance, when female workers replaced male workers in many jobs during World War II, some companies deliberately lowered the salaries to a stated percentage of the level formerly paid to men. Finally, if the company is large enough, regional comparisons may yield interesting data. In one AT&T company, an all-female job was paid at the "female, clerical" low rate, while in all other AT&T companies, the same job was all-male and paid at the much higher rate reserved for "male craftsmen."

4. 401 U.S. 424 (1971).

5. 444 F. 2d 219 (9th Cir. 1971).

6. *Bowe* v. *Colgate-Palmolive Co.*, 416 F. 2d 711 (7th Cir. 1969).

7. 29 C.F.R. §1604.2.

8. 444 F.2d 1219 (9th Cir. 1971).

9. 29 C.F.R. §§1604.2 (b) (3)-(5).

10. *Bastardo* v. *Warren*, 332 F.Supp. 501 (W.D. Wis. 1970).

11. *Burns* v. *Rohr Corporation*, 346 F.Supp. 994 (S.D. Cal. 1972).

12. *Potlatch Forests, Inc.* v. *Hays*, 465 F. 2d 1081 (8th Cir. 1972).

13. Some unions have supported the Equal Rights Amendment, the most notable example being the United Auto Workers.

14. Another possibility is to provide for voluntary overtime on the basis of seniority. That is, the most senior employees—male and female—may decline overtime, while the most junior employees must accept it (if there are not enough volunteers).

15. *Danner* v. *Phillips Petroleum Company*, 447 F.2d 159 (5th Cir. 1971). Of course, the *Danner* decision may not be extended to other union benefits. The only solution then is to make increased efforts to unionize women workers.

16. *Pittsburgh Press Co.* v. *Pittsburgh Commission on Human Relations*, 41 USLW 5055 (1973). Such laws have an added clause covering anyone who "aids or abets" someone else in discriminating; at the very least, the newspaper aids and abets discriminatory companies when it gives

them the sex-segregated column which enables them to discriminate. States with such laws include: Alaska, Arizona, California, Colorado, Connecticut, Hawaii, Illinois, Indiana, Iowa, Kansas, Kentucky, Maine, Massachusetts, Michigan, Minnesota, Missouri, New Hampshire, New Jersey, New Mexico, New York, Ohio, Oklahoma, Oregon, Pennsylvania, Rhode Island, South Dakota, Utah, and West Virginia. See Chart A, under the FEP column, for the legal citations.

17. 29 C.F.R. Part 1607.
18. 401 U.S. 424 (1971).
19. *Sontag* v. *Bronstein,* 335 N.Y.S. 2d 182 (1972). The court upheld the test, but the case is on appeal.
20. See Bem and Bem, "Case Study of A Nonconscious Ideology: Training the Woman to Know Her Place," in Bem, *Beliefs, Attitudes and Human Affairs* (1970). The Bems cite a study by Goldberg, "Are Women Prejudiced Against Women?" *Transaction* (April 1968).
21. *Ibid.* The Bems cite Brown, *Social Psychology* 162 (1965).
22. 400 U.S. 542 (1971).
23. *Bartmess* v. *Drewry's U.S.A., Inc.,* 444 F.2d 1186 (7th Cir. 1971); and *Rosen* v. *Public Services Electric and Gas Company,* 409 F.2d 775 (3rd Cir. 1969), followed by 5 FEP Cases 709 (3rd Cir. 1973).
24. 29 C.F.R. §1604.9 (f).
25. 29 C.F.R. §1604.10.
26. —— F.Supp. ——, 4 FEP Cases 885, 4 EPD ¶7773 (S.D. N.Y. 1972).
27. 29 C.F.R. §1604.9 (e). However, the Labor Department interprets the Equal Pay Act to allow smaller benefits for one sex if the employer's contribution for both sexes is equal. 29 C.F.R. §800.116(d). The Department has never applied this guideline, but women should challenge smaller benefits under Title VII alone to avoid any problems with the Equal Pay Act interpretation.
28. Women in the Minnesota Public Interest Research Group recently conducted an interesting study of employment-agency discrimination. MPIRG sent male and female applicants with identical qualifications to several agencies. Not too surprisingly, the men were treated

much better than the women. Such a study could be used by paralegal groups to get change through publicity; it would also provide good evidence for use in lawsuits against agencies. For a copy of the "MPIRG Report: Sexual Discrimination in Employment Agencies" (October 1972), write to: MPIRG, 1926 Nicollet Avenue, Minneapolis, Minnesota 55403 ([612] 376-7554).

29. Note for lawyers. The Fifth Circuit recently decided that an employee could maintain such an action prior to issuance of the "notice of right to sue." *Drew* v. *Liberty Mutual Insurance Company,* 5 FEP Cases 1077 (5th Cir. 1973). Since there is as yet no way to get a "notice of right to sue" before the lapse of one hundred eighty days, Title VII jurisdiction would be problematic in any circuit that did not agree with the *Drew* decision. In that case, a suit under the Declaratory Judgment statute might avoid the problem. Although the company would not be bound to follow such a judgment, most companies would probably hesitate to violate it.

30. *Shultz* v. *Wheaton Glass Company,* 421 F.2d 259 (3d Cir. 1970).

31. See, for example, *Hodgson* v. *Sagner, Inc.,* 326 F.Supp. 371 (D. Md. 1971).

32. If the Labor Department brings the lawsuit, it cannot win this double amount of back wages—which is an important reason for women to bring their own lawsuits. However, it can win 6 percent interest on the back wages.

33. This problem can be remedied by bringing the lawsuit under both Title VII and the Equal Pay Act because the court can order the company to raise salaries under Title VII.

III

Education

Less than one hundred forty years ago, Oberlin College opened its doors and made history by admitting both blacks and women to a college education for the first time in the United States. At first, women were considered too stupid to take the same course work as men—their minds couldn't assimilate "men's" fare, it was thought. The college preserved a clear aura of male dominance in other areas as well. Women were required to wash the male students' clothes, care for their rooms, and serve them at table. Nor were women permitted to talk in public. Lucy Stone, the famous feminist and an early Oberlin graduate, refused to write a commencement essay because only a male student would have been permitted to read it to the audience.[1]

Given this "beginning," it is not too surprising that academia is still afflicted with deep-seated and largely unrecognized sexism. Although male dominance continues today, women have recently begun to challenge it. As yet, women have only a few legal weapons, none of which reach all forms of educational discrimination. Feminists are using these laws imaginatively, but much more remains to be done, for their efforts have not yet given rise to any clearly defined rights on a national basis. Broad-based and provocative litigation can contribute significantly toward meaningful change, of course, and women must also seek new laws that will effectively insure for them equal educational opportunity.

Are there any clearly defined national rights against discrimination in education?

No. Until the spring of 1972, no Federal law specifically prohibited sex discrimination in education, although for almost a decade sex discrimination had been prohibited by national law in the field of employment. A Federal law providing for equal educational opportunity would have served as a catalyst for the number of lawsuits necessary to establish a national definition of women's rights in the academic world. Congress has now passed a law, the Education Amendments of 1972 Act, but it has glaring gaps.

Despite the absence of an adequate national law, a national definition of rights can be partially achieved now, at least as to some schools and universities. As the chapter on constitutional rights indicated, the Equal Protection clause of the Fourteenth Amendment can be used to attack discrimination carried out by state or local governments. That means that women may sue any public elementary, junior high, or senior high school, and any state college or university without further changes in the law. Since the effect of the Fourteenth Amendment on sex discrimination is not uniformly defined by the courts, there is no guarantee that any particular lawsuit will be successful. But there is enough chance of success to make it worthwhile to undertake a concerted, nationwide attack on discrimination in public schools, based on the concept of Equal Protection. In addition, the 1972 Federal law against sex discrimination in education can be used to eliminate discrimination in some public and private schools.

Part A of this chapter discusses lawsuits based on the Equal Protection clause. Even though these initial lawsuits have not yet created a coherent system of rights, they do offer valuable lessons in strategy and a sense of the possibilities for present action. Part B of the chapter discusses two new laws prohibiting educational discrimination.

A. Rights Based on the Equal Protection Clause in Public Schools and Colleges

Do women have a right to attend all-male public schools?

Sometimes yes, sometimes no. Women—and the ACLU—scored an important victory recently, when they succeeded in desegregating the previously all-male University of Virginia at Charlottesville, the most "prestigious" facility of the state university.[2] High school students knocked down the all-male barrier at prestigious Stuyvesant High School in New York City. And concerned parents recently forced the equally prestigious Boston Latin and Girls Latin public schools to use the same admissions standards for boys and girls, thus allowing some girls into the over three-hundred-year-old formerly all-male Boston Latin.[3]

But other attempts have not been so successful. Texas A&M, an all-male state university, was sued twice in the early 1960s; it remained segregated even though both cases went all the way to the United States Supreme Court. (The Court refused to review the decisions. Much later, the college voluntarily desegregated.) In early 1971, a lower Federal court refused to admit men to Winthrop College, an all-female state school in South Carolina. The Supreme Court approved the decision without even discussing the issues.[4] Thus, under the Equal Protection clause, some courts have allowed sex segregation in public schools and others have not.

The Education Amendments of 1972 Act will also affect this form of discrimination. The law allows Federal agencies to withdraw Federal funding from graduate, professional, and vocational schools, and from most undergraduate public colleges, that exclude women students. However, other schools can continue to receive Federal funding even if they remain sex-segregated. The new law is a mixed blessing but can be used to open the doors of some all-male schools, as will be seen in the next section.

Are there any differences between the successful and unsuccessful suits under the Equal Protection clause that suggest strategy and tactics for future attacks on sex-segregated school systems?

Yes. There are important lessons to be learned from comparing the successful suits with the failures. The most important single factor in explaining the women's success in desegrating the University of Virginia was the thorough documentation of the discrepancies in education available to men and to women in the state. Among the shocking differences discovered by ACLU lawyers: The men's college offered the highest average faculty salaries in the state. The state appropriation per student at the men's college was more than double that at each of the two women's colleges. Men had access to sophisticated astronomy and science facilities; women did not. Men could take degrees in astronomy, Latin-American studies, and nine foreign languages—all unavailable to women. The men's college offered a far greater variety of courses in almost every department, especially in government, astronomy, economics, English, history, physics, geology, geography, sociology, and anthropology. In short, the lawyers showed in detail that the state reserved its highest-quality educational facilities "For Men Only."

The lawyers topped this factual survey by extensive questioning of university officials to see whether they could offer any cogent reasons for excluding women. Even the judge was embarrassed by the answers the school officials gave: allowing women to use dormitories built for men would not be feasible because women need more diminutive furniture; the shower heads were set at the wrong height; and so on, *ad ridiculum*.

In contrast, lawyers for the men who unsuccessfully tried to enter Winthrop College in South Carolina apparently conceded that there was no difference between the quality of education available at Winthrop and that available at other public colleges in the state, which included the all-male Citadel and several integrated schools. Since the men failed to document any disparity, it is impossible to tell from the court's opinion whether Winthrop offered an identical education to that of the male school. However, the law establishing Winthrop had emphasized that the school should offer certain "courses thought to be especially helpful to female students." These included:

> . . . stenography, typewriting, telegraphy, bookkeeping, drawing . . . designing, engraving, sewing,

EDUCATION   121

dressmaking, millinery, art, needlework, cooking,
housekeeping and such other industrial arts as may
be suitable to their sex and conducive to their support and usefulness.

The men's school, the Citadel, is an engineering and
military school. Thus, there were clear differences between
the two schools, and, at the very least, women in South
Carolina were deprived of some forms of education available only at the Citadel. Yet the men never pointed to such
facts, and indeed may not have been able to if Winthrop
offered the same courses as the other schools. Instead, the
men sought to show that maintaining single-sex schools
was inherently lacking in rational justification and thus
violated the Equal Protection clause. This is analogous to
whites saying that "separate but equal" schools for whites
and blacks inherently violate the Equal Protection clause,
rather than showing in detail that the schools are not, *in
fact*, equal. The time may not be ripe for men—or
women—to challenge segregation per se. First, they must
build up the cases that will illustrate cogently just how
unequal *in fact* are the opportunities for women.

A second explanation for the loss of the lawsuit in South
Carolina may be that men challenged segregation at the
female school. Perhaps the suit should have instead had
women challenge segregation at the male school. As already pointed out, the Citadel did offer opportunities in
engineering and military training, which women were deprived of. Had the attack on sex segregation started with
female plaintiffs trying to enter the all-male school, the result might have been entirely different. The reason is, as
some feminists believe, that since society offers most of its
advantages to men, a lawsuit brought on behalf of men will
not evoke much sense of injustice. Courts that might be

moved to attack discrimination against women could find a man's suit a mere diversion and leave a discriminatory law standing.

Even aside from the tactical considerations, it may be counterproductive for women to use their slender legal resources for men when there is so much yet to be won for women. Other feminists believe, however, that lawsuits brought on behalf of men plaintiffs create valuable precedents and help break down sex-role stereotyping. These conflicting views should certainly be discussed.

Do girls have a right to take the same courses as boys and to refuse to take girls-only courses?

Not yet, under the Equal Protection clause.[5] A few girls have begun to challenge discriminatory course assignments —such as metalworking for boys and home economics for girls—but the courts have not yet resolved the issue.[6] In the long run, such policies should prove difficult for any board of education to defend, and girls and their parents should launch an immediate campaign to eliminate course segregation.

Do women have an equal right to participate in school athletic programs?

Sometimes yes, sometimes no. Girls in Nebraska and Minnesota recently established their right to join the all-male golf, tennis, cross-country track, and cross-country skiing teams.[7] On the other hand, girls in Illinois[8] and Connecticut have fared less well. Susan Hollander lost her

bid to run cross-country track when she appeared before
a very hostile judge, who explained:

> The present generation of our younger male popula-
> tion has not become so decadent that boys will
> experience a thrill in defeating girls in running con-
> tests. . . . In the world of sports there is ever present
> as a challenge the psychology to win. With boys vying
> with girls in cross-country running and indoor track,
> the challenge to win, and the glory of achievement, at
> least for many boys, would lose incentive and be-
> come nullified. Athletic competition builds character
> in our boys. We do not need that kind of character
> in our girls. . . .[9]

**Should women try to win more than the right to par-
ticipate on "male" athletic teams?**

Yes. Women must make some difficult strategy decisions
in seeking to establish equal rights to participate in athletic
programs. Should they ask for equal funding for separate
male and female sports, integrated sports programs, or
a combination of the two? The latter is probably the most
desirable. Integrated sports would provide the opportunity
for the most athletically talented girls to compete with
athletically talented boys. By also asking the schools to
fund sports diverse enough to attract most girls, and by
insisting that the average per-student expenditure be equal
for boys and girls, women would also provide opportunities for those girls who are not interested in, or lack the
muscular development for, some of the traditionally male
sports. More adequate funding of different sports than are
currently emphasized would also help those boys with

a similar lack of interest in or muscular development for sports like football. Eventually the schools might find themselves providing meaningful athletic programs for all students, sorting the students into sports roughly by interest and skill rather than by sex.

May a school exclude pregnant students or unwed mothers?

The answer is not completely settled. One court ordered a school to readmit an unwed mother but said the school could still exclude her if it showed she was so lacking in moral character that she would "taint the education of other students." The judge also implied that the school could exclude a pregnant girl; only after having the baby would she be entitled to return.[10] But in another case, the judge ordered school officials to permit an unwed, pregnant girl to continue regular attendance without restriction.[11]

The Women's Legal Defense Fund in Washington, D.C., is helping a Virginia student contest a school decision to expel her three months before graduation. She was pregnant but married—and had an excellent academic record. WLDF contends she should be paid damages by the school board to compensate her for future salary losses caused by her lack of a high school diploma.[12]

Do college women have the right to equal treatment in campus living rules under the Equal Protection clause?

Women at one school—Southeastern Louisiana College —have succeeded in forcing administrators to let them live off-campus in their own apartments, as men were already allowed to do. College officials claimed that they had to force all women under twenty-one to live in the dormitories to insure collecting enough money to pay off the Federal debt on the dormitories. The judge did not agree. He reasoned that the college was requiring women to shoulder more of the cost of education than it required of men. Forcing women to pay off the debt was just as arbitrary as it would be for the army to draft only blacks, he declared. Thus the school policy was irrational and in violation of the Equal Protection clause. "[A]ll must pay or none."[13]

This decision should prove useful to other women who wish to challenge similar policies. Obvious candidates for suit are the common practices of regulating women's— but not men's—hours and of furnishing college men with rooms and cleaning services at the same price women pay for rooms without cleaning services. (At the author's college, officials hired maids to make the boys' beds every morning!) A woman in Kentucky has already challenged restrictions on hours for women under twenty-one at a state college (girls could have the restriction waived with parental consent, but boys did not need parental consent). She lost her case when the judge ruled that a college could discriminate against women in order to conform to the contemporary mores of the community, but the decision is being appealed.[14]

As this hours case suggests, the decision on living off-campus may have a limited impact. This might be explained in part by the judge's consideration of financial inequities only. Charging women more than men for the same education is clearly wrong, but one's sense of moral outrage is evoked more by other considerations. The college regulation clearly implied that girls are more immature than boys and need to be closely supervised. And always, lurking in the background, is the suspicion of and the desire to regulate women's sexual conduct. College officials who are willing to make and act upon such stereotyped assumptions about girls may be just as prone to denigrate women in their educational policies. The persistent will to prevent women from assuming responsibility for their own lives is at stake in these policies—not some issue of unfair financial costs. Lawyers handling such lawsuits, and judges, must begin to confront these attitudes and the degrading impact they have on women.

What other rights should women seek to establish under the Equal Protection clause or the proposed Equal Rights Amendment?

The Citizens' Advisory Council on the Status of Women recently outlined many problems needing attention in the area of education. In any local community, the council would look for:

> . . . the degree of sex discrimination . . . with respect to (1) schools restricted to one sex; (2) courses of study in coeducational schools restricted to one sex; (3) the per-capita expenditure of funds by sex for physical-education courses and physical-education extracurricular and other extracurricular activities; (4) sex stereotyping in textbooks, library books, and other curriculum aids; (5) school activities, such as hall patrols, safety squads, room chores, etc.; and (6) promotion of teachers.[15]

Schools also use textbooks that ignore women's varied role in society. Guidance counsellors offer sex-stereotyped advice about jobs and careers to students. Many of the same problems exist in colleges and graduate schools. Additional problems at that level include restrictive quotas on the admission of women and unequal scholarship aid. Women can challenge these practices in lawsuits brought under the Equal Protection clause; and if that basis proves unsuccessful, under the Equal Rights Amendment after it is ratified. Success with respect to restrictive admissions quotas and unequal scholarship aid in public institutions seems probable. In other areas, the outcome of litigation is more problematic. Legislative measures should be sought containing prohibitions against all discriminatory practices, particularly those that are less susceptible to litigation challenges.

Should any national planning be undertaken before attempting to establish these rights?

Yes. Feminists—and particularly feminist lawyers—should definitely plan strategy for nationwide legal action to abolish discrimination in education. The lack of coordinated planning to date may already have lead to some bad losses, which will make it more difficult to win in the future. For instance, it was a mistake for men to try to desegregate a female school before solid precedent was established opening male schools to women, and the case created some extremely bad law.

Planning should define the kinds of discrimination to attack initially, the priorities thereafter, and the theoretical Equal Protection development needed. The cases adjudicated so far, and past experience in eradicating racial discrimination in education, suggest that women ought to start with—*and carefully document*—the most blatant

forms of discrimination: outright exclusion of women
from certain courses, exclusion of women from schools,
admitted restrictive quota systems, denial of access to all
athletic programs. Later they can move on to issues that
will seem less obviously discriminatory to hostile judges:
de facto quota systems on admissions, segregated athletic programs, or sex-role-biased job and career counseling
programs. Tactically, it is better to break down the segregation bars by focusing on factual comparisons of facilities
for men and women to demonstrate that the state allocates
much less money for women.[16] After that job is done, the
time may be ripe to ask judges to declare all segregation inherently illegal. Similarly, it seems wise to start the attack
with public schools and colleges since current law is so
solidly against finding state action at private schools.[17]
Finally, there should be some discussion of the tactical wis-
dom of fighting sex discrimination by the medium of suits
brought by men.

**Can the U.S. Attorney General bring an Equal Protec-
tion lawsuit on behalf of women to remedy sex discrimination in public schools and colleges?**

Yes, under a recent amendment to Title IV of the 1964
Civil Rights Act.[18]

**What kinds of discriminatory practices can be attacked
in such a lawsuit?**

To date, the Attorney General has used Title IV principally to desegregate public schools. In the course of
such lawsuits, Justice Department lawyers have also at-

tacked other forms of discrimination—both against students and teachers—but these moves have always been incidental to the main issue of desegregation. This seems to indicate that Title IV can be used against all the forms of discrimination mentioned in this chapter, but that the Justice Department may not be inclined to do so unless women raise these issues in the context of segregated schools. Women should still request the Justice Department to fight other forms of educational discrimination in integrated schools, if for no other reason than to help educate Justice Department lawyers on other sex-discrimination issues. However, requesting help is not the same as getting it, particularly from a government agency that has traditionally taken some very conservative, and sometimes sexist, stands on eradicating sex discrimination. Indeed, the Department may not even be ready to see sex segregation of schools as a denial of Equal Protection.

In theory, Title IV applies both to lower schools and to colleges, but so far the Justice Department has dealt only with elementary and secondary school education. Again, this should not preclude complaints about college-level discrimination.

How should women request the Attorney General to bring such lawsuits?

Send a letter to:

Attorney General
U. S. Department of Justice
Washington, D. C. 20537
   Attention: Education Section

At the elementary and secondary school level, the letter should be sent by the parents of affected children. At the college level, women students can raise the complaint.

Describe the school system, the discriminatory practices, and give as many facts as possible. It also helps to identify other women who share the same problem. The Justice Department will be more interested if it is a widespread problem because the Attorney General must certify that the lawsuit will further desegregation efforts. Although it is impossible to know whether the Justice Department will follow through, it is probably worthwhile to make the effort—certainly so for women who cannot find or afford their own lawyers. Even for those who have access to counsel, requests for Attorney General intervention may serve as a means of publicizing the discrimination and awakening government officials to its existence and effects.

B. Equal Educational Opportunity in both Private and Public Schools

Private schools are a major source of educational opportunities in this country, and women private-school students face the same discriminatory practices as in public schools. This section gives information on laws that can be used to reach both private and public schools—unlike the Equal Protection clause which reaches only state action. Particular discriminatory practices are not discussed since both public and private schools indulge in the kinds of discrimination discussed in Part A. The laws discussed in Part B can be used to attack all these practices.

1. *Title IX of the Education Amendments of 1972 Act*

Do women have the right to equal treatment in education in private schools?
Yes. In the spring of 1972, Congress passed the Education Amendments of 1972 Act. Title IX of that law forbids some private and public schools from discriminating on the basis of sex. However, the law is limited in scope, and women still have no specific statutory remedy against the discriminatory practices of many private schools.

What schools are prohibited from discriminating by Title IX?
Title IX covers any school—from the preschool level through graduate education—that receives Federal funds. However, it does *not* reach religious schools if a particular religion's tenets require the sex discrimination that the school practices. (If the religion's tenet does not require sex discrimination, then the school's practices are reached.) Title IX also exempts military schools, which are defined as schools training individuals for the United States military services or for the merchant marine.

What discriminatory practices does Title IX prohibit?
Discrimination is defined very broadly:

> No person in the United States shall, on the basis of
> sex, be excluded from participation in, be denied the
> benefits of, or be subject to discrimination under any
> education program or activity receiving Federal
> financial assistance. . . .

The agencies administering this law—principally, the
Department of Health, Education, and Welfare (HEW)—
will publish regulations defining the discriminatory practices much more explicitly.[19] Even without regulations,
though, one can see that this language is general enough
to include all the discriminatory practices mentioned in
Part A of this chapter, as well as any other discrimination women encounter.

What discriminatory practices does Title IX allow schools?

Title IX specifically allows many schools to engage in
discriminatory practices as to both admissions and living
facilities. First, and of principal significance, it allows
several kinds of educational institutions to discriminate in
admission policies. Presumably, this allows schools either
to exclude women completely, to set up quota systems to
limit their enrollment, or to demand that women meet
higher admissions standards than men. The schools that
may so discriminate include preschool, elementary, and
secondary schools, whether public or private*; private
undergraduate colleges (such as Harvard, Yale, or Princeton); and public undergraduate colleges that have always

---

*Vocational schools at these levels, however, may *not* discriminate in their admission policies.

been single-sex institutions.[20] In addition, any institution that was once a single-sex school and has begun to integrate under a Federally approved plan is given seven full years after the effective date of the Title (July 1, 1972) to continue to discriminate in admissions. Title IX in effect licenses many of the schools that practice the most blatant forms of discrimination to continue doing so. In fact, the only institutions prohibited from using discriminatory admissions policies are public and private vocational schools at all levels, integrated public undergraduate colleges, and public and private graduate and professional schools. Even in these categories, any school that has begun integrating under an approved plan has the seven-year grace period to continue to discriminate in admissions.[21]

Title IX specifically allows a second discriminatory practice—segregating living facilities by sex. Of course, this is not a clear-cut issue. Many students prefer segregated dormitories, and a prohibition would have eliminated the possibility of choice in this area. Others, however, want coed dorms and they will not be helped by the new law, although the law does not limit the school's option to provide integrated living facilities either for all students or for students who wish accommodations of this kind.

How are discriminatory schools punished under Title IX?

Any Federal agency that awards money—whether as grants, loans, or contracts—to a school can cancel that assistance if it finds that the school discriminates. The agency may also refuse to award such assistance in the future. Although many Federal agencies administer grant programs to educational institutions, HEW is the main grantor and as such will be the chief enforcement agency.

The threat of a cut-off of Federal money is a powerful weapon since many schools depend on this money for a major portion of their budget. Of course, HEW must be willing to make this threat and to carry through in the event of noncompliance if the law is to be effective. It remains to be seen whether HEW will be willing to do so.

It is important to understand the limitation of Title IX sanctions. There is no way for either women or HEW to force the school directly to stop discriminating—except insofar as a loss of Federal money provides leverage to achieve that. If the school is willing to forego Federal aid, it can continue discriminating. Thus, Title IX differs greatly from the Equal Protection clause, under which a court can order a school to cease discriminating if the requisite "state action" is found to exist. In some circumstances, HEW can recommend that the Justice Department bring suit against an offending school. In that case, of course, a court could order the school to stop discriminating; however, this remedy is not the normal one envisioned under Title IX.

How should women enforce their rights under Title IX?
They should send a letter detailing their charges of discriminatory practices, and naming the school involved, to:

Director, Office of Civil Rights
Department of Health, Education & Welfare
330 Independence Avenue, S.W.
Washington, D.C.

Include as many facts as possible about the school's practices, and use the advice on how to fill out complaints from the chapter on employment discrimination (see pages 105–108). For instance, list statistical evidence of discrimination; don't limit your charges to those you are sure you can prove (it should be the responsibility of HEW to investigate and prove your charges); and mention anything that you believe is discriminatory, whether or not legal authority already supports you. If possible, you should also name the Federal programs under which the school receives money. HEW will determine this fact if you don't know, though; and the department will also send your letter to the proper agency if HEW does not administer the program (or programs) at your school.

Once HEW receives your charge, it is required to investigate and conduct a hearing to determine whether the school discriminates. (Whether this requirement is more theoretical than real remains to be seen.) Women may participate in these hearings only as witnesses or as "friends of the court," but if they are unhappy with the results, they can ask a United States Court of Appeals to review the HEW action. Sometimes women's organizations may also be allowed to participate as "friends of the court," which means they can offer their opinion as to what the result should be but cannot offer evidence or control the course of the proceedings.

Should women who want to challenge discriminatory practices in public schools use both the Equal Protection clause and Title IX of the Education Amendments of 1972 Act?

Yes; because each provides a different remedy, both together would maximize the pressure on school officials. Women should remember, though, that Title IX allows many public schools to follow discriminatory admission policies. In these instances, the Equal Protection clause provides the only remedy. (Women students at private schools, of course, can use only Title IX and not the Equal Protection clause because of the lack of "state action.")

Does Title IX provide adequate protection against sex discrimination in educational opportunities?

Definitely not. In fact, some women might see the law as a sellout by Congress, particularly since Title IX was considered several weeks after the overwhelming Congressional approval of the Equal Rights Amendment. Male presidents (or their representatives) of the big-name, high-prestige schools, which are the supposed educational "leaders" in this nation, descended on Congress to plead for the right to discriminate against women students. Harvard, for example, wanted to bring its 4-1 male-female quota system slowly "down" to 3.5 to 1. Women's colleges, too, sought to preserve their present admissions practices. The schools won that "right"—which explains why the law does not even touch the admissions policies of so many kinds of schools.

Another major flaw in Title IX is its enforcement mechanism. Even though HEW has been more activist than most agencies, experience to date demonstrates that women cannot rely confidently on Federal agencies to enforce their rights.

What can women do to secure strong legislation against sex discrimination in education?

Let your Congressional representatives know that you

want strong provisions against discrimination, and you will
not settle for Title IX. When women were lobbying for
the Equal Rights Amendment, they were told repeatedly
by male lobbyists that they would have to compromise if
they wanted to get anything through Congress. The women
remained firm and got the amendment they wanted;
they realized that to settle for less was to negate completely
the principle they were striving to establish. Legislators
are used to giving up easily and to the process of compromise—but if women organize the same strong lobby for
a solid bill against discrimination, they can succeed.

**What provisions would a strong bill against discrimina-
tion in education contain?**

First, it would not exempt any school or admission
policy from coverage. Even religious schools would be
forbidden to discriminate since the law would cover only
schools receiving Federal funds. If a religious school wants
to discriminate, it should not be allowed to do so with
Federal money, particularly since part of that money
comes from female taxpayers. The same holds true for military schools. The predominantly male Congress blanches at
the idea of women in the military, but many military
schools teach valuable employment skills and offer other
benefits that cannot be acquired anywhere else. For example, commercial airlines hire almost all their pilots from
those trained by the Air Force. Since Air Force Academy
programs exclude women, women are effectively barred
from the lucrative job of commercial pilot. The prestige
private schools, like Harvard, Yale, Dartmouth, and Princeton, likewise deserve no special break. Supposedly they
provide some of the best education in this nation, and it is

outrageous that Congress is willing to continue funding, with Federal money received from female taxpayers, schools that blatantly limit women's enrollment.[22] Similarly, women's colleges receiving Federal funds should be required to open admissions to men. The price paid for maintaining all-female institutions is the maintenance of all-male institutions, and that price is too high to tolerate. All the other special exemptions for admissions policies would be eliminated—including the seven-year grace period.

Second, much stronger enforcement provisions would be built into a strong law. Women must have the right to sue directly in Federal court for a cessation of discrimination and for damages. They should also be able to sue for a cut-off of Federal funds where the agency has failed to take action. This last suggestion is crucial. The Federal bureaucracy is presently staffed at the policy level almost exclusively with males. Most of those men are indifferent to civil rights in general; even those who are interested often do not understand or care about sex discrimination. There are hundreds of ways a bureaucracy can avoid complying with the law.

Third, an effective law would provide for adequate funding and staff to make enforcement possible. HEW has named only three lawyers in its General Counsel's Office to enforce Title IX nationwide. This is absurd and shows clearly how little intention the Administration has of enforcing the law. Women's groups should study enforcement requirements and push for a formula that would guarantee sufficient staff to handle both the investigation of all charges received by HEW and a stated percentage of routine reviews of school policies.

2. *The Public Health Service Act*

Do students in the health professions have any additional rights against discrimination by their schools?

Yes. Under a recent amendment to the Public Health Service Act, two sections—§§799A and 845[23]—specifically prohibit schools and training programs in the health professions from discriminating against students on the basis of their sex. The prohibition applies only to schools and programs receiving financial assistance under Titles VII and VIII of the Public Health Service Act, but the vast majority of these schools do receive such assistance. The prohibition also applies to hospitals insofar as they operate medical schools, training programs, or even internships. Thus, women—or men—may now protest and seek legal redress if a hospital refuses to hire women interns, if a medical school limits its enrollment of women or refuses to admit people over thirty (which affects women more than men), or if a nursing school refuses to admit men.

How will the antidiscrimination provisions of the Public Health Service Act be enforced?

The Department of Health, Education, and Welfare must cancel any Federal financial assistance—whether in the form of a grant, a loan guarantee, or a subsidy on interest payments—received under Titles VII or VIII of the Public Health Service Act by a school or program that discriminates. Theoretically, cancellation can occur in three ways. If the school fails to give HEW a written as-surance that it will not discriminate, HEW *must* cut off or refuse to award the funds. HEW also conducts routine reviews to check for discrimination. Finally, someone can file a complaint with HEW, charging a program with discrimination. HEW would then conduct a hearing and cancel any financial assistance if it finds discrimination. Although women will not be allowed to participate in these hearings except as witnesses or "friends of the court," they will be able to ask a Federal court to review HEW action.

To file a complaint, send a letter detailing the charges to:

> Director, Office of Civil Rights
> Department of Health, Education, and Welfare
> 330 Independence Avenue, S.W.
> Washington, D.C.

Are there any differences between the sex-discrimination provisions of the Public Health Service Act and those of Title IX of the Education Amendments of 1972 Act?

Yes. The Public Health Service Act does not contain the numerous exceptions that Title IX does. Thus, women in the health professions who are not helped by Title IX —such as applicants to private undergraduate schools— may still be able to get relief under the Public Health Service Act. Schools are already lobbying to weaken the Public Health Service Act, so this added protection for women in the health professions may not last long. Women's groups may want to counteract this lobbying effort.

Should women who can challenge sex discrimination under both laws do so?

Yes. This may help maximize the pressure on the school, even though the remedy under both laws is of the same nature—a cut-off of Federal funds.

3. *The rights of teachers*

Are teachers and other school employees protected against employment discrimination by the sex-discrimination provisions of the Public Health Service Act and Title IX of the Education Amendments of 1972 Act?

Yes. Title IX protects all school employees. The PHSA provisions protect only those teachers and employees who work directly with the students.

Are there any other new laws that protect teachers against sex-discriminatory employment practices?

Yes. Both Title VII of the 1964 Civil Rights Act and the Equal Pay Act have recently been amended to protect teachers against sex discrimination. Both laws are discussed in the chapter on "Employment Discrimination."

Until these amendments were passed, teachers in private schools had only one very ineffective remedy against sex discrimination—Executive Order 11246, as amended by E.O. 11375. (See pages 96–99 for a discussion of its weaknesses.) Now teachers may sue in Federal court under the

Equal Pay Act and Title VII to recover lost wages and to force the school to change discriminatory policies. The Executive Order may still be used to apply additional pressure, but teachers will no longer have to rely on Federal agencies that do not wish to enforce the order.

Public school teachers already had the right to sue in Federal court under the Equal Protection clause. They too will gain from the recent amendments since courts have been much stricter about eliminating sex discrimination under Title VII than they have been under the Equal Protection clause.

Should teachers use all laws available to combat discriminatory practices?

Yes, since this maximizes the pressure on school officials. And teachers now have a wide range of remedies: court action under Titles IV and VII of the 1964 Civil Rights Act, the Equal Pay Act, and the Equal Protection clause (if they are public school employees); and differing forms of agency action under Executive Order 11246 (contract cut-off), Title IX (grant, loan, and contract cut-off), and the Public Health Service Act.

4. State laws

Do any state laws prohibit sex discrimination in education?

Yes. A few states have at least cursory provisions outlawing some forms of discrimination. They include Alaska, Illinois, Indiana, Massachusetts, and New York.

A few other states have laws prohibiting educational discrimination on the basis of race, religion, or national origin, but not sex. (See Chart B in the Appendix for the list of and citations for all such laws.) It is difficult to know how effective these state laws are. Some, administered by state civil-rights agencies, provide for a complaint procedure and full enforcement powers. Others merely forbid some forms of discrimination and provide no apparent enforcement mechanism. Even where there is a comprehensive program on paper, personnel in state agencies and courts could subvert the effectiveness of the program, as could a lack of funding. In any case, it seems worthwhile to explore using these laws, as well as to lobby for the inclusion of a nondiscrimination by sex provision in existing civil rights programs and for comprehensive laws in this area in states without any existing program.

5. Paralegal action

What can women's paralegal groups do in the education area?

As in other fields, they can teach women their rights, help them file complaints or find lawyers, and lobby for new and better laws. In addition, Title IX offers a unique organizing opportunity since it protects all the women in a particular school or campus from sex discrimination, whether the women are students, research assistants, teachers, secretaries, or maids. All these women can coalesce to study campus discrimination as it affects them all and then together file charges with HEW. This concerted action will produce a much stronger attack on discriminatory practices, and it should also help women in very different circumstances understand some of the factors that unite them. An excellent source of technical information about and assistance in action to eradicate sex discrimination on college campuses is:

The Project on the Status and Education of Women
Association of American Colleges
1818 R Street, N.W.
Washington, D.C. 20009
(202) 265-3137

Write for the project's newsletter, *On Campus with Women.*

NOTES

1. E. Flexner, *Century of Struggle* (1970), pp. 29-30 and n. 13.
2. *Kirstein* v. *Rector and Visitors of University of Virginia,* 309 F.Supp. 184 (E.D. Va. 1970).
3. *Bray* v. *Lee,* 337 F.Supp. 934 (D. Mass. 1972). A few boys are also now attending the former Girls Latin School.
4. *Williams* v. *McNair,* 316 F.Supp. 134 (D. S.Car. 1970), *aff'd.,* 401 U.S. 951 (1971).
5. State statutes in New York and Massachusetts now prohibit the exclusion of either sex from courses. See Chart B. In addition, the Pennsylvania Commissioner of Education has issued a broad directive against discrimination in education that includes a prohibition against excluding either sex from courses.
6. *Sanchez* v. *Baron,* C.A. No. 69-C-1615 (E.D. N.Y.) is one of these cases. New York City students are challenging the Board of Education's exclusion of girls from shop and metalworking classes as well as an unequal alloca-

tion of gym money on boys and girls. For further information on this case, contact:/ Nancy Stearns, Center for Constitutional Rights, 853 Broadway, New York, N.Y. 10003.

7. *Brenden* v. *Independent School District 742*, 342 F.Supp. 1224 (D. Minn. 1972); and *Reed* v. *Nebraska School Activities Association*, 341 F.Supp. 258 (D. Neb. 1972).

8. *Buchas* v. *Illinois High School Association*, 41 LW 2277 (N.D. Ill. 1972).

9. *Hollander* v. *The Connecticut Interscholastic Athletic Conference, Inc.*, No. 12 49 27 (Conn. Sup. Ct. 1971). The case is now on appeal to the Connecticut Supreme Court.

10. *Perry* v. *Granada*, 300 F.Supp. 748 (N.D. Miss. 1969). A more recent case from the same district is *Shull* v. *Columbus Municipal School District*, 338 F.Supp. 1376 (N.D. Miss. 1972).

11. *Ordway* v. *Hargraves*, 323 F.Supp. 1155 (D. Mass. 1971).

12. *Eppard* v. *Wilkerson*, C. A. No. 201-72A (E. D. Va.).

13. *Mollere* v. *Southeastern Louisiana College*, 304 F.Supp. 826 (E.D. La. 1969).

14. The woman lost on appeal. *Robinson* v. *Board of Regents*, 475 F. 2d 707 (6th Cir. 1973).

15. *Women in 1971* (1972), pp. 19-20.

16. The Citizens' Advisory Council on the Status of Women has published a pamphlet, *Need For Studies of Sex Discrimination in Public Schools*. It is available free from the council (U.S. Department of Labor, Room 1336, Washington, D.C. 20210). The Appendix lists several surveys of sex discrimination in public schools, which might be useful to women planning lawsuits.

17. Refer to the discussion of "state action" in Chapter I.

18. 42 U.S.C. §2000c *et seq.* (1973 Supp.).

19. For copies of the regulations and of Title IX (which are not yet included in the *Code of Federal Regulations* and the *United States Code*), write to: Office of Civil Rights, HEW, 330 Independence Avenue, S.W., Washington, D.C.

20. The number of single-sex public undergraduate colleges is fairly small. It includes the following all-female

schools: Texas Women's University; Mississippi State College for Women; Longwood College (Va.); Radford College (Va.); Douglass College (N.J.); and Winthrop College (S.C.). The list of all-male public under-graduate schools is larger: Maine Maritime Academy; Massachusetts Maritime Academy; New Mexico Military Institute; State University of New York Maritime College; The Citadel Military College (S.C.); Virginia Military Institute; Air Force Institute of Technology; U.S. Air Force Academy; U.S. Coast Guard Academy; U.S. Merchant Marine Academy; U.S. Naval Academy; U.S. Naval Postgraduate School; California Maritime Academy. These male schools are exempt from Title IX coverage in two ways: they are military schools; and they have always been single-sex, public undergraduate colleges.

21. The seven-year grace period comes from a technically confusing section of the Title—Section 901(a)(2). Readers interested in full details should consult the HEW regulations when they are published and, if still confused, the HEW Office of the General Counsel. For the present purpose, it is enough to know two things. First, all the schools whose discriminatory admissions policies are prohibited—professional, graduate, vocational, and integrated public undergraduate schools—had one year from the effective date of the Title, or until July 1, 1973, to continue discriminatory admissions policies. After that, discrimination in admissions was prohibited. Second, if a woman suspects discrimination in admissions, she should always file charges of sex discrimination with HEW even if the school claims it has the seven-year grace period. The school might not qualify for the grace period because it has no Federally approved plan, because it failed to submit a plan on time (by July 1, 1973), or because it began the process of integration too long ago. Or the school might not be adhering to its own plan and thus could still violate Title IX. So when in doubt, complain to HEW.

22. Women could even contend that this practice is un-constitutional. In effect, Title IX specifically allows the Federal government to give money to schools that open-

ly discriminate. Some women might want to sue the appropriate Federal agencies to prevent them from doing so and to knock out these provisions of Title IX. One could argue that the due-process guarantee of the Fifth Amendment (which makes Equal Protection concepts applicable to the Federal government) forbids government funding of discriminatory programs, especially at *public* schools, which may already be operating themselves in violation of the Equal Protection clause.

Another method is to attack the tax-exempt status of discriminatory private schools and the tax-deductibility of gifts to these institutions. Blacks recently succeeded in such a tactic, and there is no doubt that favorable rulings would have a powerful impact on schools like Harvard and Princeton. See the discussion of *Green* v. *Connally* and *McGlotten* v. *Connally* at note 7, Chapter I.

23. For copies of these sections of the law and the HEW regulations, which will be published as 45 C.F.R. Part 83, write to: Office of Civil Rights, HEW, 330 Independence Avenue, S.W., Washington, D.C.

IV

Mass Media—Radio and Television

"The Women's Rights Movement has declared war on radio and television," a leading feminist attorney wrote recently. She explained why, in terms familiar to the many women who have been outraged by the media's treatment of women: "Television is one of the largest purveyors of prejudice and contempt toward women in this country. In program after program, it presents women as flighty, frivolous, simple-minded persons, childishly in need of masculine guidance. . . . [T]elevision characterizes women as incompetent, dependent and over-emotional, [and] . . . stereotypes their social roles."[1]

Women today can take positive action against this image; they need not simply avoid the problem by flicking off the television or radio. The law governing radio and television provides several avenues of attack that can be used to force these media to change their ways.

To understand this law, some background on local stations and Federal regulation of them is in order. The television and radio industries are made up of local stations and national networks. Although the networks produce

148

most of the nationwide programing, they sell these programs to local stations, which do the actual broadcasting. It is these local stations that are regulated by the Federal Communications Commission (FCC).

Congress created this regulatory agency in the 1930s because of the problem of competing broadcasters who jammed up the airwaves so badly that no one could hear anything. To avoid this situation, the FCC was given the authority to grant particular stations a short-term monopoly to use a defined portion of the airwaves. Since only one station could use that wave length at a time, the jamming was eliminated. The stations did not acquire ownership of the airwaves—which belonged to the public—but were given a *license* to broadcast for three years. The license is granted on condition that the station operate "in the public interest, convenience, and necessity," and it must be renewed every three years for the station to continue to operate.

From this one seemingly simple condition of operation in the public interest, the FCC has defined many rights belonging to the general public. If a station does not act in certain ways, it is considered not to be acting in the "public interest, convenience and necessity," and hence will lose its license. The public has the right to demand that each station act in these ways. What then are these rights of the public?

May a radio or TV station discriminate against its women employees or applicants?

No. Most stations are already forbidden to discriminate by the laws discussed in the chapter on employment discrimination: Title VII, the Equal Pay Act, Executive

Order 11248, as amended by E.O. 11375, as well as by some state laws. But the FCC recently came up with some regulations of its own that cover much the same ground.[2] Some people might ask why these regulations should be used in addition to the other laws. The answer is that if women can make a strong showing that a station discriminates, it can be one step in challenging a station's license—and without a license, the station is out of business. The chances of revoking a station's license are in fact small, but the mere threat is a potent weapon and could lead to improvements in station policy.

What do the FCC regulations on employment discrimination require?

The FCC regulations require stations not to discriminate and to adopt affirmative action plans to end discrimination.[3] Stations must file such plans with the commission when they apply for renewal of their license. The stations must also compile annual statistics for the FCC on the breakdown by sex and minority group of employees in every job category. Both the affirmative action plan and the statistics must be kept on file for the public to see at the local station. If you want to find out how the station is doing, ask for FCC Forms 395, 303, or 315[4] (and write to the FCC if the station refuses to show them to you). Women employees can back up their claims of discrimination with this information.

If women employees and applicants at a station suspect job discrimination, what should they do?

File a complaint of job discrimination with the FCC. Address it to:

William B. Ray, Chief
Complaints and Compliance Division
Federal Communications Commission
1919 M Street, N.W.
Washington, D.C. 20554

Send a copy to the station if you want to, but this is not required.

There is no set form to follow, but the following items are good to include: the name (call numbers) of the station; all the ways in which you believe the station discriminates (see Chapter II, "Employment Discrimination"); an analysis of the station's affirmative-action program and statistics showing how inadequate its measures are; a request for an investigation; and a demand for correction of the station's job bias. Even if the FCC fails to take action immediately, you will be building a record that the station is not operating "in the public interest, convenience, and necessity," which could lead to the loss of its license.

For maximum effectiveness, and also as a basis for an alternative remedy if the FCC doesn't take action, file charges with all the other agencies authorized to handle job discrimination.

Do women have a right to have TV and radio stations broadcast news about the feminist movement fairly?

Probably. The FCC has often told stations that they have a duty to the public to broadcast fairly, under the "fairness doctrine." By this, the commission means that a station must cover controversial and important public issues, and, in doing so, it must present both sides of an issue—not just the side in which it believes. Notice that there are two steps in reaching this result: first, the issue must be controversial and of "public importance"; second, the station must present both sides.

In the past, the FCC has forced stations to broadcast both sides of many issues, including civil rights, pollution, and cigarette smoking. The fairness doctrine has never been applied to women's issues, but feminists hope that it can be used to require stations to present both sides of news about the women's movement. For example, if a station consistently editorializes, by jokes and innuendo, against women's push for the Equal Rights Amendment, the station would have to present the other side—and in a serious light.

Could the fairness doctrine be used to force coverage of both sides of feminist issues in shows other than news programs?

In theory, yes—although the FCC has never required this. The list of possible issues of interest to women takes in a wide range of concerns—from the right to abortion to whether women should be drafted.

Feminists should particularly demand that TV and radio stations treat the issue of a woman's role in the modern world more fairly. This issue is a dominant concern of a feminist movement that seeks to broaden the roles women can play. So far, the men running television and radio stations have allowed women to be portrayed in a sharply limited set of roles: as caretakers of children (mothers, teachers), servants of men (secretaries), and sex objects.

No one knows the psychic harm done to adult women by the one-dimensional model presented so continuously on TV. Growing children, too, must suffer from its impact. Both boys and girls are taught to conform to the stiff, stereotyped sex-role lines male society has mandated. This consistent treatment of women in a distorted and one-sided manner should be a prime area to challenge.

Can women force stations to present women in more diverse roles even though the stations say they merely reflect the reality of society?

Yes, providing the FCC applies the fairness doctrine to women's issues. To give a concrete example: if less than 1 percent of the nation's judges are women, must the stations ever show women judges or talk about the positive reasons for giving women judicial appointments? The answer would be yes. The issue meets the "fairness" standard of being controversial and of public importance (feminists have challenged the virtually all-male appointments to the bench to the point where candidates for the Presidency even raise it as a campaign issue). And TV has to date presented only one side of the issue—that judges are, and by implication should be, male. According to the fairness doctrine, TV should be forced to present the opposite side. A station might be required to air an interview discussing the issue with a feminist, do a documentary on women judges now on the bench, or portray judges as women in some dramatic program.

How should women raise the fairness issue?

There are several procedures to follow. The first and easiest step is to write to the broadcasting station, protesting a particularly offensive and one-sided view of some feminist issue. Identify the program and explain that the fairness standard has been violated; state what the issue is, why you believe it is a controversial issue of public importance, and that the opposite side has not been presented; request that the other viewpoint be presented. If the station fails to take satisfactory action, you can take the next step—filing a formal, legal complaint with the FCC. To do this, send a copy of your correspondence with the station to the FCC along with a separate letter of complaint. Your complaint should include everything that was included in the original letter to the station, plus the name of the station and the date and time of the broadcast.

If the FCC is unresponsive to your complaint, you can review the fairness issue in a legal proceeding to deny the station its license renewal. This last step is the most time-consuming and costly, and it will require the help of a lawyer. It will also produce the greatest results. (For a description of proceedings to deny license renewal, see pages 157–160.) Persons without time, resources, or inclination to undertake this major effort can still make a valuable contribution by letter-writing and lodging complaints with the FCC. Even the latter tactics will help build a record of women's protest nationwide—which in time may convince the FCC that fairness on women's issues is important, as well as force it occasionally to take steps against stations that consistently violate the standard.

If a TV or radio station attacks particular women or a feminist group by name, do the women have any right to reply?

Yes, under another FCC rule called the "personal attack doctrine." Basically, this rule is another aspect of the fairness doctrine. The right to reply arises when someone attacks the "honesty, character, integrity, or like personal qualities" of a person or group during the broadcast of views on a "controversial issue of public importance." Whenever this occurs, the station is required to send the person attacked a notice of the date, time, and name of the broadcast; a transcription or summary of the attack; and an offer of reply time. Two exceptions to the personal-attack rule allow news programs (except for editorials) and candidates for public office to attack others without a right to reply. With these exceptions, this right should be fairly easy to enforce because the Supreme Court has accepted it.[5]

If the station fails to send notice of the attack and an offer of reply time, what should women do to enforce their right to reply?

Write to the station. Identify the broadcast and ask for a transcript and the right to reply. If this is unsuccessful, send a copy of the correspondence to the FCC, Complaints and Compliance Division, and ask for help.

Do stations have a duty to plan programs to meet the needs of women viewers?

The answer appears to be yes. The FCC's "community ascertainment" doctrine requires stations to ascertain the needs of all segments of the community and to plan programs to meet those needs. Although the commission has never specifically required stations to consult feminist or women's groups in order to find out their view on women's needs, experts believe the commission will do so when pushed.

The FCC has defined fourteen types of programing that stations should broadcast: opportunity for local expression; development and use of local talent; programs for children; religious programs; educational programs; public-affairs programs; editorialization by licensees; political broadcasts; agricultural programs; news programs; weather and market reports; sports programs; service to minority groups; and entertainment programs. Women could demand programing to reflect women's needs in each of these areas. For instance, a station might well insist that it broadcasts sports events sufficiently to meet the needs of the public. But the events almost never depict women athletes, so girls and women who are more interested in female sports, or who need female athletes as role models, find the sports programs inadequate. Similar reasoning applies to the other programing areas. Programs for "local expression" are likely to exclude any expression by women of their interests or limit such expression to women who conform to traditional expectations about the female role. Programs for children will often overemphasize the male child (just as children's books feature little boys more than little girls). With some imagination and thought, one could set forth other needs of women not met by current or planned programs in each of the fourteen areas of required programing.

In sum, women need programing that responds to them as full human beings, participating at every level of society—rather than the current programing, which responds solely to their needs as wives and mothers. (Just as men need far more programing for their needs as husbands and fathers!)

How can women force stations to consult them on women's needs?

The only way this right can be enforced is through a lengthy legal battle over the station's right to a renewal of its broadcasting license. The legal document which starts this battle, and which raises the right to be consulted and to have responsive programing, is called a Petition to Deny License Renewal. The Petition to Deny is just what its name implies: your group will be asking the FCC to deny the station's request that its license be renewed at the end of the three-year license period; in other words, you will be asking to have the station put out of business.

Will you need a lawyer to file a Petition to Deny?

Yes, since the legal proceedings involved in filing it are fairly complicated. The proceedings are much like a lawsuit, except that they take place before the FCC instead of a court.

Must a Petition to Deny be filed within any time limit?

Yes. The station must file its application for renewal at least four months before the license expires. (All licenses in one state expire on the same date. See Note 6 at the end of this chapter for these expiration dates.) After the station applies for renewal, you must file your petition by at least thirty days prior to the license expiration date.

Are there any groups that specialize in helping others to file Petitions to Deny?

Yes. The National Organization for Women has a Task Force on the FCC, which has advised several NOW chapters on Petitions to Deny lodged against stations in New York City; Syracuse, N.Y.; Pittsburgh; Washington,

D.C.; and Florida. For further information and help, contact:

> Whitney Adams
> NOW Task Force on the FCC
> NOW National Office
> 1957 E. 73rd Street
> Chicago, Illinois 60649

Although they do not focus on women's issues, two other important public-interest groups are concerned with broadcast licensing:

> Office of Communication
> United Church of Christ
> 289 Park Avenue South
> New York, New York 10010
> (212) 475-2121

> Citizens Communications Center
> 1816 Jefferson Place, N. W.
> Washington, D.C. 20036
> (202) 296-4238

Can the attack on a station's license renewal be used to raise other issues besides the right to be consulted on women's needs and to have programing to meet those needs?

Yes. In fact, the Petition to Deny License Renewal provides the ideal opportunity to raise all of the issues already mentioned: sex discrimination in employment; unfair coverage of feminist issues; a failure to consult with women and to program to meet all of women's needs.

If women have already raised these issues in letters to the station and complaints to the FCC, their case against license renewal will be even stronger. In fact, women who plan to file a Petition to Deny in the future should coordinate a campaign of letters and complaints for the interim period in order to strengthen the final effort.

Is the FCC apt to deny license renewal to a station?

Statistically the chances are somewhat slim, although the commission has done so in a few extreme instances. But the basic point is not loss of the license. The station does not want to be tied up in expensive legal maneuvering for years in order to have its license renewed. Thus, any group challenging license renewal will have significant leverage, and can use this power to negotiate with and gain concessions from the station on all issues of women's rights.

What role can women's groups play in a Petition to Deny License Renewal?

Although women's groups should not file a Petition to Deny without the aid of a lawyer, they have a vital role in the proceedings. Women must decide which station to challenge and must monitor its programs for documentation of fairness violations and inadequate programing. This is a mammoth task, but it is essential to the success of the petition that an exhaustive feminist analysis be undertaken of all station programs for a certain period of time. The monitoring should be directed by the lawyers on the case, but the women who monitor and analyze the programs are equal partners in the endeavor. The success of the monitoring will, in large part, determine the lawyers' success in attacking the fairness and programing issues.

For more details on how to monitor, write to Whitney
Adams, the coordinator of the NOW Task Force on the
FCC (see page 158).

Could women apply to the FCC to take away a license for themselves?

Yes, although this action would require a lot of financial
backing and detailed planning. One precedent exists, a case
in which a minority group successfully pursued this route.
An interested women's group would simply compete for
the license when the existing station applied for its license
renewal. A lawyer's help would be needed, of course.

Although competition for licenses will be difficult for
women to undertake in the short run, in the long run it
may be the only real answer to the degrading fare most
stations presently feature. Minority groups have discovered
that economic development is ultimately the way to make
sure that your views prevail. Women must learn the same
lesson.

Are there any unused channels that women might apply for?

There are not very many in major cities, but small
towns and rural areas frequently have unused channels,
both commercial and noncommercial. It would be easier
to obtain unused channels than to compete for channels
already in use and often owned by the powerful major
networks. If you are interested in this option, write the
FCC for the booklet called, *How To Apply for a Broadcast License.*

Is there any way for feminists to influence the FCC on the policy decisions it makes?

Any group or individual has the right to ask the commission to make a rule—or broad policy statement—that will set standards for the broadcasters to follow. The legal document that commences this proceeding is called, appropriately enough, a Petition for Rulemaking. The National Organization for Women has already used this procedure to great effect. When the FCC first issued regulations requiring stations to cease discriminating in employment, stations were required to take two important steps. First, they were to draw up "affirmative-action" plans showing how they intended to hire and promote more minorities and women. Second, they were to file these plans with the commission. There was, however, one important difference in the second step as far as women were concerned. The station did not have to send its plan for hiring women to the commission—only its plan for hiring minorities. Naturally this made a mockery of the whole procedure as it related to women.

NOW decided not to take this exclusion sitting down and filed a Petition for Rulemaking, which proposed that the women's plan be treated the same as the minority plan—that is, that it be filed, too. Other groups, including the ACLU, supported this position. After some deliberation, the FCC finally granted NOW's petition and changed its rule. The moral of this story is that sometimes it is not difficult to get an agency to take action—partly because the agencies are so unaccustomed to citizen action. This was a relatively simple legal proceeding and did not cost much money to initiate, but it laid the groundwork for effective action: every time a station files for a renewal of its license, the FCC is now supposed to examine the station's employment program for women.

NOTES

1. Nancy E. Stanley, "Federal Communications Law and Women's Rights: Women in The Wasteland Fight Back," 23 *Hastings Law Journal* 15, 16 (1971).
2. 45 C.F.R. Part 73.
3. Chapter II, "Employment Discrimination," contains details on the definition of an affirmative action program.
4. Form 395 is the one containing the statistics. Form 303 is the station's application for license renewal, and Form 315 is its application for transfer; the affirmative-action plan is contained in section 6 of the last two forms.
5. *Red Lion Broadcasting Company v. F.C.C.*, 395 U.S. 367 (1969).
6. State license expiration dates (add three years to any date to find the next time the licenses expire in these states):

April 1, 1973—Alabama, Georgia.
June 1, 1973—Arkansas, Louisiana, Mississippi.
August 1, 1973—Indiana, Kentucky, Tennessee.
October 1, 1973—Michigan, Ohio.
December 1, 1973—Illinois, Wisconsin.
February 1, 1974—Iowa, Missouri.
April 1, 1974—Colorado, Minnesota, Montana, North Dakota, South Dakota.
June 1, 1974—Kansas, Nebraska, Oklahoma.
August 1, 1974—Texas.
October 1, 1974—Arizona, Idaho, Nevada, New Mexico, Utah, Wyoming.
December 1, 1974—California.
February 1, 1975—Alaska, Guam, Hawaii, Oregon, Washington.
April 1, 1975—Connecticut, Maine, Massachusetts, New Hampshire, Rhode Island, Vermont.
June 1, 1975—New Jersey, New York.

August 1, 1975—Delaware, Pennsylvania.
October 1, 1975—Washington, D.C., Maryland, Virginia, West Virginia.
December 1, 1975—North Carolina, South Carolina.
February 1, 1976—Florida, Puerto Rico, Virgin Islands.

V

Crimes and Juvenile Delinquency

When a woman law student asked her male law professor for leads on studying women convicted of committing crimes, his reaction was: "Women criminals? There aren't any!" He was wrong, of course. Many women and girls are convicted of committing crimes and juvenile offenses. And the laws defining these crimes and offenses, as well as the men who enforce the laws, are often biased against women. To correct these biases, we must analyze the laws, the sentences given women, and the treatment of women once they are convicted.

Criminal law itself cannot be discussed in terms of "women's rights." The brutal fact is that convicted women by and large have not yet won the right to equal treatment in the criminal and juvenile justice system. As the professor's remark indicated, this is because convicted women have been largely ignored—by the law schools, the courts, the lawyers, and the public. The first step toward fair treatment is understanding their condition.

A. Sentencing

Is a law allowing women to be given longer sentences than men for the same crime constitutional?

No. One right convicted women do have is the right to equal sentences. So far, laws providing for unequal sentences have been attacked in Connecticut, Pennsylvania, and New Jersey. Courts have struck down these laws on the ground that they violated the Fourteenth Amendment guarantee of Equal Protection.[1] In Connecticut and Pennsylvania, the courts released women who had already served sentences longer than the maximum a man could serve.

Differential sentencing laws offer a valuable lesson of the danger to women of laws that purport to accord them "favored" treatment. Most laws defining a particular crime also prescribe the maximum sentence for that crime. However, in the Connecticut and Pennsylvania cases, the women concerned were each sentenced under a law applicable to women only—one providing for what is termed indeterminate sentencing. This law provides, for example, that if a *woman* is convicted of any crime having a maximum sentence of less than three years, she must be given an indeterminate sentence of a full three years. Notice that if the crime is punishable by less than three years— say one and one half years—the maximum time she may have to serve is greater than the maximum time she would get without indeterminate sentencing. Since the indeterminate sentencing law applies only to a woman, her sentence is potentially longer than the time any *man* could serve for the same violation.

It was originally thought that indeterminate sentencing

was a progressive measure, beneficial to women. People believed that it placed more emphasis on a prisoner's behavior and that a woman, if she were a model prisoner, could get out on parole after a brief period. This procedure contrasted with the usual practice of setting both a *minimum* sentence, which a prisoner must serve before getting out, and a *maximum*. In practice, however, the parole boards that determined when a prisoner could leave for good behavior were more prone to let people stay the *maximum* time than to let them out earlier; hence, most women in states with indeterminate sentencing for women only ended up serving longer sentences than men.

Many states have indeterminate-sentencing laws for prisoners of both sexes and in these states, whatever other problems may exist with this form of sentence, sex discrimination is not an issue. However, wherever there is a special, "good" law for women, they end up in a worse position than men.[2] The moral is clear: never work for laws that apply only to women; support laws that apply equally to men and women in order to prevent later abuse of women under the guise of "beneficial" single-sex laws.

How many states have laws that permit longer sentences for women?

No one has yet made a careful study to find the answer. Experts believe, however, that a close study of the laws and their operation would reveal a high incidence of different sentencing laws and practices for men and women. Such laws are not always readily ascertainable. Some states have obscure provisions. For instance, Maine has indeterminate sentencing for both men and women. The catch is that men can be sentenced under this law only up to age twenty-six; women are subject to it up to age forty. Women aged twenty-six to forty should challenge their sentences under these laws as unconstitutional.[3]

Do any states give men longer sentences than women?
Yes, and one court has upheld this practice. A man who escaped from a Maine prison farm was sentenced to from six to twelve years, although the maximum penalty for a woman convicted of escaping from a woman's reformatory in Maine is eleven months. The Maine court upheld the difference, using stereotypical views of men and women to find that different treatment was reasonable, and the Supreme Court refused to review the case.[4]

In addition, one study suggests that courts may treat adult male criminals more harshly than adult female criminals.[5] In grand larceny and felonious assault cases during 1962, there were statistically significant differences between the treatment of men and women: a smaller percentage of men were released on bail; had their cases dismissed or were acquitted; or received suspended sentences or probation when convicted. The study has limited value, however, since there was no attempt to control for the severity of the crime. It is possible that women received less harsh treatment because they in fact stole property of less value or committed less violent assaults than did men on the average. Certainly this would accord with the social conditioning most women receive.

The study raises enough questions to merit further studies, scientifically controlled for the severity of the crime, to find out whether the enforcement of criminal laws is even-handed for men and women. If the studies showed unequal enforcement, they would reveal serious

Equal Protection issues that should be included in the defense of male defendants affected by such enforcement patterns.

B. Juvenile Delinquency

Do girl juvenile delinquents ever get longer sentences than boys?

Yes. This happens in two ways. National statistics show that girls serve longer sentences on the average than do boys, even though girls are sentenced for less serious matters.[6] This situation does not seem to arise from any laws but rather from the informal practices of courts and correction authorities, who apparently are more shocked by girls who misbehave than by boys; thus they see to it that girls serve longer sentences as a more severe punishment.

Many states, moreover, have passed juvenile-delinquency laws that make girls liable under them at a later age than boys. For example, a juvenile-delinquency law forbidding running away from home may apply to girls up to eighteen years old, but to boys only up to sixteen years. Here a seventeen- or eighteen-year-old girl is subject to punishment for conduct that is not punished at all in a boy of that age. Sometimes the discrimination under these laws runs in the opposite direction, as when the juvenile-delinquency law covers behavior that would be criminal if done by an adult. In this instance, a juvenile will receive more favorable treatment under the juvenile-delinquency law than under the adult criminal law; hence, the sixteen to eighteen age differential works in favor of the girl. But where the juvenile delinquency offense is something like

running away from home, there is no criminal penalty for
adults and the age differential thus favors boys.

**Do longer sentences for female juvenile delinquents
also violate the Equal Protection clause?**[7]

One of the courts that struck down longer sentences
for adult women later faced the same question for minors.
Connecticut law allowed girls under twenty-one to be
sentenced for three years, but boys under twenty-one
(convicted for the same offense) for only two years. The
judge said this was illegal and ordered the release of Ada
Sumrell, who had already served *more* than two years—
the maximum for a boy—for "breach of the peace."[8] In
another case, a court struck down a New York juvenile-
delinquency statute that punished girls for being "persons
in need of supervision" until age eighteen, but boys only
until sixteen. The "PINS" law did not prohibit any crimes
and thus discriminated against girls.[9] Similarly, although
a state court upheld an Oklahoma juvenile-delinquency law
that operated to discriminate against boys, saying that the
law was based on the "demonstrated facts of life," a
Federal court later found the law unconstitutional.[10]

No one has yet challenged the practices of those judges
and social workers who give longer sentences to girls than
to boys—not because a statute requires them to, but because of their biases. This is a widespread problem, and
lawyers should begin challenging the practice. They will
have to develop evidence to document the charge that
girls get longer sentences than boys, which may involve
looking into the statistical pattern of the sentencing decisions of selected judges and comparing girls' to boys'
sentences, over a period of time, for particular offenses.

This would be a good project for women's organizations
to undertake under the direction of a feminist lawyer.

May girls be convicted under juvenile-delinquency laws for acts for which boys are not punished?

Yes, in many jurisdictions. Sometimes it is blatantly
written into the law. For instance, Connecticut makes it a
crime to be an unmarried girl between sixteen and twenty-
one who is in "manifest danger of falling into habits of
vice." No boy can be convicted of this.[11]

Far more often the practice is simply a result of the
attitudes of social workers and judges. If girls run away
from home, disobey their parents, have a child without
marrying, or are promiscuous, they are branded as juvenile
delinquents. Boys engaged in the same conduct are seldom
even referred to juvenile court.

A major attack on these unjust practices should be
launched. This means educating girls to demand that their
lawyers raise the defense that boys are not punished for
these acts, and it means educating lawyers to raise that
defense. It also means working for new laws sharply
defining which acts constitute juvenile delinquency and
stipulating that the same standards must be applied to boys
and to girls. Finally, it means watching to see that new
standards are in fact enforced equally against girls and
boys.

This campaign should not be too difficult in the long
run. If judges are shocked when they learn girls receive
longer sentences than boys for the very same offense, they
will be even more shocked when they learn girls are
punished for some things boys are not punished for at all.

C. Prison Conditions

May a convicted woman be sent to a more restrictive institution than a man guilty of the same crime?

Probably not. One court has dealt with this practice and found it unconstitutional.[12] A woman sent to a state penitentiary wanted to go to the county jail, where men were sent for less serious crimes like hers. She did not want to be sent to the penitentiary where "confirmed, hardened criminals convicted of more serious crimes" were sent. She eventually won the right to the county jail sentence. Ironically, this particular problem arises out of the fact that there are so few women criminals; consequently, there are very few criminal institutions for women, and a whole range of women—from those awaiting trial to those who are hardened criminals—tend to be thrown together in one setting.

Must women prisoners be given facilities, training, and education equal to those given men?

The case mentioned in the preceding answer would seem to indicate that the answer is yes, but so far no one has won the right to equal benefits while in prison.[13] It is an important right to establish because the training and education now offered women prisoners are clearly designed to funnel them into the most low-paying jobs of our society: waitress, household worker, beautician, housewife—the classic "female" jobs. While the training at men's prisons is far from adequate, it at least offers somewhat better options. Men at some institutions can train, for instance, to be a gourmet chef or an auto mechanic—both well-paying jobs.

Training is not the only area in which women's institutions are deficient. On the surface, women's prisons are gentler and less violent places than men's prisons. It does not follow that they are better-equipped or better-staffed. Indeed, the conditions in women's prisons are usually ignored. For example, no one has yet compared the budget per prisoner in male and female prisons, even now, however, it is obvious that women lack libraries (especially law libraries) and sports and recreation facilities. Nor do women receive adequate medical and psychiatric care or individual counseling. In all these areas, lawyers should seek to bring to women prisoners the same facilities and opportunities men have. On the other hand, if women's prisons have more physical comforts and less rigid social control than men's prisons, the effort ought to be to bring the men up to par.

It is important to remember that the training facilities and care available in men's prisons are often in a deplorable state. We are not talking about unequal protection of the laws in the classic sense that men get good treatment and women bad treatment. The major reason that women should focus on the treatment of *women* prisoners is not that they receive unequal treatment. It is simply that no one else is interested in women prisoners, and their situation is usually at least as bad as, if not worse than, the situation of male prisoners.

(The effort to achieve better treatment for women prisoners should not blind us to a central fact. Most women now in prison are confined for sex-related offenses, such as prostitution, and should not be in prison at all—and if they were men, they would not be there for such offenses. So although prison-reform efforts must be made, the major thrust should be to get these women out of prison. This coincides with the broader current movement to decriminalize many activities and to eliminate prisons for nonviolent criminals.)

What can women's groups do about unequal treatment in prisons?

One of the most severe problems faced by women prisoners is isolation. No one is interested in them; no one offers to help; no one communicates. An immediate way to alleviate this condition is simply to establish contact.

In Washington, D.C., Ann Horwitz started a Visitors' Services Center at the suggestion of chaplains working in D.C. jails. People working for the center make regular visits to the prisons, help arrange transportation and baby-sitting so that families can visit the prisoners, bring reading materials and make telephone calls for the prisoners, and help provide community contact when the prisoner comes out of jail. Even more important, the center helps straighten out courtroom mixups. The center provides an invaluable service in itself, and people working there will also learn in more detail about the basic problems and needs of women's institutions. Those interested in starting such a project should contact:

Ann Horwitz
Visitors' Services Center for D.C. Jails
261 17th Street, S.E.
Washington, D.C. 20003
(202) 544-2131

It may even be possible to get Federal funding for such a project, as the Visitors' Services Center did. The Law Enforcement Assistance Administration, a Federally funded granting agency, along with private foundations and church groups, funded this project.

A second project would be to study and compare the conditions in jails, prisons, and other institutions to see how men and women, and girls and boys, are treated. This could be done under the direction of feminist lawyers and could lead to a campaign for legislative change. Where the differences between men's and women's treatment are blatant, the study might lead to a lawsuit. Feminists should be careful, though, to avoid the old pitfall of establishing different standards for men and women. Such standards can be the basis for later mistreatment of women, even unintentional mistreatment. Examples include recent concern about the sex life of male criminals and about the relationship of female criminals to their children. There has been discussion of ways to allow the men—but not the women—some heterosexual relations while in jail. This is fine, but women have sexual needs, too, and they should be equally protected. Similarly, some attention has focused on practices that deprive women prisoners of their children; no attention is paid to men, presumably on the ground that they are not interested. If methods can be established to allow a woman to keep her children, and even to see them while she is still institutionalized, the same effort should be made for men. Otherwise we are back in the old bag of setting up societal pressures that force women to care for children and teach men that they should not.

A closely related problem is that of pregnancy. Here, obviously, women have unique problems: the availability of abortions for those who do not want to give birth; the quality of health care for those who do. The indications are that practices in institutions will have to be corrected on both scores.

A third project feminists might undertake is to teach women prisoners and juvenile delinquents their legal rights. The absence of the "jailhouse lawyer" among women prisoners is conspicuous, and it is a problem that might easily be rectified. Students in a course on "Women and the Law" might assist in such efforts. Women students at Rutgers Law School in New Jersey have engaged in a project of this kind, under the direction of women lawyers. They have taught women prisoners in the Correctional Facility for Women at Clinton, New Jersey; the course covers the rights of criminal defendants and prisoners and also focuses on such issues as indeterminate sentencing and the treatment of women in women's prisons. The students report that the women prisoners are enthusiastic about the course. Similar projects are under way in Boston (The Boston Women's Law Collective does work at Framingham, Massachusetts), Philadelphia (led by Villanova students), and New York (Michele Herman supervises work at the women's prison in Bedford, New York).

For further information, contact the supervisor of the Rutgers seminar:

Rhonda Schoenbrod
Center for Constitutional Rights
853 Broadway
New York, New York 10003
(212) 674-3303

Is it legal to maintain separate prisons for women and men?

At the moment, it seems reasonably clear that no court would ever find separate prisons illegal because they violate the Equal Protection clause. If the Equal Rights Amendment passes, however, separate prisons will most certainly be illegal (except for a separation of sleeping and bathing facilities, in the interest of privacy). Ultimately, passage of the Equal Rights Amendment will probably be the fastest way both to improve the facilities and training for convicted women and, hopefully, to improve the hard-nosed attitudes toward, and social rigidity of, men's prisons.

D. Prostitution and Other Sex Offenses

Do men and women have the same legal right to engage in sexual activity?

Emphatically not—and the denial of women's rights in this area is particularly severe since she is often sent to prison or centers for juvenile delinquents if she attempts to assert her rights. This, after all, is the meaning of laws that make prostitution and solicitation a crime and that brand as juvenile delinquents young girls who are promiscuous or who become pregnant out of wedlock. Although it seems obvious that the central focus of all these laws is to punish *sexual activity*, that focus has been obscured by the technical definition of prostitution. Thus many women have not sensed as clearly as they should the

essential injustice of sending the female prostitute to prison but allowing the male customer to go free.

Of course, it is not just the laws that mandate this
result. Unequal enforcement, which results from the fact
that most officials who administer the criminal system
are male, also has its effects. Male district attorneys do
not prosecute men for "patronizing a prostitute" (often
a crime, though defined as less serious than prostitution)
or for "aiding and abetting" (always a crime) a woman
to commit prostitution. Nor are judges likely to find men
guilty under such statutes. In fact, one of the few times
this was ever attempted, the public uproar was immediate
and powerful. In the summer of 1970, the Washington,
D.C., police instituted an aggressive program of arresting
male suburban customers—but the male outcry brought
the program to a halt in four weeks. Even then the purpose of the campaign was revealing. The police basically
wanted to protect men against "dangerous" ghetto prostitutes and get the men to go to other, "safer" spots. There
was not the slightest hint that the campaign was intended
to equalize enforcement of the laws.

In response to the argument that these laws and attitudes
show a sexist bias against women, some people reply that
male homosexuals are also actively prosecuted for solicitation. If males are prosecuted, it is thought, the law must
not be biased. This response is inadequate, however, because the only males punished are those considered "deviant" by the male establishment. In fact, neither women
nor "deviant" men should be punished for solicitation that
leads to sex between consenting adults—just as "normal"
men are never punished for such activity.[14]

Is there any way to establish an equal right to sexual activity?

Yes, but the solutions are long-term ones. First, push for legislative repeal of the laws that make women's participation in sex illegal, that is, all prostitution, solicitation, and juvenile delinquency laws used to punish females, but not males, for sexual activity.

Second, litigation strategy warrants attention. Lawyers for women prosecuted under these laws could try to establish that the laws violate the Equal Protection clause. It will be a difficult issue to win, so firm is the conviction that the act of receiving money, rather than giving money for sex makes a difference. Lawyers could also argue that the laws are invalid because they violate the constitutional rights to privacy, to freedom of expression, and to freedom of association, and they are unconstitutionally vague and overbroad. One judge recently accepted all these arguments in a landmark decision invalidating the District of Columbia's solicitation laws, which had been used solely to prosecute women prostitutes. The case is *United States* v. *Moses.*[15]

It may be easier to win the right to sexual activity for juvenile girls than for adult women, since most of the laws girls are sentenced under theoretically apply equally to boys. If the lawyers can prove that more girls than boys are punished under these laws, then it will be clear that the law is being enforced unequally, which should be a violation of the Equal Protection clause.

A third strategy for establishing an equal right to sexual activity for both girls and women might be to push for enforcement of aiding and abetting and "patronizing a prostitute" laws against men. A really firm campaign to do this—instead of challenging enforcement of the laws directed against women—would probably enrage men so much that they might even join in the effort to get rid of the laws altogether.

If the laws against prostitution and solicitation were repealed or struck down, would any problems remain?

Perhaps. Men who talk about legalizing prostitution often want to set up special centers for prostitutes and certify them medically safe for the customer. In other words, there is still a strong urge, among those who oppose the laws, to impose restrictive conditions on women prostitutes but not on men customers. In fact, it is rarely the women professionals who spread VD. (The *Moses* decision cites several sources that point this out.) Here, as elsewhere, the guiding principle should be to seek equal treatment. If a woman must have periodic health examinations to protect the men from VD, then the male customers should also be screened for VD in order to protect the women. If the male customer is exempted, then so too should the woman professional.

E. The Crime of Rape

Does the law protect women against rape?

Theoretically, yes; in reality, very little. The reasons stem from a complex of mutually contradictory male ideologies about women, which have been enshrined in the law of rape. Ideology number one is that women are vindictive and/or psychopathic creatures who frequently turn in an innocent sex partner to the police as a rapist out of spite or revenge. A prominent legal authority on rules of evidence asserts, for instance:

> Modern psychiatrists have amply studied the behavior of errant young girls and women coming before the courts in all sorts of cases. Their psychic complexes are multifarious, distorted partly by inherent defects, partly by diseased derangements or abnormal instincts, partly by bad social environment, partly by temporary physiological or emotional conditions. One form taken by these complexes is that of contriving false charges of sexual offences by men.[16]

Ideology number two is that most women want to be raped, and ask for it by wearing sexually suggestive clothing and by walking around in strange places instead of staying home. This helps account for the popularity of the suggestion, frequently advanced when a rash of rapes occurs, that a curfew ought to be imposed—but on the female victims rather than the male aggressors!

Ideology number three is that only a "pure" woman can be raped; if she has ever indulged in sex before, particularly with the accused rapist, she could not possibly have been raped. If she doesn't drink or smoke, this will strongly support her story.

Ideology number four is that woman are chaste, delicate creatures, belonging to particular men, and that rape is thus a particularly heinous crime since it involves a violation of both the woman's unique purity and the man's property rights. In Bangladesh, for instance, husbands refused en masse, out of a sense of outraged male ownership, to remain with wives who had been raped by the invading Pakistanis.

These ideologies form the basis for several legal doctrines that have the net effect of making it extraordinarily difficult to convict a man of rape, but that subject the woman victim to humiliating treatment by the police and the courts. All kinds of special evidence rules, unique to the crime of rape, are set up in order to protect the accused male against women's vindictive spirit. These rules reflect two basic assumptions about women and rape: that "the woman will usually lie," and that "the woman really consented, so it wasn't rape."

"The woman will usually lie."

The most important manifestation of this assumption comes with the requirement that various aspects of the crime—unlike any other crime—be corroborated by evidence other than the victim's testimony, since it is presumed that the woman victim will lie. The word of the victim is not enough, as it is in other crimes. Thus in many states, to convict a man the prosecutor must prove through evidence independent of the woman's testimony that she was penetrated, that force was used, and/or that the man accused was the actual person who did it. In some cases, these things are difficult, if not impossible, to prove. Many women's first step after being raped will be to douche themselves, thus destroying the sperm which is the proof of penetration. In addition, many rapists are ejaculatory impotents and do not deposit sperm in the woman's vagina even when there is penetration. Proof of penetration, in these cases, is never possible. Proving force is even more difficult. A woman victim can point to her bruises to show that force was used, but many men, including judges, believe that women enjoy a little violence as part of normal sex—and thus refuse to consider bruises as evidence of sex without consent. Finally, corroborating the identity of the assailant is a third difficult problem. This rule practically requires that a third-party eyewitness be present at the rape—and that, of course, is quite rare. Such strict standards of corroboration make a conviction for the crime of rape almost impossible. The statistics for New York City show the depth of the problem: in 1971, out of 1085 arrests for rape, the state secured only eighteen convictions.

The belief that the woman will lie leads to other legal doctrines besides corroboration. A woman's failure to go to the police promptly can be used to attack her credibility on the witness stand. So deep is this distrust of women that in some states the court can allow the defendant's lawyer to have the *victim* subjected to psychiatric examination and present the results to the jury. Victims of other crimes are not normally subjected to such treatment.

"She really consented so it wasn't rape."

The second element of protection for the accused male lies in inferences the law permits in determining whether the woman was a willing partner. A woman's prior lack of virginity or her reputation for unchastity can be used by the accused rapist's lawyer as evidence to cast doubt on her claim that she did not consent. Her prior consent to intercourse with the accused male also can be used in the same way to disprove a rape. In practical effect, this can amount to licensing any man who has once slept with a woman to rape her in the future with impunity. And finally, some states require that the woman must have resisted before the state will say she did not consent to the act. This is absurd in a day when most women are told by the police themselves—and have ample reason to believe—that it is best not to resist in order to save one's life.

In conclusion, it must be said that some of these defenses have probably been created because the penalties for rape are often unreasonably high. Rape has been equated with murder in terms of the sentences imposed; understandably, this harshness contributes to an extreme reluctance to find a man guilty.

What is the practical effect of these evidence rules for the rape victim?

The rules discussed above are not mere abstract injustices. Because these rules exist, both the police and lawyers will ask the woman probing and humiliating questions about her past sex life, whether she ever slept with the accused, what kind of clothes she was wearing, what she was doing in that part of town anyway, and on and on. If the woman decides to go to court to testify against the rapist, much of this questioning will take place on the witness stand, often with much publicity. The best tactic the accused man's lawyer can use is to throw doubt on the woman's every word. He will do everything he can to make her appear promiscuous or vindictive or hostile toward men, or perhaps even sexually disturbed. What would a nice girl be doing at that time of day, in that part of town, with that clothing on? This will be the implication behind

every question. And while it is theoretically the duty of
the prosecuting lawyer to object to those questions, most
of the prosecuting lawyers are men, who may secretly
believe in the implications behind the questions and therefore not object to improper questioning. The net result
will be that the rapist goes free, the woman suffers unnecessary humiliation, and other women learn the lesson:
don't bother to report a rape or attempted assault to the
police, because neither the police nor the courts will help
you.

**What can be done to make the laws more effective in
protecting women against rape?**

All special rules applied solely in rape trials must be
done away with. This means doing away with the assumption that women will lie: there should be no special corroboration requirements, no inferences drawn from the
fact that a woman didn't go to the police right away, and
no suggestion that the victim be psychoanalyzed.[17] Reform also requires a realistic notion of consent: there should
be no requirement that a woman resist, and no inference
drawn because she has slept with other men or even, in
the past, with the rapist himself.

The requirement that a woman be penetrated should also
be abolished. Whether or not a man merely touches his
genitals to an unwilling woman or penetrates her makes no
difference in terms of the intended humiliation and invasion of her privacy that lie at the core of the crime of
rape. And the requirement of penetration leads to degrading and meaningless searches for sperm—meaningless if the
man is an ejaculatory impotent or if the victim douches
before she goes to the police.

By itself, abolishing these rules will do much to eliminate the unjust treatment a woman now receives when she is raped. Today, the woman victim is subjected to intense humiliation from the salacious inquiries the police sometimes indulge in to the outrageous cross-examination the woman is often subjected to when she testifies about the crime in court. If the special evidence rules were abolished, these humilating questions would no longer be relevant and therefore should no longer be asked.

How do women go about changing these rules?

The first effort should take place in actual trials, where lawyers can ask the court to change judge-made rules. Feminist groups should contact prosecutors to try to convince them to raise these issues. Women victims should try to retain their own lawyers to represent them while they are testifying, and these lawyers should also challenge special rules applied solely to rape. If change cannot be achieved through the courts, a drive should be launched in the state legislatures to abolish special rules for rape.

Women should also seek new laws setting lower penalties for rape, penalties parallel to those imposed for aggravated assault, for instance. Although it sounds anomalous to urge lower sentences, actually this should help to assure more convictions. Experts are convinced that one reason the special evidence rules have been created, and so few convictions obtained, is the legitimate reluctance to give a man a life sentence or the death penalty for the act of rape. If the penalties are lowered to a more realistic level, the emotional climate in favor of the accused will be reduced.

Can any practical measures be adopted to help the rape victim?

There are several practical steps women can take to avoid some of the humiliating treatment they now receive from the time they first report the crime to the police to the time they testify in court. Until these measures are undertaken, women will remain victims—victims of the police, the lawyers, and the judges.

First, when you report the crime, take a strong friend along—possibly one who is a lawyer or law student. You want someone who is cool, calm, sure of herself, and will stand up for your rights at a time when you may be least able to do so. The role of the friend will be to help you assert your rights and to protect you against salacious questioning (such as forcing you to repeat all the details of the rape over and over to inordinately curious male police officers).

Second, refuse to answer questions about your past sex life. This is no one's business, and it is irrelevant to whether or not you have been raped. Even if the police insist that your sexual experience is relevant because of the special evidence rules, reply that you will be challenging those rules and will not answer. Go to the inquiring officers' superiors, if necessary.

Third, take a friend with you when the police send you to a doctor or hospital. The friend will help you object to improper treatment. One of the most frequent complaints rape victims make concerns the rude, abrupt, and hostile medical examinations they are given by police doctors. Such doctors often refuse to treat the victim but merely examine her to make sure that she has been raped.

You should also go to your own doctor for treatment afterward, including getting an antipregnancy pill.

An important service that women's groups could perform in this area would be to meet with the police medical authorities to explain the problems with present procedures and attitudes in order to get considerate treatment for rape victims. Another service would be to set up a panel of doctors (and especially women doctors) who would be willing to give post-rape treatment in cases where police medical treatment is inadequate and women do not have family doctors they can go to immediately. The women's groups could publicize a phone number for rape victims; women who called would be given the name of a doctor who would see them. A number of trained women could also be on hand to accompany any victim when she made her report to the police; their services could be offered at the same time the woman calls in for a doctor's name. Women's groups would thus develop relationships with sympathetic doctors and gain firsthand knowledge of the kinds of abuse most prevalent at police stations. Experience in developing a service of the kind suggested could provide ammunition for later organizational efforts to make the police change their practices.

Fourth, discuss with the prosecutor the evidence he will be using at the trial and the kinds of questions you will be asked, both by him and by the lawyer for the accused rapist. If the questions are humiliating or unnecessary, explain to him why and request that the questions not be asked or that he object to such questions by the defendant's lawyer. Go over his head, if necessary.

Fifth, try to get your own lawyer for the actual trial. You want someone who will object if improper questions, based on the special evidence rules, are asked of you by the defendant's lawyer. Of course, you will have to answer if the court orders you to do so—that is, if your lawyer has been unsuccessful in getting the court to rule that the particular questions are unnecessary.

Theoretically the prosecutor should raise objections, but he often will not, and the result can be humiliating if you don't have a lawyer whose special role is to protect your interests. Your lawyer, in fact, should explain to the judge that he or she is there to protect your reputation. Your lawyer should also discuss with you in advance the kinds of evidence that will be used at the trial so that you understand what will happen once you are in the courtroom.

Sixth, women's groups should meet with the police and prosecuting attorneys to explain what women find objectionable about present procedures, and they should seek institutional change in these procedures. The Washington, D.C., NOW group is doing just that. Contact: Carol Burris, 1345 G Street, S.E., Washington, D.C. 20003 ([202] 547-0082) for suggestions.

Seventh, use the employment-discrimination laws to get more women into the police forces, the district attorney's office, and on the bench. A major part of the problem is that the rape victim faces an essentially all-male system from the moment she reports the crime to the day of the trial. Men in our society frequently believe that all women have secret fantasies of being raped; there is seldom a discussion of male fantasies of raping women. Men with such beliefs or fantasies cannot help but be biased against the woman rape victim.

Change in this area will not be accomplished easily. Women will be dealing with very conservative forces. Policemen, lawyers, and judges are accustomed to handling rape cases in one way. They will not welcome reports from women that they themselves are mistreating rape victims, and that reforms are necessary to correct that mistreatment. Nevertheless, if women organize, they should be able to effect change in this area as in others.

NOTES

1. *Robinson* v. *York*, 281 F.Supp. 8 (D. Conn. 1968); *Commonwealth* v. *Daniel*, 430 Pa. 642, 243 A.2d 400 (1968); *State* v. *Chambers*, 13 Cr.L. 2330 (N.J. Sup. Ct. June 26, 1973).

2. For a parallel situation, see the discussion of state labor laws that regulate women's employment in the chapter on "Employment Discrimination," pp. 42-45.

3. Another important lesson to draw from indeterminate sentencing is that, at this stage in society's development, it does not help women—or anyone—to do away with the strict standards that lawyers refer to as "procedural due process." Indeterminate sentencing has been part of a broad social reform movement, which thought that giving discretion to parole boards and social workers would be beneficial to both women and children. We have come to see the disastrous consequences this approach has for children, and concerned people are working to reinstate strict standards for the treatment of juvenile offenses. The consequences are equally disastrous for adults, and we must also work to reverse the unbridled discretion given parole boards over convicted women—and men—under indeterminate-sentencing laws.

4. *Wark* v. *State*, 266 A.2d 62 (1970), *cert. denied*, 400 U.S. 952 (1970).

5. Nagel & Weitzman, "Women as Litigants," 23 *Hastings Law Journal* 171 (1971).

6. W. Lunden, *Statistics on Delinquents and Delinquency* (1964), pp. 258, 259; U.S. Children's Bureau, *Statistics on Public Institutions for Delinquent Children—1964* (1964), p. 1; President's Commission on Law Enforcement, *The Challenge of Crime in a Free Society* (1967),

p. 56; all cited in S. Gold, "Equal Protection for Juvenile Girls in Need of Supervision," 17 *N.Y. Law Forum* 570, 582-584 (1971). Of course, individual judges may favor girls over boys rather than vice versa. On a nationwide basis, however, girls are serving longer sentences than boys, on the average, even though the majority of girls are confined for running away from home, sexual activity, or having a child without being married; while the majority of boys are confined for serious offenses, such as larceny and breaking and entering.

7. See generally S. Gold, n. 6, *supra*.
8. *Sumrell* v. *York*, 288 F.Supp. 955 (D. Conn. 1968).
9. *A.* v. *City of New York*, 31 N.Y. 2d 83, 335 N.Y.S. 2d 33 (1972).
10. *Lamb* v. *State*, 475 P.2d 829, 830 (Okla. 1970); *Lamb* v. *Brown*, 456 F.2d 18 (10th Cir. 1972).
11. On the other hand, in Massachusetts it is a crime to cause the conception of an out-of-wedlock child, although this law is probably never enforced.
12. *Commonwealth* v. *Stauffer*, 214 Pa. Super. 113, 251 A.2d 718 (1969).
13. Lawyers in Washington, D.C., have filed a lawsuit to establish better conditions at the Women's Detention Center. Some of their arguments focus on Equal Protection violations (there are youth facilities for boys, but not for girls; male prisoners can have contact with their visitors, but female prisoners are sealed off by a glass partition). On most issues, however, the lawyers will not settle for the standard prevalent at the men's prison. For further information, write about *Garnes* v. *Taylor*, C.A. No. 159-72 (*complaint filed* Jan. 1972, D. D.C.), to: Al Bronstein, National Prison Project, 1424 16th Street, N.W., Suite 404, Washington, D.C., (202) 234-9345.
14. Some people contend that solicitation by either men or women constitutes an offensive invasion of privacy. However, punishing such conduct runs into difficult issues of freedom of speech and association under the First Amendment. Even if there were no First Amendment problems with punishing solicitation, a serious

Equal Protection problem would remain. Those people who fear invasion of privacy and would like to punish solicitation seldom discuss seriously the need to punish the "normal" male solicitation, which thousands of women encounter every day on the street. It seems obvious that elementary Equal Protection theory cannot sanction punishing the female and the "deviant" male for actions undertaken by "normal" males without the remotest fear of punishment.

15. *United States* v. *Moses,* Crim. Nos. 17778-72, 21346-72 (D.C. Super.Ct., Nov. 3, 1972). This is an exceptionally well-written and thorough opinion, based in large part on the work of two law students, and it should be read by all people interested in this issue.

16. Wigmore, 3A *Evidence* §924a at 736 (1970).

17. It is of course true that there may be rape cases where women complainants do not tell the truth, just as there are robbery cases where complainants do not tell the truth. However, the credibility of the witness in rape cases can be tested in the same way as in other cases. There is no need for a special presumption that rape victims will lie. In one particularly shocking case, where the court reversed a rape conviction even though the victim had identified both the man's ring and his car, a dissenting judge pointed out: "Our system of jurisprudence relies on a jury to distinguish truth from falsehood, after hearing evidence and giving due weight to the requirement that one must be considered innocent until proven guilty beyond a reasonable doubt. Since these safeguards suffice for murder, robbery or burglary cases, there is no cogent reason why they should fail when the crime charged is a sex offense." *People* v. *Linzey,* 31 N.Y. 2d 99, 335 N.Y.S. 2d 45, 52 (1972).

VI

A Woman's Right to Control Her Body

No book on women's rights would be complete without a discussion of abortion, birth control, and sterilization.[1] Abortion, particularly, is one area where enormous changes have occurred in the last five years alone. In the late 1960s many states passed new laws increasing the grounds for abortion or making abortion available on request. Courts, both Federal and state, struck down restrictive laws. And in early 1973, the Supreme Court invalidated the abortion laws of most states. The net result is that many women in the United States can now get an abortion with relative ease. But important issues remain to be resolved before all women will have the access to abortion, birth control, and sterilization that is needed in order to control their own bodies. This chapter will discuss some of these issues.

What kinds of state laws have been used to regulate a woman's right to have an abortion?

There are four basic kinds of state laws. The first is

extremely restrictive, and allows abortion only when necessary to preserve the life of the mother. The second is only slightly less restrictive; it permits abortions to preserve both the life and health of the mother. The third type of statute was pushed by reform forces in the mid-1960s and is called an American Law Institute (ALI) statute. It allows abortion for a number of reasons: saving the mother's life, preserving her physical or mental health, fetal deformity, rape, and incest. The following states have passed ALI laws: Arkansas, California, Colorado, Delaware, Florida, Georgia, Kansas, Maryland, New Mexico, North Carolina, Oregon, South Carolina, and Virginia. The fourth type of law provides for repeal of the restrictive laws; it allows abortion on request, generally with certain time restrictions (up to the twenty-fourth week of pregnancy, for example) and sometimes with residency requirements. Alaska, Hawaii, New York, and Washington have passed laws of the fourth kind.

Are these abortion laws unconstitutional?

Yes. From the late 1960s on, women and doctors litigated this issue on a massive scale in both state and Federal courts. Initially they had mixed success. Some courts found the laws unconstitutional because they interfere with a woman's right to control her body, and thus with her right to privacy. Other courts found the laws valid and enforceable.

In 1971, the Supreme Court had a chance to resolve the conflict in the case of the *United States* v. *Vuitch*,[2] but instead it avoided direct confrontation of the issue. The Court ruled that a "life and health" abortion law was not so vague as to be invalid, but it did so in a way that nullified the practical effect of the law. The decision involved a District of Columbia doctor who was prosecuted under the Washington, D.C., law forbidding abortions unless they are necessary to preserve the life or health of the mother. The Court ruled that health includes both physical and mental health, and that the District of Columbia would have to prove that a woman's health was not in danger in order to get a valid conviction against a doctor performing an abortion. These two conditions made it extremely difficult for the District of Columbia to secure convictions; as a result, D. C. hospitals and clinics now make abortions generally available to women, ·although this did not happen in the rest of the country.

Finally in 1973, the Court met the issue head-on. In the historic opinions of *Roe* v. *Wade*[3] and *Doe* v. *Bolton*,[4] it ruled that abortion laws—both the more restrictive and the ALI model—are unconstitutional because they interfere with the right to privacy, which includes "a woman's decision whether or not to terminate her pregnancy." The Court also invalidated many of the procedural regulations that on a practical level had rendered abortions difficult to procure.

What are the full implications of the Supreme Court's abortion decisions?

In *Roe* v. *Wade*, the Court set the basic structure for future state laws. States may not prohibit abortions during the first trimester of pregnancy. From then until viability (the twenty-fourth to twenty-eighth week of pregnancy), the state can establish medical regulations designed to make abortions safe, but it cannot prohibit them. After viability, the state can prohibit abortions except where they are necessary to protect the life or health of the woman.

The rationale for this timetable turns on the competing interests of the woman and the state. The woman has a right to privacy; the state has an interest in protecting the health of the woman and the potentiality of human life. However, until the end of the first trimester, the mortality rate for childbirth is higher than for abortion; thus, the state's interest in preserving a woman's health is not served by outlawing abortions during this time. Viability means that the fetus is potentially able to survive outside the mother's womb; thus, after that point the state's interest in the potentiality of human life takes precedence over the mother's right to privacy and abortions can be prohibited except to preserve her life or health. Even though abortions may thus be proscribed after viability, this limit will probably not be very effective because the Court's 1971 *Vuitch* decision interprets "life or health" so broadly.

In the second decision, *Doe* v. *Bolton,* the Court struck down several procedural regulations in a Georgia ALI statute. States may not require that abortions be performed in a specially accredited hospital (in Georgia's case, by the Joint Commission on Accreditation); and during the first trimester the state cannot even require that abortions be performed in hospitals. After the first trimester, the state can set standards for licensing abortion facilities, but the Court left open the question of whether hospitals can be required during this time period. Approval of abortions by a hospital abortion committee and concurrence with the patient's doctor by two other doctors that the abortion is necessary are both invalid regulations throughout the pregnancy. Finally, the state cannot require that the patient be a state resident.

Thus, the first three kinds of abortion laws described above are unconstitutional, and even the repeal laws have some unconstitutional requirements. The net effect of the Court's decisions will be to force almost all the states to rewrite their abortion laws.

In which states are abortions now freely available?

Women can of course obtain abortions readily in the states that passed repeal bills: Alaska, Hawaii, New York, and Washington. The District of Columbia also offers abortions freely because of the *Vuitch* decision. Although both California and Oregon have ALI abortion laws (now unconstitutional), the medical profession in those two states has interpreted the law much more liberally than in other ALI states. As a result, virtually all requested abortions in California and Oregon were already being performed prior to the Supreme Court decisions. Finally, because of some legal maneuvering after a favorable court decision, abortion clinics operate openly in Madison, Wisconsin.

Among the states where abortions are generally available as this book goes to press, New York State provides them most readily. There is no residency requirement, the abortion does not have to be performed in a hospital, and it can be done up to the twenty-fourth week of pregnancy. In contrast, Alaska, Hawaii, and Washington have set up residency requirements, now unconstitutional (of thirty, ninety, and ninety days, respectively); and the fetus must be nonviable in Alaska, and not have quickened (also unconstitutional) in Washington. If states are still enforcing the unconstitutional residency requirements, women have often by-passed them by registering as living with a friend or relative in the state. There is no residency requirement in the District of Columbia, California, or Wisconsin, but there is in Oregon.

As this book goes to press, the situation in other states is still very much in flux. Most states have balked at immediate implementation of the abortion decisions by refusing to pass constitutional abortion laws, by re-enacting unconstitutional laws, or by issuing Attorney General opinions that unconstitutional laws are constitutional. Given this situation, many doctors and hospitals have refused to give abortions. However, a drop in the abortion rate of states where abortions were already freely available prior to the decisions indicates that other doctors and hospitals have begun providing abortions more readily. Eventually abortions should be freely available throughout the United States, but this will take time —time to lobby for new laws and to litigate against unconstitutional laws and practices in recalcitrant states.

Where can women find details about obtaining abortions?

Most states now have referral groups, and there are national organizations as well. Two sources that list many such groups are: *Everywoman's Guide To Abortion,* edited by Martin Ebon (Pocket Books, 1971, $1.25); and "A Guide To Abortion Laws in the United States," by Lawrence Lader, in the June 1971 issue of *Redbook* (reprints available for $.35 and a stamped, business-size, self-addressed envelope, from Department A-45, Redbook Magazine, 230 Park Avenue, New York, N.Y. 10017). A useful article giving information about New York abortions is "New York Handbook: Abortions In New York, What You Need To Know," *New York Magazine*

(July 1972); reprints are available for $1.25 from Department H, New York Magazine, 207 E. 32nd Street, New York, N.Y. 10016.

For quick help, contact the Family Planning Information Service, 300 Park Avenue South, New York, N.Y. 10010 ([212] 677-3040). The service is operated by Planned Parenthood of New York City on behalf of the New York City Interagency Council on Family Planning; it gives complete information on abortion referral for New York City and on other aspects of family planning as well. The Abortion Rights Association of New York (250 West 57th Street, New York, N.Y. 10019; [212] 541-8887) provides a "Listing of Selected New York State Abortion Clinics," including prices and the kind of care. In Washington, D.C., the Women's Health and Abortion Project (Washington Area Women's Center, P.O. Box 13098, Washington, D.C. 20009; [202] 483-4632) provides comprehensive abortion referral and birth-control information for the District of Columbia. For help in other areas of the country, consult the Ebon and Lader guides or the National Clergy Consultation Service (55 Washington Square South, New York, N.Y. 10012; [212] 477-0034)—the New York branch of the NCCS should be able to refer women to one of its many branches in other states.

What problems remain to be resolved after the Supreme Court decisions?

The chief one is implementation of the decisions. It will probably take several years to force all the states to begin permitting abortions. Beyond that, women have encountered a number of problems, even in states with repeal laws, under the laws themselves, city regulations, hospital restrictions, or insurance policies. Consent of the husband, or of the parents for girls under eighteen to twenty-one years old, is often required, and the Supreme Court expressly refused to rule on this issue. Sometimes doctors are not allowed to perform abortions in their offices but must do so in a hospital or a clinic connected to a hospital; since the abortion decisions left the hospital issue open after the first trimester, this issue will still have to be litigated. In hospitals, abortions are sometimes subject to the approval of hospital review committees, often dominated by hostile doctors; this is clearly unconstitutional and will be easy to attack. Only doctors are allowed to give abortions, and some women believe that the procedure, at least in the early weeks of pregnancy, is so simple that nurses and medical paraprofessionals could be trained to do it. Arbitrary time limits are set, and abortions are not available after a certain month of pregnancy; again, restrictions prior to viability will be easy to attack. The availability of Medicaid to pay for an abortion is uncertain in some states, and insurance coverage sometimes does not include abortion, especially for single women. Women are often required to be state residents (clearly unconstitutional), and psychiatric counseling is sometimes required.

All of these restrictions can be tested in the courts. Women have had success contesting some issues already. A woman in the District of Columbia won the right to have an abortion (or sterilization) without her husband's consent, and a minor in California successfully challenged a parental-consent requirement.[5] Limitations of abortions to hospitals have been struck down in some New York towns and in Kansas.[6]

Lawyers from the Center for Constitutional Rights in New York City helped win reversal of the policy of the state commissioner of social services stating that Medicaid could only be used for abortions necessary to preserve the mother's life.[7] Women interested in challenging such restrictions in their states should consult feminist lawyers.

Are there any restrictions on the right to birth control for either married or single adult women?

None that are legally enforceable. There are two clear-cut Supreme Court decisions on this issue: *Griswold* v. *Connecticut*;[8] and *Eisenstadt* v. *Baird*.[9] In the first case, the Court invalidated a Connecticut law that prohibited any person from using birth control, because the law interfered with a married couple's right to privacy. In the second case, the Court struck down the Massachusetts law that forbade distributing contraception to unmarried persons as a denial of Equal Protection to the unmarried. This leaves only one state, Wisconsin, with a law that forbids single people to obtain birth-control information and devices. Wisconsin is apparently still enforcing the law, but it should now be easy to contest.

Do minors have a right to practice birth control without parental consent?

As the question implies, minors who have their parents' consent should have no problem obtaining birth-control prescriptions. Minors who do not have parental consent will find it more difficult. An old common-law rule makes many doctors reluctant to give out birth-control prescriptions without the consent of the parents. Under this rule, doctors could be sued for damages if they treated minors without parental consent. There are several exceptions to this rule, so that in theory minor girls who are emancipated or mature should be able to get birth-control prescriptions. Nor are there any reported cases where doctors have been held liable for providing birth-control prescriptions to minors without parental consent. In addition, state laws and regulations often affirmatively provide that minors under twenty-one may have access to birth-control devices without parental consent, and no statute prohibits a doctor from providing or prescribing birth control for a minor. Despite all these factors, many doctors and clinics remain reluctant to provide birth-control assistance to minors without parental consent for fear of being sued. One major exception is Planned Parenthood. The Planned Parenthood clinics are willing to prescribe birth control without parental consent, and this fact should be well publicized.

There are several ways to combat the reluctance of doctors and clinics to provide birth control. First, they should be educated as to the extreme unlikelihood of a lawsuit, and girls should be prepared to explain this when they seek birth-control assistance. Second, any minor girl who does fit one of the exceptions—particularly emancipation—should take advantage of it. Third, in states that do not yet have laws or regulations explicitly authorizing a doctor to give birth-control prescriptions to minors without parental consent, such laws should be passed. Finally, women could consider suing on constitutional grounds any institution receiving public funds for its refusal to grant birth control to minors without parental consent.

Paralegal groups should research state law to find out the common-law exceptions to the need for parental consent, how they are defined, and whether there is any state law permitting birth control for minors without parental consent. The results should be publicized in order to educate both medical institutions on their ability to pro-

vide birth-control assistance to minors without fearing
legal consequences and minor girls on their right to obtain
birth-control assistance. For more information on these
subjects, women should read: H. Pilpel and Wechsler,
"Birth Control, Teenagers and the Law: A New Look,
1971," 3 *Family Planning Perspectives* 37 (No. 3, 1971);
H. Pilpel and Wechsler, "Birth Control, Teenagers and the
Law," 1 *Family Planning Perspectives* 29 (No. 1, 1969);
and *Contraception, Family Planning and Voluntary Ster-*
ilization: Laws and Policies of the United States, Each
State and Jurisdiction, published by the National Center
for Family Planning Services, Health Service and Mental
Health Administration, HEW. The HEW study is available
from the Superintendent of Documents, United States
Government Printing Office, Washington, D.C. 20402.

**Do minors have a right to get abortions without parental
consent?**

Even though the Supreme Court has declared that restrictive abortion laws are unconstitutional, the common-
law rule that doctors can be sued for treatment of minors
without parental consent causes the same problem for
abortion as it does for birth control. However, it can be
rectified in the same ways—that is, through education
emphasizing the unlikelihood of suit and the utilization of
exceptions in appropriate situations.

A second factor causing problems is state abortion laws
specifically requiring parental consent. Among the seventeen ALI and "repeal-law" states, eleven require that
minors obtain parental consent (or, in some cases spousal
consent).[10] Other states may add parental-consent requirements to new abortion laws because the Supreme

Court expressly refused to decide whether the requirement is unconstitutional. Thus, girls in states with this requirement will have to bring lawsuits to win the right to an abortion without parental consent. They could urge either constitutional rights or, in some states, that state laws allowing minors to consent to medical care or treatment related to pregnancy necessarily allow them to consent to abortion.[11] One girl has already succeeded in winning an abortion without parental consent in California, based on this last argument.[12]

Besides filing lawsuits, women can lobby for new laws to erase any existing parental-consent requirements and to provide, affirmatively, that abortion be available to minors without parental consent. Readers interested in pursuing either route should read Pilpel and Zuckerman, "Abortion and the Rights of Minors," 23 *Case Western Reserve Law Review* 779 (No. 4, 1972).

Do women have a right to voluntary sterilizations?

Sterilization is now legal in all fifty states, but women still have problems obtaining the operation because of restrictive hospital regulations. Many hospitals require the husband's consent or impose the Rule of One Hundred Twenty or similar requirements. The Rule of One Hundred Twenty is that the woman's age times the number of children she has must equal one hundred twenty in order for her to get the operation; thus, a woman twenty-five years old would have to have at least five children in order to be sterilized! Hospital review committees and an insistence on hospital, rather than office, operations also pose problems—although both practices should be easy to attack under the *Doe* v. *Bolton* abortion decisions. All the practices mentioned can be combated through litigation against any hospital that receives public funds.

So far, there is only one clear decision ordering a hospital to perform the operation, because hospitals usually cave in as soon as suit is filed. In this one case, a court ordered a Catholic hospital to perform a tubal ligation because the hospital was the only one providing maternity facilities in the area.[13] Another case in New York State indicates that courts will be sympathetic to the issue. The case involved Linda McCabe, a young mother who had been pregnant six times and had four children. She and her husband decided not to have any more children, but the local public hospital refused to perform the sterilization operation because she did not have five children. After she sued the hospital, medical officials changed their mind. Despite the fact that she already had had the operation by the time the lawsuit progressed, a Federal appellate court allowed her suit to continue, saying that she might well be able to recover damages for the hospital's actions.[14]

Is it legal for a state to force women to be sterilized?

No court has yet decided this issue. As this book goes to press, the ACLU Women's Rights Project is preparing a lawsuit attacking this shocking practice. The case will seek to invalidate North Carolina's Eugenic Sterilization Act, under which the state has forced people—mostly young, poor, and/or black women—to undergo sterilization. Since the Supreme Court has already invalidated an Oklahoma forced-sterilization law, used in the 1940s against some criminals but not others, it seems likely that the North Carolina practice will not survive constitutional attack, either.

What can paralegal groups do in this area of the right to control one's body?

If there is no local abortion-referral and birth-control-information group, they can establish one. This includes monitoring and warning women about profit-making referral groups, which often charge women money for information that is available free elsewhere. The paralegal groups can also research and publicize information on local law relating to the right of minors to get birth-control assistance and abortions without parental consent. They should publicize fee schedules for abortions in order to help keep fees down; in doing this, they should work in conjunction with abortion reform groups.

They should be aware of the nationwide efforts of Right To Life groups to reinstate restrictive abortion laws and be prepared to help lobby to fight these efforts where necessary. In New York State, for instance, women's groups were caught unaware in the 1971-72 Right To Life effort to reinstate the old New York law. The old law was actually reinstated by the New York State legislature, and only Governor Rockefeller's veto saved the situation. With the support of the Catholic Church, these groups are now lobbying for a constitutional amendment prohibiting abortions throughout the United States. Women must combat this effort.

Finally, paralegal groups can join the drive to conform their state's laws to the Supreme Court decisions. This too will require lobbying, as well as litigation in particularly recalcitrant states. They can also join state coalition groups in establishing high-quality, low-cost clinics, and in pressuring hospitals to allow outpatient abortions.

What additional sources can women turn to for information and help in litigating or lobbying on abortion issues?

Besides the materials already mentioned in this chapter, readers might be interested in a series of articles on abortion found in "Symposium: Abortion and the Law," 23 *Case Western Reserve Law Review* 705-895 (No. 4, 1972). For the feminist legal arguments on why abortion laws are unconstitutional, a brief filed by feminist groups in the two recent Supreme Court cases would be of interest. The *Amicus Curiae* ("Friend of the Court") brief in the cases of *Roe* v. *Wade* and *Doe* v. *Bolton,* filed on behalf of New Women Lawyers, Women's Health and Abortion Project, and Women's National Abortion Action Coalition, is available for $2.50 from The Center for Constitutional Rights (853 Broadway, New York, N. Y. 10003). Lawyers at the center are experienced in litigation in the abortion area and would be helpful to groups undertaking such litigation.

The Association for the Study of Abortion (120 W. 57th Street, New York, N.Y. [212] 245-2360) maintains a current chart on abortion law in each state; it also sends out an excellent newsletter on current cases and developments. For help in lobbying to repeal abortion laws, contact the National Association for Repeal of Abortion Laws (250 West 57th Street, New York, N.Y. 10019 [212] 265-5125). The Women's National Abortion Action Coalition (150 Fifth Avenue, Suite 1104, New York, N. Y. 10011; [212] 675-9150) also offers help in organizing and litigating against abortion laws.

NOTES

1. See generally Lister, "The Right to Control the Use of One's Body," in N. Dorsen, ed., *The Rights of Americans* (1971).
2. 402 U.S. 62 (1971).
3. —— U.S. ——, 93 S. Ct. 705, 35 L. Ed. 2d 147 (1973).
4. —— U.S. ——, 93 S. Ct. 739, 35 L. Ed. 2d 201 (1973).
5. *Coe* v. *D.C. General Hospital,* C.A. No. 1477-71 (D. D.C. June 5, 1972); and *Ballard* v. *Anderson,* 484 P.2d 1345, 95 Cal. Rptr. 1 (1971).
6. *Robin* v. *Hempstead,* 334 N.Y.S. 2d 129 (1972) is the New York case.
7. *Klein* v. *Nassau County Medical Center,* 347 F.Supp. 496 (E.D. N.Y. 1972).
8. 381 U.S. 479 (1965).
9. 405 U.S. 439 (1972).
10. The ALI states requiring parental consent, and the respective age limits of minority, are Arkansas, twenty-one; Colorado, eighteen; Delaware, nineteen; Florida, eighteen and unmarried; New Mexico, eighteen; North Carolina, twenty-one; Oregon, twenty-one and unmarried; South Carolina, twenty-one; and Virginia, eighteen. The repeal-law states are Washington, eighteen and unmarried; Alaska, eighteen and unmarried.
11. The states with such laws are: Alabama, California, Delaware, Georgia, Kansas, Maryland, Minnesota, Mississippi, New Jersey, Pennsylvania, and Virginia. Hawaii and Missouri also have such laws, but they specifically exclude abortion.
12. *Ballard* v. *Anderson,* 484 P.2d 1345, 95 Cal. Rptr. 1 (1971).
13. *Taylor* v. *St. Vincents Hospital,* Civil No. 1090 (D. Mont. 1972).
14. *McCabe* v. *Nassau County Medical Center,* 453 F.2d 698 (2nd Cir. 1971).

VII

Divorce

For many women, the most difficult legal problem they ever face is getting a divorce. Emotional and legal problems mingle, exacerbating each other. The husband may threaten to harm the wife or take the children away; he may remove all the money from the joint savings account. The wife may feel lonely and scared, yet find that this is the time when she is most under pressure to cope, to find a lawyer, to protect herself. Many feminist lawyers report getting phone calls from women who have acute marital problems and are on the verge of hysteria: they often believe there is nothing they can do to protect themselves. This is not true. Women who are about to be divorced can get help and they can protect themselves.

This chapter is not designed to enable women to get their own divorces or to learn the legal grounds for divorce. Rather, it is designed to show women the kinds of issues they should be concerned with in the divorce situation, and to convince them that they can and should protect their own interests.

Do most people have to go through a long, drawn-out courtroom battle in order to get a divorce?

No. Most divorces are negotiated between the parties, who make only a pro forma courtroom appearance to finalize the breakup. Only in a small fraction of all divorces do the parties actually engage in courtroom dramatics. In those few cases, each side presents evidence, and the judge makes the final decision on whether to grant a divorce, on who gets custody of the children, and on the amount of alimony and child support that should be awarded. In most cases, however, the parties make their own decisions about these details, to which the judge merely gives formal approval.

Does a woman need her own lawyer for divorce proceedings even when she and her husband have a friendly agreement to negotiate the details?

Yes. No matter how amicable your relationship with your husband is, once you agree to a divorce you have interests separate from his and you should be represented separately. *This is vital.*

Should a woman retain a lawyer to whom she is referred by her husband's lawyer?

Definitely not. This will be a tempting course to follow for any woman who has had little or no exposure to lawyers before, has no idea of how to get one, and feels bewildered and scared by the whole process. Avoid the temptation. The person your husband's lawyer recommends might be a fine attorney, but, if he is brought into the case in this way, he may be more sympathetic toward your husband's interests than he should be. This may happen for several reasons. The lawyer you are referred to might need the business, and may find that the other lawyer ceases to refer business if he or she represents your interests too firmly; therefore, this lawyer may make certain compromises in advocating your side, perhaps even at a subconscious level. Or the lawyers might simply be good friends, and your lawyer may find himself or herself swayed too much by the arguments of a good friend. It is even possible that there is a formal kickback arrangement between the two lawyers, whereby your lawyer pays some of his or her own fee to the original lawyer for the favor of sending the business. This is grossly unethical, of course, but it does sometimes occur.

The fact that these things can happen does not mean that in any particular case they will happen. However, there is no reason to tempt fate by accepting a referral arrangement that can lead to problems. Most husbands and wives have at least some conflicting interests. Each party considering a divorce should get a lawyer who will represent those interests fully, without any possibility of a conflict in loyalties.

How should a woman go about finding a divorce lawyer?
There are a number of ways. Probably one of the best is to ask other friends or acquaintances who have obtained divorces whether they were satisfied with their lawyer's services. If they were, this may be a good recommendation.

If you are poor, you should check with the Legal Aid Society or a legal services program; they usually do divorce work and should be listed in the telephone directory under those names. Check with them even if you are not sure whether you would qualify for free help; they might be able to refer you to a lawyer even if they can't provide free services.

Another way to find information is to contact a women's paralegal group. Such groups often counsel women who are getting divorces, and this includes helping you find a lawyer. The best way to locate such a group would be to look in the telephone book for a Women's Center, a local chapter of NOW (the National Organization for Women), or WEAL (the Women's Equity Action League). Or, you could just ask around to find someone in the feminist movement who could lead you to any of the existing groups in your community. (Groups that are already formed are listed in Chart D in the Appendix.)

A more traditional way to find a lawyer is through the local bar association. Such groups usually maintain a lawyer-referral service, which will give out a list of names to anyone who needs a lawyer. Use this service only as a last resort—and with caution. The bar association does not guarantee that the lawyers are competent; it simply gives the names of all lawyers who ask to be placed on the list. You should, therefore, shop around before you finally choose the lawyer you wish to retain. Arrange a short interview before making your decision, so that you can find out whether you like the lawyer and his or her manner of dealing with your questions. There is usually no fee for such a preliminary interview, but check ahead of time to make sure.

Are there any books that it would be helpful to read before seeing a lawyer?

Yes. Reading a book on divorce written for nonlawyers will help give you a clearer idea of what is going on and what to expect during the legal process. Two books that are fairly good, despite some sexist overtones, are: *Making the Best of It: A Common-Sense Guide to Negotiating A Divorce*, by Newton Frohlich (Harper & Row, 1971); and *The Divorced Mother: A Guide to Readjustment*, by Carol Mindey (McGraw-Hill, 1969). The Frohlich book emphasizes the process of negotiating divorce settlements and explains what each side should bargain for (although the woman's side is often not thought out adequately). The Mindey book offers advice on problems such as jobs, loneliness, and finances. An excellent book is *Women's Survival Manual, A Feminist Handbook on Separation and Divorce*, available from its authors, Women in Transition (see Chart D, Section C).

How much does a divorce cost?

When you pay for a divorce, you are paying mainly for the lawyer's time. Divorce fees tend to be standardized, with different fees charged in different parts of the country. Shop around to find out the range of fees usually charged in your area. This will help you choose a lawyer who will not overcharge. Generally a divorce that is uncontested—that is, one your husband agrees to, and in which you can negotiate all the details before going to court—costs less than a contested divorce. A fairly standard range is three hundred to five hundred dollars for a simple, uncontested divorce; this fee covers simple negotiations, drafting of a simple settlement, and standard courtroom procedures. For a contested divorce, the fee might start in the same range and then require an hourly fee of twenty-five to fifty dollars (or one hundred dollars for a high-priced lawyer) after you have used up the initial fee at that rate. Some court costs will also be charged, perhaps in the range of twenty-five to fifty dollars.

You should also realize that most lawyers will charge you something every time you call him or her up, usually in fifteen-minute increments. So remember this: if you need to keep costs down, but are tempted to call the lawyer for emotional support, call your friends instead. They won't charge you, and they'll probably do a better job of comforting you, anyway.

Who pays the attorney's fees for the wife's lawyer?

It depends on your situation. If you qualify for Legal Aid or a legal services program, there is no charge. If you have your own income, you'll pay for your attorney. If you have no independent income, your husband will be forced to pay your attorney; and your lawyer can collect this fee when he arranges for temporary alimony and child support.

If you are unhappy with your lawyer and don't believe that he or she is representing you fairly, what can you do?

You can fire the lawyer. Many women do not realize that the relationship between a lawyer and a client is that of employer and employee. You are the employer and you have a perfect right to fire your employee at any time.

Firing your lawyer may present tricky financial problems, though. First, if the lawyer required a retainer ahead of time, he or she may try to keep it, whether or not any work has been done. The lawyer is entitled to payment only for work actually done, however, and must refund unearned portions. Ask for an itemized bill, setting forth hours worked and the nature of work done in that time. If the retainer seems unjustified, ask for the refund. Your next lawyer may be able to help you collect it if the first lawyer proves recalcitrant.

Second, some lawyers will try to keep any original papers you have given them for the divorce, under what is called a lawyer's lien, unless you pay them the agreed-upon fee. Since you need the papers to get the divorce, the lawyer has you over a barrel until you pay the fee. Your new lawyer can also help negotiate this matter, but the best thing is to avoid the situation altogether by giving lawyers only copies of original documents. In that way, you always have the papers you need, and papers can never be withheld as a way to force you to pay an unearned fee. If your lawyer does need the originals for the courtroom proceedings, you can hand them over at that stage. You can always explain the copy by saying you want the original for sentimental reasons.

A less drastic method than firing your attorney might be to tell him or her clearly and calmly what you are unhappy about, and see whether this produces any changes.

If you believe your lawyer has acted unethically, or has failed to represent you fully, report this to any feminist group that you know of and to the bar association. The more feedback women's groups get on divorce lawyers, the more they can do something about the present situation in which many women have voiced very strong complaints about the way they are being treated by lawyers.

How can you tell if your lawyer is representing you adequately?

There are no hard and fast rules, but there are a few things to look out for. The lawyer should send you itemized bills for his or her services, detailed by the hour, and should explain any item you do not understand. You should get copies of all papers and letters prepared for your case. The lawyer should be willing to explain what is happening in terms that make sense to you. The lawyer should insist on fair property and custody arrangements on your behalf (there will be some discussion of these concepts later in the chapter), and you should feel totally confident that he or she will go to bat for you. From a feminist perspective, the lawyer should be able to perceive you as a person with individual strengths and weaknesses, not as a stereotyped "woman" whose needs he or she automatically understands, without question. For instance, a lawyer might assume automatically that you want custody of the children; or he or she might not check to see whether you need alimony to cover expenses for additional training or education, thinking you would be satisfied to work at a low-paid job or not to work at all. Finally, your lawyer should have time to talk with you. Feel suspicious if he or she doesn't return your calls or asks you to repeat the same things over and over. If it seems your lawyer has no time, it is better to find one who does have time to devote to your case.

If your husband mistreats you physically or threatens to harm you, can you do anything?

Definitely. Your lawyer can go to court immediately and get a court order forbidding your husband to do these things. If your husband persists, he can be thrown into jail for disobeying the court order. If you have the feeling that your husband is all-powerful, just remember that he is not. In this situation, the law will be on your side.

Does the husband have the right to kick his wife out of the house?

No. Courts will almost always allow the wife to remain in the house, and you can legally enforce this right the same way you enforce your right to physical safety.

Is it all right to sleep with your husband once you have decided to get a divorce?

Never. First, in many states sleeping with your husband may prevent you from getting the divorce at all. If you have established your husband's adultery as grounds for divorce, sleeping with him after the adultery occurred is legally construed as forgiving him for his actions. Thus you lose your right to divorce him.

Second, even if the divorce is uncontested (so that you don't need to prove adultery, or any other grounds for divorce, in court), the fact that you do have strong legal grounds for divorce can put you in a strong bargaining position in negotiations over the details of the divorce. You may, for example, get a better settlement on issues like child custody and alimony simply because your husband's lawyer knows you would win in court on the question of the divorce itself. Thus your husband may have even been advised to sleep with you for just this reason: to destroy your legal grounds for divorce and thereby weaken your position in the negotiations.

Should you ask for alimony?

Probably, if you are in the situation of most wives. Many women have begun to feel guilty about asking for alimony—perhaps in response to those men who are clamoring that alimony is "anti" women's liberation and oppresses men. The fact that these same men have not taken up any other banner of women's liberation provides a definite clue to their real motives. They want to get out of their marriages with as much money as possible, while absolving themselves of responsibility for the financial situation of their wives.

Whether men want to admit it or not, marriage still places women at a tremendous financial disadvantage. It is still the exceptional women who escapes that disadvantage. Most women do not get enough training or education before marriage to maximize their wage-earning capacity; they are told that their husbands will take care of them and that they need not plan for a career. Then society encourages women to bear and rear children. This further decreases a woman's wage-earning capacity; for even when she has somehow managed to acquire education or training, she loses work experience and her own self-confidence during the years of child-rearing. Many women work to put their husbands through medical school or other kinds of extended education without ever receiving comparable training themselves, or even a repayment of the money. Nor are women paid for their years of work in the home even though this work has real economic value. Thus, they have no way to acquire property unless the husband "gives" it to them. Finally, society also encourages most women to take custody of the children upon divorce—again without compensation. Put all these factors together, and it is clear that alimony is one way of compensating women for those financial disabilities aggravated, or caused, by marriage: unequal educational opportunities; unequal employment opportunities; and an unequal division of family responsibilities, with no compensation for the spouse who works in the home.

A husband may argue, of course, that society, and not he, is responsible for any discrimination his wife faces in education or employment. This may be true. The husband, however, benefits from the *system's discrimination in his favor,* and there is no valid reason to allow him to carry away the fruits of an unfair bias. Moreover, the husband is often responsible for any unequal division of housekeeping responsibilities and lack of pay for the "housekeeper." After all, husbands acquiesce in the societal demand that the wife stay home; and it is a rare man indeed who would even consider staying home himself with the children so the wife could advance her career. If the husband would help rear the children, he and his wife could come much closer to equalizing their wage-earning capacities. Unfortunately most men don't see it this way. When married, they expect their wives to assume most of the responsibility for rearing the children. When divorced, many of them expect their wives to take custody of the children, again without conceding that their wives ought to be compensated for the extra work the men are avoiding.

Thus, women should not be cowed into believing that to ask for alimony is to be unliberated, or that their husbands provide alimony out of the largesse of their noble hearts. Women have earned alimony and will continue to earn it—they should receive it as well. It's a different story, of course, for women who have been married only briefly and have suffered no change in earning capacity, or for those few women who do have equal wage-earning capacity, whose husbands have shared equally in the responsibilities of home life, and whose husbands will continue to carry an equal burden with the children after the divorce. But until other women achieve that status, they still deserve alimony.

Should the woman ever pay alimony?

Yes, if she has the greater wage-earning capacity, and if the husband has taken and will continue to take the primary burden for rearing the children. If the partners are equal in both respects, presumably neither should pay alimony and each should pay an equal proportion of the child-support costs.

What kinds of expenses does alimony cover?

Alimony covers household and personal expenses, work-related costs, training and educational expenses, and recreation for the spouse.

Is a woman entitled to child-support payments?

Of course, if she has custody of the children. Again, women should not hesitate to ask that the husband contribute his fair share. Recent studies have shown that women usually contribute a greater share of child-support costs than do their husbands.

What should be included in child support?

The standard items are fairly obvious: food, clothing, shelter, education, medicine, medical insurance (it is usually cheaper for the kids to stay on the husband's Blue Cross program). If it is financially feasible, one should also negotiate for the costs of a college education and even the cost of graduate school (although the latter is hard to get).

Will it help the lawyer increase the amount of alimony and child support if a woman documents her past budget needs and the family assets?

Yes, in fact it can't be done without your help. You must itemize all expenses that you will need covered and document them with past bills wherever possible. The lawyer must have this information in order to make a convincing case of your need for alimony and child support. Standard budget items would include rent or mortgage payments; repair bills; utility and phone bills; household supplies; furniture replacements; transportation (including

car and public transportation); insurance premiums (for
health and life insurance); psychiatric, medical, and dental
care expenses; food; clothing; recreation, including vacations; such work-related expenses as lunches, extra clothes,
day-care, and cleaning and laundry services; education and
training costs; and taxes.

You should make special arrangements for the life insurance to insure that there will be a viable policy to cover
alimony and child support if your husband should die.
One arrangement is for your husband to give you the
incidents of ownership on the policy, so that he cannot use
the policy as security for a loan or change the named
beneficiaries. Another approach is to request alimony
money to make the premium payments yourself; this in-
sures that your husband will not let the insurance policy
lapse.

Work and education-related expenses should also be
emphasized because they are the kinds of expenses most
lawyers tend to overlook for a woman. Both are important for your own well-being, too, because being busy
will make it easier to adjust to the change and because
the vast majority of women will never receive enough alimony to live on comfortably. Most men simply do not
make enough money to support two families, and few
men keep the payments up anyway.[1] It is best to face
these facts from the start. Thus, you will have a real need
to improve your education or training. Additional training
will increase your wage-earning capacity and your ability
to provide the kind of living you would like on your own.
Having the training also reduces the pressure to remarry
for economic reasons and allows you the time to find someone you really care about if you do want to remarry.
Don't think, though, that education eliminates the need
for alimony. Always plan for the worst. A BA is no

guarantee of a good job to a forty-five-year-old woman
who has been out of the labor market for a long time.

In addition to preparing a solid budget, you will need
to list the family assets. You should get the original or
copies of all legal documents showing property of any kind
owned by either or both of you and tax returns showing
your husband's income. You should do these things as soon
as there is any indication of trouble in the marriage because some husbands hide these documents or change real
estate, stocks, bonds, cash, and other property owned in
your joint names to their own name alone.

What other legal documents will your lawyer need?

He or she will need your marriage certificate and documentation of any former marriages and divorces.

Is there any reason to collect budget, property, and income information quickly?

Yes. First, as mentioned above, your husband may be
acting to hide the information in order to reduce his payments; you should get copies before he does so. In fact,
it wouldn't hurt if women began collecting duplicate copies
of such information as a matter of course in case the
husband ever does walk out on them without much advance warning. This information would also be useful in
case of sudden death and just to make you more independent.

Second, you will need this information for the temporary alimony payments your lawyer will get for the
interval before the divorce takes place. It is extremely

important to have accurate information for this round, because what you get as temporary alimony will set the tone for how much you receive as permanent alimony. If you are unsure of the exact amount for any particular item and have no documentation, it is best to err on the generous side since the judge will almost always cut back on the figures.

Is there a difference between alimony and property?

Alimony and property are two separate concepts. Property includes all physical possessions—cash, house, furnishings, jewels, boat, land, stocks, bonds, etc.—which have been acquired in the family up to the time of divorce. Alimony consists of *future* payments of support money, after the end of the marriage.

How much alimony, child support, and property should a good lawyer be able to get for a woman?

There is no one correct answer. At present, one third to one half of the property, plus one third to one half of the husband's *net* income as *gross* alimony and child support is considered the upper limit. Women ought to debate whether this is in fact a good standard.

Other views are certainly possible. Those who strongly view marriage as a partnership, in which each partner does work that is equally valuable, might like to see women get one half of all property and enough alimony to leave each party with equal cash on hand after both deduct certain fixed expenses such as money used solely for the children (child support) and taxes. That is, wife and husband will have equal *net* incomes after the divorce.

Other women might prefer to examine the economic situation of the parties more closely. This view would use property settlement and alimony to compensate women only for financial damages incurred through marriage. Women who have stayed home for years rearing the family and doing elaborate housework would charge damages for each year of loss of wages, loss of associated fringe benefits (paid vacations, sick leave, medical-insurance coverage, pension plans), and decrease in wage-earning capacity, plus any continued loss of these items after the divorce. Conversely, the woman who has been married for only a few years, has had no children, has continued the career she had prior to the marriage, and whose husband has shared the housework equally, has suffered no financial loss through the marriage. She would not receive alimony, although she would still be entitled to one half of the property acquired through joint effort during the marriage.

What is the practical difference between the use of gross- and net-income figures in computing alimony and child support?

Lawyers often compare the gross income a woman receives—including any salary she earns, plus alimony and child support—to the net income the man is left with after deducting taxes, alimony, child support, and other expenses. This makes their relative economic positions look much more equitable than they really are, and thus leads the woman to ask for less. For instance, in *Making the Best of It* Newton Frolich advises the husband to deduct from his gross income the following expenses: taxes, computed at the higher post-divorce rate; life, medical, and hospital insurance premiums; contribution to children's college education fund; and retirement- and pension-fund contributions. He then further deducts one half of the remaining net figure as alimony and child support.

Frolich's figures, in one example, are as follows:

Husband's Income		$15,000
Deductions		
Post-divorce taxes	$2650	
Retirement fund payment	1200	
Life, disability, hospital and		
medical insurance premiums	850	
College fund payment	500	
Total:	$5200	
		-5,200
		$ 9,800
Alimony and child support	$4900	-4,900
Total:		$ 4,900

This computation appears reasonable since each is left with $4,900. After all, the man does not have the personal use of all the deductions, so it is only fair that the woman get one half of his usable income. The flaw in this reasoning is that she will not have the personal use of much of her income, either. Frolich has actually compared the husband's net income of $4,900 to the wife's *gross* income of $4,900. When she deducts income not available for her personal use, such as taxes and child support, her net income will be considerably smaller than $4,900.

If the husband deducts taxes, medical insurance, child support, and other expenses from his gross income, the wife should deduct comparable expenses and then compare their net incomes. For instance, she will have to pay taxes on alimony, she will have to use most of the child-support money for actual child-rearing expenses, and she may have to pay medical-care expenses, too. (The portion of child-support money that benefits her should not be deducted since it is available for her personal use. For example, if the child-support money covers rent for a large house, some of that rent should be counted as benefiting her.) The husband's claim is that he will not have the personal use of the money that must be spent to meet all these expenses. The wife's claim is the same. It is important to remember this point, especially in connection with the child-support payment. The child-support money is intended to cover the *actual cost* of rearing the children. It does not matter whether it is the husband or wife who actually walks into the store and lays out this money; it will still not be available for other purposes. Thus, a principal point to keep in mind while negotiating divorce settlements is to compare, and strive to achieve equality in, the net incomes of husband and wife.

This same approach can be used where the wife works. It would compensate the woman whose wage-earning capacity has suffered because she stayed home for a time to rear the children. Why should the man continue to be able to enjoy a larger net income just because he had the privilege of working for pay during the entire marriage while the woman worked for free during many years? In such a case, each would deduct taxes, retirement payments, insurance premiums, college-fund payments, and child-support expense money. The wife would then be entitled to one half of the difference between their two net incomes as alimony—in order to equalize their net incomes. This compensates her fairly for her earlier contribution to the family, any sacrifice of career, and continued work in caring for the children. The formula also rewards the husband who is willing to take on his share of the care of the children after the divorce and who did not demand that his wife stay home at the cost of her career. In this situation, if their net incomes are roughly comparable, there may be no alimony.

Are there any qualifications to this discussion of the need to equalize the post-divorce incomes of the husband and wife?

Two provisos to this discussion are needed. First, courts do not accept the views set forth and would not use this standard in awarding alimony and child support to the woman. However, this fact need not prevent a woman from convincing her husband that equal net incomes would be the egalitarian solution and from obtaining a divorce settlement along the suggested lines.

Second, the answer has assumed a strong partnership view of marriage and is intended to stimulate discussion on the issue of how to compensate women fairly in the divorce situation.[2] To date, most discussions of the issue have looked at the woman's income as determined by her needs, and the man's as determined by his right to keep as much of his "own" income as possible. The author believes that marriage should be legally viewed as a partnership, which implies that the husband and wife have equal economic rights, no matter which one chooses to stay home or work outside the home or in what combination they do these things. The assumption is that working outside the home for pay is, in a moral sense, a privilege, not a right, and that the person who has the privilege is not automatically entitled to all the benefits of that status—including the pay. Most people assume that the man has the right to support the family by working outside the home for pay and that whatever is left after expenses are met is his. If the husband's work is a privilege and if the wife's work in the home is seen as a necessary half of an important partnership, obviously both partners should get one half of the proceeds. Where the partnership continues after a divorce because the woman still takes care of the children, or where the wife works outside the home for pay, but the partnership has previously crippled her ability to earn money, she should still be entitled to one half of the proceeds, although her own earnings will be added into the communal pot for division purposes.

Is it important to get good alimony and property arrangements in the interim before the final divorce is secured?

Definitely. The amount of temporary alimony you receive usually sets the standard for the amount of permanent alimony you'll receive. This holds true for child-support payments also. Thus, the effort to secure temporary payments is just as important as the final divorce proceeding itself.

If the husband has a small income at the time of the divorce, is there any way to get an increase in alimony in the future?

Yes. You can request an escalation clause in the separation agreement, which will provide for a stated increase in alimony for every stated increase in your husband's income.

What are the tax differences between alimony and child support?

The husband can deduct alimony from his income for income-tax purposes; he cannot deduct child support. Similarly, the wife must pay taxes on alimony; she does not have to pay taxes on child support.

What are the practical consequences of the tax difference?

The tax difference induces husbands to try to disguise child-support payments as alimony. For instance, Newton Frohlich makes a big pitch in his book that it saves men money to pay alimony. He does not mean that a man should pay adequate child support and then some extra money as alimony. Instead, he literally means that the husband should take the same amount of money he will have to pay anyway as child support, and call some of it alimony in order to get the income-tax deduction. Women should be extremely wary of this tactic since child-support money, whether called child support or alimony, is still money that must be used for the children. It cannot be used for personal needs. Since the woman does need alimony for her own support, she should bargain for it as a separate item.

Accepting a large alimony payment in lieu of adequate child support can lead to real financial hardship for the wife and children. First, as already noted, the wife must pay taxes on alimony. This means that while an alimony settlement is a tax advantage for the man, it is a decided disadvantage for the woman. Second, alimony ceases upon remarriage, but child support ceases only when the children come of age. If you have agreed to call some child support alimony, you will lose it when you remarry, even though your children may still need the money. Your new husband may not be able to support your children since he may already have children of his own. Lack of adequate child support might even discourage him from marrying you.

On the other hand, it is important to bargain for enough alimony to meet your own personal needs. If you fail to do this and rely instead on child support, you may find yourself really destitute when the children grow up and the child support ceases. A recent study by the Rand Corporation in California showed that some former wives of wealthy doctors and lawyers were living on welfare[3]— a sad commentary on how well their lawyers had bargained for them. The rule of thumb, then, in bargaining for alimony and child support, is to *keep the two as separate items.* If you get the right amount of money for each category, you insure that your children will have the money they need as long as they need it, and that you will have the personal income you need as long as you need it. Of course, if you can get more money by departing from this rule, you should do it—provided you are clear about your financial needs once either alimony or child support ceases.

Should you negotiate with your husband about alimony, child support, property, or other matters before seeing your own lawyer?

Emphatically not. You should know your rights before making any agreement—financial or otherwise. You might be entitled to much more than you realize, or you might not have seriously analyzed your future situation—and it is always best to have the facts before making a decision.

Should you leave your money or securities in a joint account if you are thinking about a divorce or you suspect your husband wants a divorce?

No. Take out the money you think is your own. Men are often advised to take all the money out of a joint account as a way of preventing their wives from getting any of it. If you have even the slightest suspicion that your husband would do such a thing, out of bitterness or anger, and if you need the money, it is best to take precautionary measures.

If your husband has cleaned out the joint savings or checking account, or sold joint property, is there anything you can do?

Yes. Your lawyer can get a court order forcing your husband to reimburse you in a property settlement. If he has not taken property or funds, but you suspect he plans to do so, your lawyer can also get an order forbidding any

such action. This would prevent your husband from re-
moving or selling any assets until the divorce.

**Do many men default on alimony and child-support
payments?**

So far, no one has conducted an in-depth study in this
area. The surveys available to date, however, indicate that
most men do default, starting even in the first year after
the divorce.[4]

**Can any laws be passed to prevent default on alimony
and child support?**

Women's groups can begin lobbying for a law that would
require courts to order automatic payroll deductions for
all alimony and child-support payments. The New York
City NOW chapter has already begun a campaign for
such a law. Under this system, the husband's employer
would make the payments directly to the wife. Since the
husband would have no choice in the process, it would be
difficult for him to default—except by changing jobs and
moving to another state where it would be hard to locate
him. For a copy of the NOW divorce-reform bill, write to:

Betty Berry
541 East 20th Street, Apt. 7C
New York, N. Y. 10010.

**Once a husband has defaulted on payments, can anything
be done to get the money?**

Definitely, although many lawyers do not like to institute collection proceedings because they can't make very

much money on these kinds of cases. In many states, a
lawyer can have the man's salary garnished if he defaults
on payments. Other judicial proceedings are also available
to collect overdue alimony and child support. One way
to make collection easier would be for your lawyer to
negotiate for a provision in the settlement whereby the
husband agrees to pay your attorney's fees for any default
proceedings, as well as court costs. The maximum interest
allowable on the default payments under state usury laws
should also be included. It would be difficult for the
husband's lawyer to object to these provisions since that
would be tantamount to admitting that the husband intended to default. If the agreement sets the lawyer's fee
high enough, your lawyer or another one should find it
worthwhile to take the case in the event your husband
defaults.

**Do you need a full-scale trial to get the best property
settlement, alimony, and child-support payments?**

No. In fact, the full-scale trial is a bad idea. It sends attorneys' fees skyrocketing because preparation for trial
and a trial itself are very time-consuming. In addition, a
trial brings a private controversy out into the open. It
makes both parties anxious to show the world that the
other side was at fault, and it usually ends with bitterness and hostility on all sides. If at all possible, it is much
better to negotiate the details of your divorce, and then
go through a pro forma court hearing.

This said, it must still be emphasized that there will undoubtedly be some divorces that women will want to litigate. If a husband will not negotiate, a trial may be
the only way the wife can secure the financial arrange-

ments that are her due. In this situation, she should not hesitate to go forward to a full-scale court hearing.

What can a woman do if both she and her husband are so poor that they cannot afford to live apart?

Many families have such a small income that they cannot afford to set up two separate households. In this situation, the woman should think about obtaining welfare; another book in this series, *The Rights of the Very Poor*, explains in detail what one's rights to welfare are and how to go about asserting them. An alternative for families that cannot afford to live apart on the present income is for the wife to work for pay if she is not yet doing so. This might increase the family income enough so the parties can afford to separate. There may be government training and day-care programs available to help the wife, particularly if the President doesn't veto the next day-care bill as he vetoed the bill passed by Congress in 1971.

If the woman wants custody of the children, are there any special steps she should take?

Yes. She should be very discreet about any relationship with another man. The legal system still imposes a double standard, and a mother will be judged much more harshly for extramarital affairs than will a father. If your husband is trying to get custody of the children and you want to retain custody, it would be wise to avoid any affairs with men for the interim period. Of course, whenever possible, women should fight the issue openly in order to establish precedents to help other women in the same predicament;

however, the risk you take is losing custody of your children. Before deciding to fight the issue, you should consider the risks carefully.

Some states require that persons seeking divorce see a social worker, a friend of the court, or a marriage counselor before the divorce is granted. Be as discreet as possible with any of them. This includes being careful about what is on display in your home as well as what you say. Talk to your lawyer about these matters before any interviews or visits. As a practical matter, these people are very powerful. Judges rarely overturn their recommendations on child custody; so if you offend them on matters related to sexual behavior, it is likely to have serious consequences.

Is it important to maintain custody of your children in the period preceding the actual divorce?
Definitely. Just as the amount of temporary alimony you receive sets a precedent for the award of permanent alimony, the party who has temporary custody of the children is often granted permanent custody as well.

If your husband's visits upset the children, can you prevent them after the divorce is final?
Yes. The question of visitation rights can be reopened and new arrangements made if the old arrangements prove unsatisfactory.

What can women's paralegal groups do to help women who are in the process of getting a divorce?

Women in several cities—including Chicago, Los Angeles, New Haven, Philadelphia, Seattle, and Washington, D.C.—have already undertaken paralegal divorce projects. For further information, contact one of the groups listed in Chart D, subsection C (Divorce), in the Appendix.

Paralegal workers in these projects have provided women with general counseling on coping with new life situations and have given them a chance to talk with other women who have been through a divorce. Counseling might also include information on welfare, housing, day-care, job opportunities, and managing finances on one's own. Another valuable service is educating women on their legal rights in the divorce situation so that they will know what they can seek in negotiations. Still another service is providing the names of lawyers who have a good reputation and who do not shortchange a woman's needs. In the case of poor women who cannot locate free legal help and who need a default divorce (one the husband is not contesting, either because he has left town or because he doesn't care) a counseling service might show the woman the ropes so she can go into court and get her own divorce.

Another extremely valuable service a paralegal group could provide is to give bar associations and feminist lawyers feedback on complaints women have about the way their lawyers treat them. This action might lead to some meetings with the local bar association, to press for change and reeducation of the bar, but such meetings should not take place without the help of a feminist lawyer. As to the complaints, the group's lawyer should give careful thought to the problem of libel; for if an individual lawyer is charged with failure to fulfill his duty to female divorce clients, he will almost surely respond with a lawsuit against the accusers. This is not to say that the real problems of poor representation cannot be confronted, but rather that such an effort must be carefully planned with the help of feminist lawyers.

NOTES

1. Eckhardt, "Deviance, Visibility, and Legal Action: The Duty to Support," in *Social Problems* (1968); see also Note 4.
2. For questions discussing fair compensation during the marriage, see pages 267-273.
3. Winston and Forsher, "Non-Support of Legitimate Children by Affluent Fathers as a Cause of Poverty and Welfare Dependence." The report is available for $2 from: Rand Corporation, 1700 Main Street, Santa Monica, Cal. 90406.
4. See generally Nagel & Weitzman, "Women as Litigants," 23 *Hastings Law Journal* 171, 187-192 (1971); and Citizens' Advisory Council on the Status of Women, *Women In 1971* (1972), pp. 42-48. Both sources cite a particularly interesting study: Eckhardt, "Deviance, Visibility, and Legal Action: The Duty to Support," *Social Problems* (1968). Eckhardt compiled statistics from a 1955 sample of fathers ordered to pay child support in a metropolitan Wisconsin county. He found that after one year 38 percent of the fathers had complied fully, 20 percent were in partial compliance, and 42 percent were in total noncompliance. By the sixth year, 17 percent were in full compliance, 12 percent in partial compliance, and 71 percent in total noncom-

pliance. Nagel and Weitzman suggest that noncompliance is probably even higher on alimony awards; and they point out that, in any case and contrary to popular mythology, alimony is awarded very infrequently. They cite a study of twelve thousand Chicago divorces, where the wives waived post-divorce alimony in 93 percent of the cases. The study cited is M. Virtue, *Family Cases In Court* (1956).

VIII

Names and Name Change—
Symbols of a New Identity

Names symbolize a person's identity, so it is not surprising that the subject of names has become increasingly important to feminists. The present system for naming people reflects women's status today. Almost every woman in this country uses the name of a man, whether father or husband, as her last name. Symbolically, then, every woman's identity is still tied to a man.

Many women have begun searching for ways around this male-oriented system. A few refuse to use either their father's or their husband's name.[1] These women choose surnames that are not related to any man: a beautiful word that seizes their fancy; the name of a city; their mother's first name, combined with "child," as in Sara-child. Other women choose to use their father's name, both before and after marriage. Still others prefer a husband's name to the father's, or combine and hyphenate the two. Some decide with or convince their husbands that both should take a new name—whether a combination of their fathers' names or an unrelated third name.

Each solution has advantages and disadvantages. Choos-

239

ing a name apart from either the father's or husband's allows one to express the greatest disagreement with the male orientation of the present system, but it takes time and effort to reeducate friends, parents, and officials to call you by a name social custom has not sanctioned. Using the father's name allows a woman to retain the identity she grew up with and symbolizes equality upon marriage since the man also retains his father's name. However, every woman who chooses to do this still carries a symbolic tie to her father only—but none to her mother—and if she has children, they will have the same problem. Some women prefer to use their husband's name because they like it better or feel they have some choice in taking it, even though the choice is between identification with one male and identification with another male. Married couples who hyphenate their fathers' names or take a third name also opt for a symbol of equality, and each partner contributes to the children's surname, but it sets off the family unit in a way some do not wish to perpetuate.

Ideally, we need a new system for naming people. Children should be given surnames that either reflect the names of both parents or the names of neither. When these children marry in turn, both men and women could keep their surnames, combine them,[2] or choose a third name. None of these choices would carry a sexist connotation since none would favor a male's name over a female's name.

Instituting a new system means passing new laws, though, and this may require prolonged effort. Meanwhile many women—and some men—want to deviate from tradition by taking names that reflect a more egalitarian view of the relationship between men and women. These people are sometimes told that the difficulties are insurmountable, or that they will lose important legal rights if they do so.

This is not really so. Although there will be no perfect solutions until laws are changed, there are ways of coping with the present system.

Do women and men have the right to use any name they choose?

Yes. Under the common law, our legal system has long recognized the right of any person to use any name she or he likes, as long as he or she is not doing so in order to defraud someone else. To exercise this right in most states, one simply begins using a new name. In addition, most states have passed laws to establish formal name-change procedures, but it is usually not necessary to use these procedures. They are merely a convenient formality. However, in a few states, the only legal way to change your name is by complying with the statutory procedures. (See Appendix, Chart C, "Explanation of Chart," to learn of the states in which one must use the statutory procedure.)

Must a woman take her husband's surname as her last name when she marries?

Not necessarily. Many legal cases and treatises state categorically that women must take the husband's name. When one examines these statutes and decisions more closely, it appears closer to the truth to state that women generally use their husband's name as a matter of social custom and not because the law requires it. In fact, only one state—Hawaii—and Puerto Rico have a law stating clearly and unequivocally that the wife (and children) must use the husband's name. A group of law students who recently researched the law on this question could not find a single case where a judge ordered a woman to use her husband's name for all purposes. However, a few married women who have refused to use their husband's name have been penalized by the loss of some other right (see next question).

What penalties have been or can be imposed on women for refusing to use their husband's surname?

Penalties have generally been imposed under state laws requiring people to reregister or notify authorities when their name changes "by marriage or otherwise." Such persons must generally reregister in order to vote and must notify officials to retain a valid driver's license, motor vehicle registration, or certificate of title to a car, and even to remain a notary public. In theory if one does not do so, one can no longer vote, legally drive a car, etc., although laws often do not explicitly prescribe a penalty for failure to register. (For a detailed list showing which laws your state has passed, see the Appendix, Chart C, "Name Change.") Despite the large number of states with these laws, however, only five or six reported cases could be found where a woman was actually penalized for refusing to reregister under her husband's name. In a few cases, these women were denied the right to vote; in one case, a woman who sued to get a driver's license issued in her maiden name was unsuccessful; and in a case in the 1930s, a woman artist was unable to obtain naturalization papers issued in her maiden name.[3]

The number of reported penalties is so low, in part, because most of the laws are ambiguous. They require a woman to reregister when her name changes by marriage, but they do not tell her if her name changes automatically upon marriage or whether the change is voluntary. If it is the latter, any married woman who does not actually change her name cannot be penalized for a refusal to reregister. In order to avoid penalties, then, women need to convince officials and judges to interpret reregistration laws in the second way. Some women have already done so. The best example is a 1961 Ohio case involving a woman named Krupansky, who had not changed her name for any purpose when she married and had voted in the name of Krupansky in three elections. When she decided to run for a local office, a taxpayer sued to have her name taken off the ballot because it was not the name of her husband. The judge refused to do so, stating that: "It is only by custom, in English speaking countries, that a woman, upon marriage, adopts the surname of her husband in place of the surname of her father. The state of Ohio follows this custom but there exists no law compelling it. . . . A wife may continue to use her maiden, married, or any other name she wishes to be known by. . . ."[4] Thus, even though Ohio has a reregistration law, the woman was not penalized in any way because Ohio judges interpret the law to mean that a woman has the option to use whatever name she likes.

On the other hand, some states have taken the opposite approach. Illinois has refused to allow a married woman to vote in her maiden name.[5] And recently the Maryland attorney general ruled that a married woman must use her husband's surname as a matter of law. Relying on this interpretation, a Maryland voting registrar deregistered a married woman who refused to reregister, claiming she never used her husband's name. Fortunately, the case was reversed on appeal.[6] Most states have not reached such clear interpretations of the reregistration laws, although their position can sometimes be implied or predicted from other laws or cases.

Other kinds of penalties are more widespread but are not compelled by any law. Many married women report difficulties in obtaining a passport in their father's name, although passport officials do not act uniformly on this matter. Sometimes they will issue women passports under the names of both the father and husband; other officials will issue them in the father's name alone if the woman presents affidavits that she has always been known by that name. Other people, such as employers and bank or department store officers, may also penalize the married woman who refuses to use her husband's surname. They may refuse to issue mortgages, credit cards, or paychecks in the name a woman chooses, or harass her at length before doing so.

If a married woman exercises her common-law right to use a name other than her husband's, will she be penalized in all these ways?

No. In fact, the chances are slim that she will lose any of the legal rights mentioned. This is so whether the woman decides to retain her father's name when she marries, chooses a third name, or decides after first using her husband's name to resume her father's name or adopt a new name. In all of these situations, however, the chances of encountering resistance by banks, department stores, and employers run high.

Will going through a state's formal name-change procedure help a married woman avoid the imposition of
penalties, whether formal or informal?

Yes. Once a woman obtains a legal document setting
forth her legal surname, state officials cannot penalize her
for refusing to use her husband's name. (Of course, the
woman who *does* change her name—whether to her husband's name when she marries, back to her father's name
after using her husband's name, or to a third name—should
comply with reregistration and notification laws.) Women
report that a legal document also works like magic in
eliminating the objections of bank, department store, and
employer personnel.

What are the disadvantages of using the name-change
procedure?

First, it symbolizes inequality since no man need use the
procedure in order to retain his father's name after marriage. Second, the procedure does cost money and take
some effort. The amount varies from state to state and
includes a court filing fee (perhaps ten dollars or so), the
cost of publishing a notice in the newspaper in some states
(which can run as high as one hundred dollars in some
states), and perhaps the services of an attorney (anywhere
from twenty-five to one hundred dollars, unless one quali-
fies for free legal help from an OEO legal-services program).

Is use of the name-change procedure mandatory for any married woman who does not want to use her husband's name?

No, except in those states where this is the only legal method to change one's name (see Chart C). Any woman who is willing to risk the penalties can simply continue or commence using any name she likes. Even if she is then faced with a penalty, she can almost always avoid it by reregistering in her husband's name. Where officials remain adamant, though, the only choices are turning to the name-change procedure, using the husband's name in the contested circumstance, or losing the right involved. Of course, if the state has no reregistration or notification laws, the chances of being penalized for using a name other than the husband's are slim.

Is there any way to know whether use of the formal procedures is really necessary?

There is no definitive guide, but the chart on "Name Change" gives some assistance. The last column indicates states whose laws or decisions provide a clue as to whether the state will take the position that a woman's name changes automatically upon marriage as a matter of law (L), or whether women have an option to use any name because it is only customary (C) for them to change their names. In states with an L, or where the formal procedures are the exclusive method for changing anyone's name, it would probably be wise to use these procedures. Where there is a C, women may not have to use the procedures. (Blanks indicate states where research has not turned up any clues, one way or the other.) In all states, though, use of the name-change procedure is still valuable to protect against harassment and the imposition of penalties.

Can all married women use the name-change procedures?

No. In a few states (see the chart), married women are prohibited from using the procedures, or the wording of the law strongly implies that they cannot. Married women in these states may have to bring a lawsuit to establish their right to use a name other than their husband's.

Do all men and all single women have the right to use the name-change procedure?

Without question. Men and single women who wish to change from their father's name to another name should have little difficulty in doing so. In one or two states, though, a married man may need his wife's consent.

What do the formal name-change procedures entail?

The procedures vary slightly from state to state but are generally not complicated. Most women could follow them on their own if they want to save money by avoiding a lawyer's fee.

Some states will not allow anyone to use the procedures

unless she or he has been a county resident for six months or a year, but most do not impose this limitation. Usually one must first go to a courthouse and fill out a paper—often called a Petition for Change of Name—listing such standard items as current name, name desired, age, residence, and reason for change. Then the court clerk files this paper, usually for a nominal fee of perhaps ten dollars or so. Sometimes one must publish a notice of the proceedings in a local newspaper and present copies to the court to prove that this was done. Unfortunately the cost of newspaper publication can be expensive—up to one hundred dollars. The final step in some states is a short hearing before a judge, who will ask a few questions. If all goes smoothly, one then receives a legal document setting forth one's legal surname.

Chart C in the Appendix tells the kind of court that will grant this name change for each state. For more details on the procedure, call the clerk of the court, who is listed in the phone book for the named court. If there is no such court in the phone book, call any court and ask how to locate the correct one for name changing.

Two cautionary notes should be added. First, the court will probably be most concerned with your reasons for changing your name; it may probe to find out whether you have any intent to defraud someone by the change of name. To avoid this problem, it may be wise, in addition to your setting forth the reasons for change, to state that you have no intention to defraud anyone. The reasons for seeking a change should be phrased somewhat conservatively in order not to alienate the judge, for some judges have strong feelings about a woman's "proper name." A good tactic might be to emphasize a desire to maintain a separate identity from one's husband or father for work purposes, rather than blatantly stating that one does not wish to be identified with a man. Nor does a woman have to state that she changed her name when she married, if she did not. She can state that she wishes to establish her legal right to *continue* using her father's name rather than change back to it.

The second note of caution is that if the judge turns down your petition, you should definitely get a lawyer before proceeding further. An appeal can be taken to a higher court to reverse the judge's decision, but appeals are more complicated and require a lawyer's assistance.

What projects could women's groups undertake to help other women change or keep their names?

An ideal project would be to study the state procedures, publicize them, and help women file their own petitions. This would save women the cost of hiring an attorney, which is the major cost in formalizing a name change. Publicity should include a description of the procedures, information on where to go for the proper forms and for filing them, and an offer of assistance in filling them out. Members of the group could also accompany anyone to court if she so desires and help get a notice published in a newspaper, where this is necessary.

The Women's Legal Defense Fund recently undertook a project like this. Interested readers should write (for the address, see Chart D, Section A) for a copy of the fund's pamphlet, "Name Change Information for the Washington Area"; the cost is $.50. They should also read the applicable state statute, citations for which are given in Chart C.

As a second project, the group could find a lawyer to research state law in more depth than was possible for this book. If the lawyer discovers cases or laws that make

it clear that married women can use any name they like in
that state, the group should widely publicize the results
of her research. Armed with this information, women can
take advantage of their legal right to establish their name
by usage, without the cost of formal procedures or the
fear of penalty. If the law remains ambiguous, the group
should consider suing state officials for what is called a
"class-action declaratory judgment." In such a lawsuit, the
women request the judge to declare what their rights are.
Here they want a declaration that the class of all married
women in the state have the option of using any name they
like, as the Ohio judge declared in Ms. Krupansky's case.
Lawsuits like this could also be brought in states where
married women are barred from using the name-change
procedures. If the women win the suit, they can use the
decision to force state or business officials to deal with
women under their chosen name.

Another option—especially where the state forces married women to use their husband's name—is to lobby for
legislative change. The new law would eliminate forced
use of the husband's name and the bar to change of name
by married women.

**Does a married woman with a surname different from
that of her husband have any right to give her surname
to her child?**

Sometimes. Generally a child's surname is that of his
or her father. When the father changes his name, the
child's name changes at the same time, at least while he
or she is a young child. Thus, if the father contests the
mother's right to name the child, he will almost always
win in legal proceedings. Of course, if the father agrees,

the couple can give the child the mother's surname; although there is always the risk that government officials or businessmen will insist that the child use the father's name, just as they insist that the mother use her husband's name.

Is there any practical way for a woman to insure that her children will use a surname that she has helped choose?

Yes. The woman and her husband can choose as their common name a joint surname to which both contribute. This might be a hyphenated combination of their fathers' names or a third, mutually satisfactory, name or even her father's name instead of his. Whatever choice they make, both should change their names through the name-change procedure. Their children would then automatically acquire the new name, obviating any later problems about who gets to name the child. This procedure will even work for couples who already have children.

Some women prefer not to set off the family unit with a family surname. The only way they can insure their right to give the child their surname is to secure the husband's agreement. The problem with this solution is that there is no way to enforce it if the man changes his mind.

Does a divorced woman have a right to resume using her father's name or to take on another name?

Usually. Many states have passed laws that provide that a divorced woman may use any name she likes. Some states, however, allow a divorced woman to do so only if she

is considered the blameless party in the divorce, or if she
has no children or does not have custody of the children.
(See Chart C.) But even if a judge tells her that she must
continue to use her husband's name, as a practical matter,
his decision is probably not enforceable. Certainly once
the woman moves to another state, no one will force her
to resume her husband's name, and even within the state,
enforcement is highly unlikely. To avoid any problems,
women seeking divorce who want to change their name
should ask their lawyer to get this approved in the final
court decree.

**May a divorced woman have her children's name
changed?**

Sometimes. Some women have done so under the name-
change statutes, even where the father objected. Most
women who have done so, though, have simply changed
the children's name from that of husband one to that
of husband two.

**Do boys and girls have an equal right to change from
their father's name to another name?**

In many states they do not because of the variation
in the age when they achieve majority. Here it should
work to the girl's advantage, since generally she is said
to become an adult for some purposes, like marriage or
legal drinking, at age eighteen, while the boy must wait
until twenty or twenty-one. In those states, a girl will be
able to use the name-change procedure without parental

permission sooner than a boy will. In other states, the age of majority is the same for both.

What new laws are needed to achieve equality of names for men and women—both in naming children and upon marriage?

Two kinds of laws are needed. The first would establish the right of any woman, whether single or married, to use any name she likes. The second would create a new nonmale-oriented system for naming children. Although many feminists have begun lobbying for the first kind of law, there has been little thought devoted to the second. Until this is done, the law will continue to symbolize a woman's tie to a man, for most women will continue to use their father's name and to have no say in the naming of their children.

What other sources are there on names and name change?

Two interesting law-review articles are Carlsson, "Surnames of Married Women and Legitimate Children," 17 *New York Law Forum* 552 (1971); and Hughes, "And Then There Were Two," 23 *Hastings Law Journal* 233 (1971). The Women's Rights Project of the American Civil Liberties Union has published a memorandum on the "Right of Married Women to Retain or Regain Their Birth Names." The project also wrote the brief in the Maryland case in which a woman established her right to vote using her birth name.[7] For copies of both the memorandum and the brief, write to the project (see Chart D, Section A, for the address). As this book goes to press, an article on name change by Priscilla McDougall is expected in issue number 3 of the *Women's Rights Law Reporter.*

NOTES

1. One of the greatest sources of controversy among friends who read over this chapter was what to call a woman's surname: maiden name, birth name, or father's name? All have disadvantages. Each is inaccurate in some circumstances. Thus, some women using a "maiden name" are married; some women using a "birth name" have changed the surname they acquired at birth (referring to any woman—married or single—who changes her name because she wants another name); and some women using a "father's name" in fact acquired their surname from their mother. Moreover, each name has ideological connotations that other women dislike.

   The author finally decided on "father's name" because she wished to emphasize that most people in our society still give their children the surname of the father. Many feminists have been combating the custom of a woman's changing her name to that of the husband at marriage, but they have ignored the male-oriented system for naming children. By using the term "father's name," the author hopes to encourage more women to see and combat the second problem.

2. If a combined name is elected, modification will be required in the next generation. It would take mean parents to burden a child with four names! Perhaps one name could be dropped from each parent's side, the name to be determined by alphabetical order.

3. A special note for lawyers: this 1930s case, *In Re Kayaloff*, 9 F.Supp. 176 (S.D. N.Y. 1936), illustrates the harm that can be caused by the sloppy use of precedents. The Federal court cited two New York cases for the proposition that married women must take their husband's surname; however, the cases cited had not

imposed penalties on married women who refused to take the husband's name. The first cited decision refused to uphold the validity of a lawsuit against a married woman *who in fact used her husband's name*, where notice of the suit was sent to her in her maiden name and she never received the notice. In the second suit, the court refused a wife's request for an injunction forbidding another woman from using the wife's name. Clearly the judge's passing reference that, in his opinion, the common law required married women to use their husband's surname was not justified by the cases he cited. In representing women seeking to raise these issues, then, the lawyer must carefully read past precedent; most of it can be distinguished or dismissed as *dictum*.

4. *Krupa* v. *Green,* 114 Ohio App. 497, 177 N.E. 2d 616 (1961).

5. *People ex rel Rago* v. *Lipsky,* 327 Ill. App. 63, 63 N.E. 2d 642 (1945).

6. *Stuart* v. *Board of Supervisors of Elections,* 295 A.2d 223 (1972).

7. *Stuart* v. *Board of Supervisors of Elections,* 295 A.2d 223 (1972).

IX

A Miscellany of Sex-Discrimination Problems

This is a grab-bag chapter. Women still need new laws passed to remedy the problems they face in many areas. The questions that follow are primarily designed to remind readers of these areas, and to encourage them to press for new laws and for test litigation to establish new rights. The questions also point to some encouraging developments. A few laws have already been passed, and a few cases won.

May a public bar refuse to serve women?
Probably not, ever since the day Faith Seidenberg, a feminist attorney from Syracuse, New York, won the right to buy a drink at McSorleys' Old Ale House in New York City. McSorleys' has long been famous among New Yorkers for liederkranz cheese and onions served with ale and, likewise, for a refusal to serve women. When Ms. Seidenberg decided to have a sip of ale there, too, she narrowly escaped physical attack for her temerity. The

policeman who arrived on the scene threatened to arrest her rather than the men who initiated the violence, and she flew the scene. But she had the last word when she sued McSorleys' and won the right to have her drink.[1]

It is important to understand the court's legal theory because it broke new ground and can be applied elsewhere. Usually private companies like McSorleys' are not covered by the Equal Protection clause of the Fourteenth Amendment. In this case the court decided that when the state chose to regulate the sale of liquor, it became so involved in the McSorleys' business that the business reflected "state action." Once the state is involved, the refusal to sell liquor to women must survive the Equal Protection test—and this, McSorleys' policy could not do. Even McSorleys' could hardly claim with a straight face that serving liquor to women is going to upset the moral equilibrium of the nation, as people once justified this policy. Thus, this case can be used in other states to challenge similar policies; if litigation doesn't work, women can then lobby for new laws. (A recent Supreme Court decision, *Moose Lodge No. 107* v. *Irvis,* casts doubts on whether the McSorleys' decision will help women in other states. See the discussion of the *Moose Lodge* case below.)

May a private club refuse to admit women?

Yes, under the Equal Protection law, but women may be able to get the state to withdraw a club's liquor license unless it will admit women. There's the rub, as they found to their surprise down at Mory's, when some Yale law students decided they had had enough of the club's grand old all-male traditions. The women petitioned the Connecticut Liquor Control Commission to withdraw Mory's liquor license under two Connecticut laws: one defining private clubs, the other bidding state agencies to use their licensing power to combat discrimination. The commission accepted the women's contention that Mory's was not private and that the commission should not give a liquor license to a club that discriminates, and it withdrew the license under the authority of both laws. This action has been postponed, pending the outcome of an appeal by Mory's. If the women prevail, however, Mory's will either have to admit women or try to continue business as usual without serving alcohol to its male customers. Other women (and men) are trying to take away the liquor license of the Harvard Club in New York City.

Women elsewhere should look for similar state laws that can be used to harass and build up pressure on many so-called private clubs. Even if state authorities won't condition a liquor license on admitting women, as Connecticut was willing to do, examining the club's bona fides as a private club could open up alternative attack routes. For instance, if the club doesn't fit the state definition of being private, it may have to get a public liquor license and admit the general male public. As a *public* accommodation, the *McSorleys'* precedent or state public-accommodation laws could be used to attack the exclusion of women.

If a club is really private, this tactic will not work. But many so-called private clubs may have some embarrassing questions to answer. How closely, for instance, are new members screened? Are all males automatically qualified for membership, simply by virtue of their sex? Are elections ever held to select a board of directors? Do the members really own the club?

Genuinely private clubs *will* be immune to attack (unless the state has a law like Connecticut's, telling the state liquor control agency to use its licensing power to combat discrimination). That is because the Supreme Court recently decided that state regulation of liquor did not create enough state action in a private club to bring the club under the Fourteenth Amendment and prohibit it from excluding black guests.[2] The case involved a local Moose lodge.

We don't yet know whether the Supreme Court would reach the same conclusion about bars like McSorleys' that are not private but are open to the general public. Until the Court decides that issue, women should still try attacking public bars and restaurants under the *McSorleys'* precedent.

What other methods can be used to combat discrimination practiced by private clubs and fraternal orders?

Women can seek to take away from such groups various forms of government financial aid, including: tax-exempt status, both Federal and state; the deductibility of gifts to such groups; and government grants or subsidies. The Portland City Club in Portland, Oregon, currently faces such an attack; the ACLU is helping women and men to contest the club's tax-exempt status.[3] Using this approach, blacks have already succeeded in a number of suits against the Elks.[4] None of these cases force clubs or fraternal orders to cease discriminating. They do increase the costs of discriminating, and thus provide powerful leverage for change.

Are there any state or city laws forbidding public bars, restaurants, and hotels from discriminating against women?

Yes. A few states and cities have already passed such

laws, generally referred to as public accommodation laws. More are needed. Chart B in the Appendix shows the states with these laws, as well as the much larger category of states with public-accommodations laws that do not outlaw sex discrimination. The Federal government is in the latter category, for Title II of the 1964 Civil Rights Act forbids only discrimination based on race, religion, color, and national origin.

The issues raised under these laws are sometimes complex. For instance, New York City has decided that residential hotels for women should open their doors to men, and that barber and beauty shops should serve all clients. Some women may not desire this result, because of an instinct for privacy, and others may not think the issue important. But for women who want to mingle with men and who believe it is insulting to be excluded from any public area, the passage of new public-accommodations laws and the inclusion of sex discrimination in existing laws should be a pressing concern.

May a landlord refuse to rent or sell an apartment or house because of a person's sex?

The answer to this question is almost everywhere still yes. And although the press has given little publicity to this problem, many women find themselves virtually unable to get housing. Many landlords suspect single women of being prostitutes and separated women with children of being unable to support themselves. In a few states, legislation has been passed to forbid the practice. Women in these few states (see Chart B) should begin to avail themselves of the remedy; in other states, they must seek new laws.

Is it legal for a bank or lending institution to refuse to give women mortgages or other financing for housing?

Again, very few states prohibit this practice (see Chart B). There are many variants on the basic discrimination. The bank may refuse to give all women mortgages, so that single or separated women find it practically impossible to purchase their own home. The bank may refuse to count a married woman's income, or count only a fraction of her income, in deciding whether the couple's income level is high enough to grant a mortgage. The assumption is that she will have children and cease working; even women who have young children and are presently working find themselves faced with this assumption.

New laws are clearly needed in this area, as in others. Women should also press the various Federal agencies that regulate banks and other lending institutions to adopt stringent regulations prohibiting sex discrimination in lending policies. The relevant agencies are the Federal Reserve Board, the Federal Home Loan Bank Board, the Federal Deposit Insurance Corporation, the Comptroller of the Currency, and the Federal Housing Administration. One quasi-governmental agency, the Federal National Mortgage Association, recently took a small step in the right direction by informing lending institutions that it would buy mortgages granted to couples where the institution counted the wife's income. The keynote is reasonableness—would it be reasonable, given the past history and circumstances of the couple, to assume that the wife would continue working? This should help counter the policy of banks which still insist on discounting all or most of the wife's income. If a woman encounters this, she should inform the bank of the FNMA policy and complain to FNMA about the bank. (The FNMA national office is located at 1133 15th Street, N.W., Washington, D.C.)

Is it legal for a bank to grant a mortgage to a couple on the condition that they sign an agreement not to have children?

Although no law prohibits a bank from doing this, no court is apt to enforce such an agreement because it would be against public policy to do so. If you face this situation, the best thing to do is just to sign the agreement, take your mortgage, and go right ahead and have children if you so desire. As long as you keep up your payments, there is little the bank can do about it. After all, bank officials will hardly want to sue you for a forced abortion or adoption. Nor can they repossess the house if you have not defaulted on the payments.

In Washington, D.C., the Women's Legal Defense Fund was faced with this precise situation, and gave that advice. The fund may help the couple sue for a "declaratory judgment" that the agreement not to have children is legally unenforceable. Ask your lawyer about bringing such a lawsuit if faced with this problem.

How should women protest discrimination in public accommodations, housing, and financing under the various state and city laws?

Many of these laws provide for comprehensive enforcement schemes under the same state agency that regulates employment discrimination. It is not possible to explain in this handbook the various procedures under all these laws, but some general advice would be to call the state employment discrimination agency (see Appendix, Chart A) and ask for information about where to go and what to do next. If the agency cannot help, women could try reading the law itself (see Chart B for the legal citations for all such state laws). If this is not informative, the help of a lawyer will be needed.

An obvious project for paralegal counseling groups would be to research the local laws and write and distribute pamphlets explaining how to use these laws. Lawyers or law students should help—both to locate laws that may not be included in the chart (city laws, or ones passed after publication of this book) and to check the accuracy of the legal advice proposed by the counseling group.

Can the Federal government and the states discriminate against women in job-training programs?

The answer is not settled, but this should be an easy issue to win because it is connected to employment rights, and courts have been very strict in eliminating employment discrimination. The Federal government, in conjunction with state governments, offers a multitude of job training programs, such as Job Corps, Manpower Development and Training Act programs (MDTA), and Work Incentive (WIN). Many of the programs are sex-segregated, quotas are used to keep women's enrollment down, women are trained predominantly for low-paying, traditionally "female" jobs, and some programs have given priority to male applicants. This last provision has been successfully challenged under both the Equal Protection clause and Title VII of the 1964 Civil Rights Act.[5] The decision suggests that the widespread sex discrimination in these programs is ripe for challenge. The government will return the challenge, of course—as was shown when Congress re-enacted the WIN preference for men after the successful decision.

Can parents legally establish day-care centers for their children?

It depends. This question is presented to highlight the fact that states and cities throughout the country have enacted a variety of extremely restrictive day-care regulations. By requiring a higher standard of care than most parents achieve in their own home, they raise costs so high that most parents cannot afford to start any day-care center at all.

Typically restrictive features include these: only women can take care of very young children; centers may not accept children below the age of two or three; the center must have plenty of park space, and a defined amount of space per child (even in big cities where land is costly and the children serviced would never have such space at home, anyway). There are many other restrictions, too varied to detail at length here, but these few indicate the general problem. Authorities who would prefer that mothers stay home to tend their children have imposed such unrealistic and costly conditions on day-care centers that parents are forced to resort to totally unregulated centers or homes since they must find some place to leave their children while they work. These regulations should be challenged, and new, more realistic ones enacted.

Where can parents get help in establishing day-care centers?

One source of information is the Day Care and Child Development Council of America. The council publishes a pamphlet, *Basic Facts About Licensing of Day Care,* which is available for $.50, and a newsletter, *Action For Children.* Both can be obtained by writing to;

> Day Care & Child Development Council of America
> 1426 H Street, N.W.
> Washington, D.C. 20005

The council also has three organizers who will help interested local groups start day-care centers.

Other sources include: *Day Care: How To Plan, Develop and Operate a Day Care Center,* by E. Belle Evans, Beth Schub, and Marlene Weinstein (Beacon Press, $6.95); and *So You're Going to Run a Day Care Service.* The last is available from the:

> Day Care Council of New York, Inc.
> 114 East 32nd Street
> New York, N.Y. 10016

Can most parents afford to establish the quality day-care centers that are needed?

Probably not. Realistically, parents need Federal aid to establish the quantity and quality of day-care centers needed. President Nixon recently vetoed a bill designed to make a substantial start toward Federally supported, comprehensive child-care facilities, and pressure is needed to get a new bill. One feature feminists should be especially wary of is the tendency to make such care available only to the poor. Parents of all income levels need this program, and an absence of quality day care keeps the middle-income woman tied to her home just as much as the lower-income woman. The solution may be to make day care available to all, but on a sliding-fee scale. Women will have to fight for this provision, though, since it faces the opposition of both conservative and liberal Congressmen.

Is there any income-tax relief for parents who do use day-care centers?

Yes. Congress has passed a law giving a substantial deduction—for the first time—for the costs of day care. Parents with a joint income of eighteen thousand dollars or less can now deduct up to four hundred dollars per month from their income for day-care expenses within the home for children under fourteen. (They are allowed two hundred dollars per month for one child, three thundred dollars for two children, and four hundred dollars for three or more for care outside the home). Where the couple's adjusted gross income exceeds eighteen thousand dollars, the amount of the annual deduction is reduced by one half of the excess income over eighteen thousand dollars. Although this provision is a substantial improvement, many women feel that there should be no limit on upper income or on the amount of the deduction. After all, the wealthy businessman who gets to deduct the cost of his yacht as a business expense is not told that he cannot do this if he makes more than eighteen thousand dollars a year, nor is he limited on the cost of the yacht. On the other hand, some people would prefer to give a tax credit, rather than a deduction, for child-care expenses in order to avoid subsidizing child care most heavily for the rich.

Should housewives be entitled to wages, vacations, sick leave, medical insurance, unemployment compensation, workman's compensation, and pension plans?

Why not? Paying housewives a salary and fringe benefits might resolve the contradiction now found in society's attitude. Rhetorically, the housewife is praised, told that motherhood and care of the home are the backbone of our society, and that this is the finest role she can ever fulfill. But financially, she is told that the job is worthless. Any money she gets is a gift from her husband. It is support —money she has not earned, but which he chooses to give her. She is also informed that she doesn't really work; work is something done only for pay. Thus when her husband gets home from a hard day at the plant or office, she is supposed to wait on him, on the theory that she has not been working all day. The average housewife has been working just as hard as her husband, and they should both share the household duties at night, after both have finished their daytime activities; they should both be compensated; they should both receive fringe benefits.

Compensating the housewife might increase a woman's sense of self-worth. Earnings are a measure of pride and independence in this society. The woman who works in the home does many important things, and she deserves to be rewarded in the same way as are other people in our society.

Is there any practical way for housewives to receive pay?

Yes. The simplest way to pay housewives (or men who take the same job) would be to institute a modified community-property system nationwide. Community property is the law in eight states. It declares that all property acquired by either the man or the woman during marriage belongs to both equally, thus recognizing that the woman's contribution to the family unit is just as valuable as the man's. However, most of the eight community-property states reserve management and control rights to the husband.[6] He can unilaterally decide to sell the house belonging to them both or to splurge the jointly owned paycheck.

For practical purposes, management and control rights are equivalent to ownership rights, so this aspect of the system must be changed by giving the woman co-equal management and control rights over the community property. In addition, she should be given the right to sue the husband (and vice versa where appropriate) to acquire her half of the income and the property, even if the marriage is ongoing and the parties are living together. The right to sue is vital if her ownership and control of half the family income is to mean anything. This right also represents a radical departure from current legal concepts of the relationship between husband and wife. By and large, courts refuse to interfere in an ongoing relationship between the two—they will leave the couple to work it out in private. (This is why the right to "support" is an illusion; it remains a gift the husband can choose to give. There is no way a woman who wants to live with her stingy husband can sue him for the money. The courts don't want to interfere.) Thus, the concept of intervening—particularly in order to take away what most judges will see as "his" income, to give it to an "undeserving" woman who doesn't even "work"—will be hard to achieve.

Are there any problems with compensating the house-wife through a modified community-property system?

There may be problems with this scheme, of course. The suggestions above are intended primarily to stimulate discussion of the issue. Some feminists would disagree with the proposed solution for several reasons.

First, they would argue that we should not encourage women to stay home, and that this scheme would have the effect of doing so. Other feminists would reply that women who are going to stay home anyway should at least be compensated for the work they do, and that paying for this work might encourage more men to stay home for some of the years of child-rearing.

Second, giving a woman a salary based on the husband's income deemphasizes the idea of being paid for the value of one's work. On the other hand, it emphasizes that marriage is a partnership, in a world where many people—both men and women—still believe that young children should be reared by a parent.

Third, some would argue that the housewife married to a rich man can employ household workers to do much of the traditional housewife's job, and therefore gets paid more for doing less than the housewife married to a poor man. On the other hand, the woman with a rich husband may perform other services of a valuable nature, such as entertaining and elaborate garden work. Perhaps this work, too, deserves compensation.

Finally, some people believe that the scheme does not help the woman who works outside the home and still does all the housework; although she does two jobs, she gets paid for only one. But in reply, one can point out that at least community property would increase the amount of money and property owned by most women holding down two jobs. The average woman is statistically apt to earn less than her husband because of employment discrimination. Since community property gives her one half of the combined incomes, the system would indeed compensate her in some degree for her "two" jobs; for one half of the combined incomes would be greater than the outside salary alone for most women working outside the home.

How can women achieve a modified community-property system with co-equal management and control rights?

They should lobby for new laws instituting the community-property system—modified to give women co-equal management and control rights—throughout the nation. Women in the eight community-property states should bring lawsuits based on the Equal Protection clause to obtain co-equal management and control rights over their community property.

In the interim, women may be able to negotiate contracts with their husbands to accomplish the same result. The courts are not likely to uphold such contracts, although the chances are greater if the parties enter into them before marriage rather than after. In either case, many people should still find it worth doing for the psychological effect of formally agreeing to be equal partners.

Women should also explore the possibility of getting a law passed to validate such contracts in states where it is impossible to pass a community-property law. Such a contract would provide that both parties equally own and control one half of all income and property acquired during the marriage, and that if one party retains control over the other party's half, the second person could sue the first for his or her rightful share. A provision that the wrongful party pay for attorneys' fees, court costs, and interest should also be included in order to make it easier to get a lawyer to bring such a lawsuit.

Is there another way in which women might equalize the financial situation in marriage?

Yes. Women could make written agreements with their husbands to loan them money for certain expenses to be repaid at standard interest rates. For example, a young wife who finances her husband's graduate or professional education by working while he goes to school could at least insure repayment of this money. Such a loan agreement would be legally enforceable.

Is there any way for women to insure that their husbands share the work of maintaining the house and rearing the children?

No, but women might want to make a second kind of contract, setting forth the duties of each party during the marriage. Lawyers refer to this kind of contract as one dealing with the incidents of marriage, that is, the duties and obligations legally imposed on each partner under marriage law. It is clear that judges will not enforce a contract that seeks to change the common-law incidents of marriage, so this contract is useful only for its psychological effect. Women might also lobby for laws to validate these contracts—although the prospect of suing one's husband for breaking his contract by not doing the dishes has some troublesome overtones. In any case, women should keep these contracts separate from those providing for equal rights in income and property; the latter have a greater chance of being enforced, and if the two are mingled the court might find both invalid.

A "personal incidents" contract would detail the household duties for each party to the marriage, including care of the children. It could also provide for vacations, free evenings and weekends, and so forth, for each party. This would reinforce the point that the wife (or rare husband) who stays home does work all day and deserves some respite from that work.

For a good example of such a contract, read "How To Write Your Own Marriage Contract," by Susan Edmiston in the Spring 1972 issue of *Ms*. The article includes the "Shulman's Marriage Agreement," whose guiding principle is especially interesting:

> We reject the notion that the work which brings in more money is more valuable. The ability to earn more money is a privilege which must not be compounded by enabling the larger earner to buy out of his/her duties and put the burden on the partner who earns less or on another person hired from outside.

What ideas might be explored for providing fringe benefits for housewives?

Housewives will find it more difficult to get the other fringe benefits mentioned—sick leave, medical insurance, unemployment compensation, workman's compensation, and pension plans. Some women have suggested adding a component to existing social-insurance programs for women, or men, who work in the home. For example, if the housewife were injured while working, she would receive compensatory payments under the Workman's Compensation Act. If she were ill, she would be entitled to state payments from the Temporary Disability Insurance Program, in states with such a program. If she were divorced and the husband defaulted on alimony and child support, she would receive unemployment compensation. And she would be entitled to Social Security benefits in her own right, not as someone's wife; she would receive credit for income earned as a housewife during the years in the home, just as she would for income as a paid worker in the outside labor force for those years.

Of course, in-depth economic research is needed before we can know whether these ideas are feasible. Other important problems would also need to be resolved. For instance, under these programs who would be deemed the woman's employer? Should the woman who works both inside and outside the home receive double benefits? But the important thing is for women to begin exploring ways to better the economic position of the housewife. If real solutions can be developed, perhaps even men would become more willing to share the job with their wives.

What can women's paralegal projects do in this area?

They can work with attorneys on drawing up model contracts for women and help individual women write their own contracts. The legal effect of such contracts must be explained, of course, and the group should ask attorneys to research state laws thoroughly on this question. Finally, women's groups can work with attorneys to prepare model legislation for all the problem areas mentioned in this chapter, and then help lobby for passage of such laws.

NOTES

1. *Seidenberg* v. *McSorleys' Old Ale House,* 317 F.Supp. 593 (S.D. N.Y. 1970). A more recent decision is *Bennett* v. *Dyer's Chop House,* 41 U.S. Law Week 2243 (N.D. Ohio, Oct. 26, 1972).
2. *Moose Lodge No. 107* v. *Irvis,* 92 S.Ct. 1965 (1972).
3. *McCoy* v. *Schultz,* C.A. No. 1580-72 (D. D.C.). For information, contact: Roger L. Meyer, ACLU, 1111 Wilcox Building, Portland, Oregon 97204.
4. *Falkenstein* v. *Department of Revenue for the State of Oregon,* Civ. No. 71-816 (D. Ore., Nov. 20, 1972); *McGlotten* v. *Connally,* 338 F.Supp. 448 (D. D.C. 1972); *Pitts* v. *Department of Revenue for the State of Wisconsin,* 333 F.Supp. 662 (E.D. Wis. 1971).
5. *Thorn* v. *Richardson,* 4 FEP Cases 299 (W.D. Wash. 1971).
6. The eight states are: Arizona, California, Idaho, Louisiana, Nevada, New Mexico, Texas, and Washington. Texas recently modified its law to provide that each partner manages the money he or she earns on the outside until the marriage terminates. This does not help the woman who stays home to rear children; she still has no management or control over her half of the community property.

X

The Legal System

For many persons, law appears to be black magic—
an obscure domain that can be fathomed only by the professional initiated into its mysteries. Women who might use
the law to their advantage sometimes avoid the effort out
of excess awe for its intricacies. But the main lines of the
legal system, and of the law in a particular area, can be
explained in terms clear to the layperson.

Many women are seeking to improve their lot in life
generally or are searching for solutions to specific problems. Often they have legal rights to better treatment
but don't know about these rights or how to assert them.
The purpose of this book has been to describe in direct,
concrete fashion the legal rights of women and the ways
in which these rights can be implemented so that women
can use law to achieve their goals. In this concluding
chapter, however, the nature of the legal system and some
of its key concepts are described to render more useful
the specific information about women's rights.

What does a lawyer mean by saying that a person has a legal right?

Having a right means that society has given a person permission—through the legal system—to secure some action or to act in some way that she or he desires. A woman might have a right to an abortion, a right to employment free from discrimination, or a right to use whatever name she likes.

How does one enforce a legal right?

The concept of *enforcing* a right gives meaning to the concept of the right itself. While the abstract right may be significant to a particular woman because it carries some connotation of morality and justice, enforcing the right yields something concrete—the abortion, the job, the name.

A woman enforces her right by going to some appropriate authority—often, a judge—who has the power to take certain action. The judge can order the people who are refusing to grant the right to start doing so, on pain of going to jail if they disobey. The judge can also order the people to pay the woman money to compensate her for the loss of the right. Sometimes she will turn to other authorities such as Federal and state administrative agencies (see below for definition) or a labor arbitrator.

The problem with the enforcement process is that it will often be lengthy, time-consuming, expensive, frustrating, and arouse hostility in others—in short, it may not be worth the effort. On the other hand, in some cases you

may not need to go to an enforcement authority in order
to implement your right. The concerned persons or officials
may not realize that you have a particular right and may
voluntarily change their actions once you explain your
rights. Then, too, they may not want to go through the
legal process either—it may be as expensive and frustrating
for them as it is for you.

If you understand what your rights are, you will be
equipped to convince others to recognize them. Should
your explanation and effort at persuasion fail to achieve
the desired result, knowledge of your rights and their
significance will enable you to decide whether to go forward with enforcement. The time and expense may be
justified in terms of your own self-dignity or the importance of the right to other women.

What is a moral right?

This question emphasizes the point that although the
formal legal system does not always give you important
rights, you may still be entitled to them in the sense of a
larger justice. Arguably, it may still be legal for Harvard
University to admit undergraduate students in the ratio
of four men to every one woman. But in a larger, moral
sense, we can believe that a woman has a right to an
equal chance for admission, and that Harvard has acted
arbitrarily and unjustly in its preference for men and its
maintenance of a restrictive quota for women. The conviction that the woman has a moral right to fair treatment should then lead us to fight for new laws that will
secure for her the legal right as well.

An underlying philosophy of this book is that women do
have the moral right to equal treatment with men in every

facet of life. The preceding chapters have both identified existing legal rights and explored those areas in which women have moral rights with uncertain, if any, legal support—areas in which they should press for corrective legislation.

Where are legal rights defined?

There are several sources. Rights are defined in the statutes or laws passed by the United States Congress and by state and city legislatures. They are also set forth in the written decisions of judges—both Federal and state. Congress and state and local legislatures have also created institutions called administrative agencies to enforce certain laws, and these agencies interpret the laws in written decisions and rules that further define people's rights.

Are rights always clearly defined and evenly applied to all people?

Not at all, although this is one of the great myths about law. Because so many different sources define people's rights, and because persons of diverse backgrounds and beliefs implement and enforce the law, there is virtually no way to assure uniformity. Nor do statutes that set forth rights always do so with clarity or in great detail. It remains for judges or personnel in administrative agencies to provide interpretation and to flesh out the details; and in the process of doing so, many of the interpreters reach different solutions. For example, the Equal Protection clause of the Fourteenth Amendment affirms that all citizens are entitled to equal treatment from the state, but it fails to define equal treatment. At different times, two groups of women seeking to be admitted to all-male schools sued state officials on the grounds that they were not getting equal treatment. The first suit witnessed the first time in its then ninety-year-old history that women had ever used the Fourteenth Amendment to attack sex-segregated public universities. The judge—a state judge—who interpreted the Equal Protection clause in this first situation found that the equal treatment requirement did not extend to exclusion of women from a public university; the prospective students lost their lawsuit.[1] Ten years later, a second court—a Federal court in a different part of the country—read the same Fourteenth Amendment, decided it does include sex discrimination, and declared that school officials were required to admit women.[2] So do women have an equal right to go to public universities? The answer, based on these two decisions, is: sometimes yes, sometimes no.

The situation is not always this ambiguous. The more times a particular issue is decided, the more guidance you have in predicting what other judges or administrative personnel will decide. Similarly, the importance of the court or agency deciding a case or the persuasiveness of its reasoning will help determine the effect of its decisions on other authorities. A decision of the Supreme Court will affect other judges' interpretation of the law much more than that of a state court; someone who articulates thoughtful reasons for a decision will have more influence than one who offers no reasons. There are degrees of predictability to rights; some that have been presented in this book will be more certain of attainment than others, but in all cases there will be some solid ground for an effort directed toward recognition of the right in question. But even though one can predict, one can never *know* in advance what the final result of a lawsuit will be—a very important point to keep in mind in reading this book and contemplating legal action.

Law then is not a preordained set of doctrines, applied rigidly and unswervingly in every situation. Rather, law is molded from the arguments and decisions of thousands of persons. It is very much a human process, a game of trying to convince others—a judge, a jury, an administrator, the lawyer for the other side—that your view of what the law requires is correct. The game of convincing others is carried out in a clearly defined forum with clearly defined ground rules, but otherwise it is not really that different from trying to convince people in general that your position is correct and that they ought to act accordingly. Once women understand that law is a process of convincing others, rather than formalized rules dropped from on high, they will be able to use law as an instrument to create change.

What is a decision or case?

Lawyers often use these words interchangeably, although technically they do not mean the same thing. A case means the lawsuit started by one person against another, and it can refer to that lawsuit at any time from the moment it is started until the final result is reached. A decision means the written memorandum in which the judge declares who wins the lawsuit and why.

What is meant by precedent?

Precedent means past decisions. Lawyers use precedent

to influence the decision a judge reaches today. If the facts involved in the prior decision are close to the facts in the present case, the judge will be strongly tempted to follow the former decision. He is not, however, bound to do so and, if persuasive reasons are presented to show that the prior decision was wrong or ill-suited to changed conditions in society, he may not follow precedent.

What is the relationship between decisions and statutes?
In our legal system, most legal concepts originally were defined in the decisions of judges. In deciding what legal doctrine to apply to any case, each judge kept building on what other judges had done before him. The body of legal doctrines created in this way is called the common law.

The common law still applies in many situations, but increasingly state legislatures and the Congress pass laws, or statutes, to define the legal concepts that judges or agencies should use in deciding cases. The written decisions of individual judges are still very important even where there is a statute because the statute is generally not specific enough to cover every set of facts. The judges have to interpret the meaning of the statute, apply it to the facts at hand, and write a decision; that decision will then be considered by other judges when they deal with the same statute in another case. Thus, it is generally not enough to know what a relevant statute defines as illegal; you also have to know how the judges have interpreted that statute in specific fact situations. For instance, the Civil Rights Act of 1964 says it is illegal to discriminate on the basis of sex in employment. If an employer fires a pregnant woman because she is pregnant, even though she is physically able to work, has he violated this law? You can't tell just by reading the words of the statute, which do not mention pregnancy. Instead, you must read the guidelines and decisions of administrators and judges interpreting the statute in that fact situation or in a closely related situation. (So far, the agency and most judges have said the policy is illegal.)

What different kinds of courts are there?

The United States is unique for its variety of courts. Broadly speaking, there are two distinct court systems: Federal and state. Both are located physically throughout the country, but each is limited to certain kinds of cases, with substantial areas of overlap. Most crimes are prosecuted in state courts, for instance, although there are a number of Federal crimes prosecuted in Federal court. People must always use state courts to get a divorce, but they must sue in Federal courts to establish their rights under certain Federal laws, such as the 1964 Civil Rights Act.

A distinction present in both Federal and state court systems is that between trial and appellate courts. In either system, one starts out at the trial-court level, where the facts are "tried." This means that a judge or jury listens and watches as the lawyers for each side present evidence of the facts that each side seeks to prove. Evidence can take many forms: written documents, the testimony of a witness on the stand, photographs, charts. Once the judge or jury has listened to or observed all the evidence presented by each side, it will choose the version of the facts it believes, apply the applicable legal doctrine to these facts, and decide which side has won. If either side is unhappy with the results, that side may be able to take the case to the next, higher-level court and argue that the judge or the jury applied the wrong legal concept to the facts, or that no reasonable jury or judge could have found the facts as they were found in the trial court, and that the result was therefore wrong. The process of contesting your initial loss is called an appeal because you are "appealing" to a higher authority to tell the lower court that it was wrong. All courts above the trial court are called appellate courts. Although there is generally only one level of court that conducts a trial, hearing evidence and deciding the facts, there may be two or more tiers of appellate courts.

In the Federal system, the trial courts are called District Courts. The first tier of Federal appellate courts is the Court of Appeals; above that is the United States Supreme Court. Geographically the country is broken into ten circuits, with one Court of Appeals in each numbered circuit. The Court of Appeals is generally referred to by the number of the circuit—e.g., the Second Circuit (abbreviated as 2d Cir.). Each circuit is in turn divided into several districts, and the Court of Appeals for the circuit hears the appeals from all the District Courts within its boundaries. The District Courts are given geographic names, e.g., the Southern District of New York (abbreviated, S.D. N.Y.), the Northern District of California (N.D. Cal.).

In the state system, each state sets up its own series of trial and appellate courts. The number and the names of these courts differ in each state. For example, New York State has a trial court called the Supreme Court (notice that the lowest court here has the same name as the highest Federal court), followed by the Appellate Division of the Supreme Court as the first appellate-level court. The Court of Appeals is the highest appellate level in New York. Litigants can sometimes appeal a de-

cision of the highest state appellate court to the United
States Supreme Court.

In addition to these general courts, there are special
courts that handle exclusively cases involving a particular
subject matter, such as tax. Another example is the United
States Court of Claims, which only handles lawsuits in
which people assert a claim against the government.

In general the higher the court in either the Federal or
the state system, the more influential the decisions of its
judges will be within that system. Thus, a United States
Supreme Court decision will have enormous impact on
both state and Federal judges, who will feel bound to try to
follow it; the highest state appellate court will have a
similar impact on lower-court decisions within that state.
High state- and Federal-court decisions may be influential
in other states and circuits or in the other system, but in
most cases courts of another system will not feel bound in
the same way as they do by decisions of a court in a direct
line of authority over them. Finally, certain judges acquire a reputation for being better than others and, consequently, their decisions have a greater influence on other
courts.

Weighing all these factors can help women interpret the
effect of any given decision. By knowing how high a court
voiced a decision, how respected a judge issued it, and
whether most cases involving the issue will be brought
in that system, you can decide whether the results are
likely to affect the rights of many women or of just a few.
A United States Supreme Court decision will always affect
the rights of many; a first-level state appellate-court decision written by an obscure judge and dealing with an
issue normally decided in the Federal court system will
affect the rights of very few women. You should be aware
of these distinctions when trying to convince others of

your rights, and you should probe for these factors in evaluating what others tell you about your rights.

What are plaintiffs and defendants?

The plaintiff is the person who sues—that is, who com*plains* that someone has wronged her and asks the court to remedy this situation. The defendant is the person sued —or the one who *defends* herself against the charges of the plaintiff. The legal writing in which the plaintiff articulates her basic grievance is the com*plaint,* and a lawsuit is generally commenced by filing this document with the clerk at the courthouse. The defendant then responds to these charges in a document appropriately named an *answer.*

One refers to a particular lawsuit by giving the names of the plaintiff and defendant. If Mary Jones sues Smith Corporation for refusing to hire her because she is a woman, her case will be called *Jones* v. *Smith Corporation* (v. stands for versus, or against).

What is an administrative agency?

Agencies are institutions established by both state and Federal legislatures to administer or enforce a particular law or series of laws and are distinct from both courts and legislatures. They often regulate a particular industry. For example, the Federal Communications Commission regulates the broadcasting industry (radio and television stations and networks) and the telephone and telegraph industry, in accordance with the legal standards set forth in the Federal Communications Act. Or the Interstate Commerce Commission regulates the ground-transportation industry.

The personnel in these agencies establish broad legal principles, referred to as rules, regulations, or guidelines. Rules are interpretations of a statute and are designed to function in the same way as a statute does—to define people's rights and obligations on a general scale, although in somewhat more detailed fashion than the statute itself. Agencies also issue specific decisions in particular cases, applying, as does a judge, a broad law or rule to the factual dispute between particular parties.

In essence, an administrative agency is an institution that works parallel to, and sometimes subordinate to, the courts. People must often take their dispute to an agency first in order to establish some right, but may then appeal the agency's decision to a court. In that instance, the agency functions as an informal trial court.

Women should learn about agencies—they have figured prominently in this book, particularly in the chapters on employment rights and on the mass media—because these institutions administer laws that give women important rights.

How does one find and read court decisions, statutes, and agency rules and decisions?

All these materials are published and can be found in law libraries. In order to find the item desired, one should understand the system lawyers use for referring to, or citing, these materials. Some examples will help clarify the system. A case might be cited as *Watson* v. *Limbach Company,* 333 F.Supp. 754 (S.D. Ohio 1971); a law, as 42 U.S.C. §1983; a regulation, as 29 C.F.R. §1604.10(b). The unifying factor in all three citations is that the first number denotes the particular volume in a series of books with the same title; the words or letters that follow represent the name of the book; and the second number represents either the page or the section in the identified volume. In the examples above, the case is found in the 333rd volume of the series of books called *Federal Supplement* at page 754; the statute is found in volume 42 of the series called *United States Code* at section 1983; the regulation is in volume 29 of the *Code of Federal Regulations* at section 1604.10(b). Once you understand the system, all you need do is find out from the librarian where any particular series of books is kept, then look up the proper volume and page or section. It is also important to look for the same page or section in the paper insert at the back of the book, since many legal materials are periodically updated by this insert. The librarian will tell you what any abbreviations stand for if you are unfamiliar with that series.

The other information given in the citation to a decision includes the last names of the parties to the lawsuit, the name of the court, and the year the decision was written. In the example, Mr. Watson sued the Limbach Company; the court that reached this decision was the U.S. District Court for the Southern District of Ohio, and the year was 1971.

Series of legal volumes are often organized to reflect the institution responsible for the laws or legal doctrines found in those books. The decisions of District Court judges are found in the *Federal Supplement* (F.Supp.) series; all laws passed by the United States Congress are found in the *United States Code* (U.S.C.); and all regulations issued by Federal agencies are found in the *Code of Federal Regulations* (C.F.R.). Another way that legal books are organized is by subject matter. One publisher issues a series of books called *Fair Employment Practice Cases*. These books cover all cases in which discrimination in employment is involved —no matter what kind of court or agency issued the decision.

Given this basic information, anyone can locate and read important cases, statutes, and regulations. Throughout the book, such materials have been cited when deemed particularly important, and women are urged to read them. Although lawyers often use overly technical language, the references cited in this book can be comprehended without serious difficulty, and reading the original legal materials will give women greater self-confidence and a deeper understanding of their rights. Paralegal groups who want to help other women learn and assert their rights would be particularly advised to read these materials in order to get a more fundamental grasp of the law.

Where can one find a law library?

The biggest and best ones will be found at law schools. Another source would be the libraries of bar associations, although access to these by laypersons may be restricted. Ask a lawyer for suggestions if all else fails.

What is the role of the lawyer in the legal system?

A lawyer understands the intricacies and technicalities of the legal system, can maneuver within it efficiently, and helps other people by doing so. Thus, the lawyer knows where to find out about the leading legal doctrines in any given area and how to predict the outcome of your case, based on a knowledge of those doctrines. A lawyer can advise you what to do: forget about the case; take it to an administrative agency; sue in court; make a will; and so on.

The lawyer then helps you take the legal actions that you determine are necessary.

For an in-depth exploration of a lawyer's roles, readers might like to consult Johnstone and Hopson, *Lawyers and Their Work* (Bobbs-Merrill, 1967).

How are legal costs determined and how do they affect people's rights?

The cost of using the legal system is predominantly the cost of paying the lawyer for her or his time. Since the cost has become prohibitive for even middle-class individuals, many people are not able to assert their rights, even though they might ultimately win if they had the money to pay a lawyer for doing the job.

This poses a severe problem for women, many of whom have little or no money of their own. One of the aims of this book has been to present ideas for areas where paralegal women's groups can help other women to assert their legal rights on their own. However, there is a fine line between actually acting as another woman's lawyer—which may be illegal—and lending a supporting hand to help other women assert their rights by themselves. One way to draw that line is to question whether the activity of a paralegal group takes money away from a lawyer. If so, some lawyers might consider the activity to be unauthorized, and this could get the group in trouble. Participation of or cooperation with a lawyer sympathetic to the aims of the group can help to avoid problems of this nature.

Is legal action the only way to win one's legal rights?

By no means. Negotiation, education, consciousness-raising, publicity, demonstrations, organization, and lobbying are all ways to achieve rights, often more effectively than through the standard but costly and time-consuming resort to the courts.[3] In all these areas, though, it helps to have secure knowledge of the legal underpinning of your rights. One has a great deal more authority if one is protesting illegal action. The refrain, "that's illegal," may move some people in and of itself; or it may convince those with whom you are dealing that you're serious enough to do something about the situation—by starting a lawsuit, for instance.

This book, of course, does focus on rights and how to assert them through legal action. This is not because law is the only way, or even the best way, to change women's status; however, it is *one* way to achieve change, and a way women could utilize more than they have in the past. Women have often not acted forcefully enough because of a lack of knowledge. This book has been designed to fill that knowledge gap and, also, to inspire women to assert their legal rights. For if women actually try to enforce the rights now on the books, they could achieve enormous change in our society. It only requires the will to do so.

NOTES

1. *Allred* v. *Heaton*, 336 S.W. 2d 251, *cert. denied*, 364 U.S. 517 (1960).
2. *Kirstein* v. *Rectors and Visitors of University of Virginia*, 309 F.Supp. 184 (E.D. Va. 1970).
3. For the effective use of other methods, see D. K. Ross, *A Public Citizen's Action Manual* (Grossman, 1973), especially Chapters 3 and 6.

APPENDIX

Chart A:*

State Laws Forbidding Employment Discrimination

Explanation of Chart. Most states have passed a wide variety of laws forbidding employment discrimination. This chart is provided as a supplement to Chapter II in order to enable women to apply the maximum amount of pressure by using all remedies available to them at the state level as well as the Federal level. The end of that chapter outlined reasons why it is important to know how many different laws there are and what the differences are among them. Although much of that discussion re-

---

*The research for this chart, as well as for the charts that follow, may be incomplete. Readers—and especially paralegal groups—are cautioned to do follow-up research on their own state's laws.

lates to Federal laws, the same themes can be applied to the differences among state laws.

For each state, in turn, the first horizontal column in the chart lists five kinds of laws and the citation for each. The laws covered: fair-employment-practice laws, which are generally modeled on Title VII and offer the same kind of broad coverage; equal pay laws, modeled on the Equal Pay Act; state contracts laws, which are modeled on Executive Order 11246, as amended by E.O. 11375, and which generally protect the employees of companies that hold contracts with the state government; state employees laws, which are sometimes modeled on Executive Order 11478 and prohibit the state government from discriminating against its own employees; and age discrimination laws, which are sometimes modeled on the Federal Age Discrimination Act or which may be included within other state antidiscrimination laws.

The second horizontal column tells whether the state law prohibits sex discrimination ("yes," if it does; "no," if it does not) and, in the case of age discrimination laws, what age groups are protected. Women should lobby to have sex added to the coverage of laws that do not presently reach sex discrimination. They should also check periodically for changes because states frequently pass new laws or amend existing laws in this field. The Equal Employment Opportunity Commission will help accelerate this trend because it is pressuring states to add sex-discrimination provisions to existing laws. In fact, the commission will no longer defer to states that have not prohibited sex discrimination after July 1, 1973. (For an explanation of deferral, see page 64.) This may force a lot of states to change their laws.

The third horizontal column gives the agency (along with its address and telephone number) that enforces the particular law, if that information was readily available to researchers. The FEP agency is always listed. If other agencies are not listed, women should try contacting the state FEP agency to help in locating them. Although the state contracts and state employees laws often do not indicate the agency that enforces the law, the appropriate agency will usually be the one holding the contract with the offending company (referred to as the Contracting Agency, where the law expressly indicates it) or the agency that employs the woman who is charging discrimination (referred to as the State Agency, where the law expressly indicates it). Since the governor often issues both of these laws, his office would be another source of information on how to assert one's rights under these laws.

The fourth horizontal column states the time limit within which employees must assert their rights. Generally this applies to the time they have to file a complaint with the agency. For example, Alaska's FEP law says ninety days; an employee there must file a complaint of discrimination with the State Commission for Human Rights within ninety days after the discrimination occurs. Time limits are extremely important because they can be used to prevent women from asserting their rights. Sometimes the time limit applies to the time women have to file a lawsuit; again, failure to comply can cause the loss of the lawsuit. This column also tells the number of employees an employer must have in order to be covered by the law. If a time limit or a number of employees is not listed, the applicable law does not give them. However, there may be a general state law that establishes time limits for bringing lawsuits, so it is important to complain about discrimination as soon as possible in all states.

The fifth horizontal column gives a code for the kind

of enforcement process that applicable state law establishes. This information will help women know the steps they need to take to enforce their rights and the options they have among the different processes.

Code one stands for a cease-and-desist enforcement process, under which the agency generally investigates the complaint, holds a hearing, and can order the company or union to cease discriminating and to pay back wages. The orders of the agency may be reviewed by the courts, but a new trial would not be held in court. If the agency enforces the law vigorously, this would be one of the best options for women since it requires the least time, effort, and money.

Code two stands for the right of an aggrieved individual to bring a lawsuit against the company or union; the court generally can order a cessation of discrimination and back wages. This option requires more from women complainants, but it could be a better choice in a state where the state agency is pro-business or fails to enforce the law effectively. At the Federal level, both Title VII and the Equal Pay Act are enforced in this way.

Code three stands for an agency lawsuit, which means that the agency itself goes into court on behalf of women complainants. Again, both Title VII and the Equal Pay Act can be enforced in this way. This process is also good for women with scant resources, but it depends on effective action by state-agency personnel—which is not always forthcoming.

Code four stands for criminal enforcement, with fines in the range of five hundred dollars and jail sentences of up to one year. This method depends on local officials prosecuting offending companies and unions, which they rarely ever do, so as a practical matter the method is virtually useless even though it sounds more severe than the others.

Code five stands for laws that do not expressly set forth any obvious enforcement scheme, or that are limited to encouraging or recommending compliance, or under which the state agency is supposed to discipline itself or cut off state contracts. State laws in this category are also virtually useless. In theory, state-agency personnel might discipline themselves or cut off contracts of state contractors who discriminate against women employees, but in practice they rarely do. (The code is summarized below.)

Women can use the information in this last column by lobbying for more effective enforcement where necessary. It is important to look at more than the paper enforcement scheme, though, since even the best plan can be sabotaged by a lack of state funding, an orientation of agency heads toward business interests, or a lack of education among agency personnel as to the full scope and meaning of discrimination. Women's groups should explore all these questions and begin pressuring state agencies to become more effective. Such action will become increasingly important, for the EEOC is likely to leave more and more of the individual discrimination complaints for state agencies to resolve while reserving class-wide complaints dealing with the rights of many employees for itself, as a way of maximizing the commission's slender resources.

A few general caveats about Chart A should be added. First, it is always better to read the laws themselves. The chart gives women the starting point for doing so. Second, the research for the chart was done in the spring of 1972; as the field is a rapidly changing one, women's groups should check for new laws or amendments to existing laws. Third, some of the legal citations are to little-used sources, particularly for state contracts and state-employees laws. If you cannot find a law in the official reporter system for that state's laws, try either the *Fair Employment Practice Manual* (Bureau of National Affairs), or 2 *Employment Practices Guide* (Commerce Clearing House). Both reproduce each state's employment discrimination laws, except that BNA does not include equal pay laws. Fourth, there has been no attempt to list city or local antidiscrimination agencies even though there are many of these, some of which are more effective than the state agency. For a list of such agencies, write for the *Directory of State and Local Anti-discrimination Agencies,* published by EEOC and updated on January 1 and July 1 of each year. It is available from: Office of State and Community Affairs, EEOC, 1800 G Street, N.W., Washington, D.C. 20506. Fifth, the kinds of employees who are protected vary widely from statute to statute. Depending on the law, the following categories of employees may be excluded: employees of a relative; domestic employees; employees of religious associations; employees of social, fraternal, and other nonprofit organizations; and/or employees of educational institutions. State employees are sometimes protected by the FEP, equal-pay, or age-discrimination laws, and sometimes they are not. The protection for employees of state contractors may be narrowed by limiting the kinds of contracts covered or by requiring that the contract reach a certain dollar level for coverage. Obviously, all these exclusions and limitations can dramatically affect the number of people protected by the laws, and lobbying should be undertaken to eliminate such gaps.

Finally, many state laws allow specific discriminatory practices that Federal courts have found to violate Title VII. Business interests have often lobbied for the inclusion of provisions such as those permitting different retirement ages for men and women. Women's groups should study state laws and lobby for amendments to eliminate those blatantly pro-business exceptions.

Summary of Enforcement Process Code

1—The state agency has the power to issue cease and desist orders, subject to judicial review.
2—Women have the right to file lawsuits in court against discriminators.
3—The state agency has the power to file lawsuits in court on behalf of complainants.
4—The discriminating company or union may be punished by criminal sanctions—either by fine or imprisonment.
5—There is no enforcement scheme, or the "enforcement" is limited to voluntary compliance, or a state is supposed to monitor its own employment practices or those of its contractors (and enforce the law by cutting off the contract).

CHART A

	FEP	Equal Pay	State Contracts	State Employees	Age Discrimination
1. Alaska	Alas. Stat. §§18.80.010 to 18.80.300, 22.10.20, 23.10.192	§§23.10.155 to 23.10.185	Gov. Code of Fair Prac., Art. II, 8-11-67	Gov. Code of Fair Prac., Art. I, 8-11-67	included in FEP, State Contracts, and State Employes laws
Sex; Age Limits	Yes	Yes	Yes	Yes	
Agency	State Comm'n. for Human Rights 520 MacKay Bldg. 338 Denali St. Anchorage 99501 (907)272-9504	Dept. of Labor E.S.D. Bldg. Box 1149 Juneau 99801	Contracting Agency	State Agency	
Time Limit; Number of Employees	90 days; 1 employee				
Process	1, 2, 4	2 or 3, 4	5	5	

	FEP	Equal Pay	State Contracts	State Employees	Age Discrimination
2. Arizona	Ariz. Rev. Stat. Ann. §§41-1401 to 41-1403, 41-1461 to 41-1466, 41-1481 to 41-1485	§§23-301 et seq., 23-340, 23-341	§23-373	none	none
Sex; Age Limits	Yes	Yes	No		
Agency	Ariz. Civil Rts. Comm'n. 1502 W. Jefferson St. Phoenix 85007 (602)271-5266	Industrial Comm'n. of Ariz. 2933 N. Central Ave. Phoenix	Bd. of Regents- Budget 411 N. Central Ave. Phoenix (and then, Ariz. Civ. Rts. Comm'n.)		
Time Limit; Number of Employees	60 days; 20 employees	6 months; 21 employees			
Process	1, 4	1, 2, 4	1 (by Civ. Rts. Comm'n.)		

	FEP	Equal Pay	State Contracts	State Employees	Age Discrimination
3. Arkansas	none	Ark. Stat. §§81-623 to 81-629	none	none	none
Sex; Age Limits		Yes			
Agency		Comm'n. of Labor Dept. of Labor Little Rock			
Time Limit; Number of Employees		2 years			
Process		2 or 3, 4			

	FEP	Equal Pay	State Contracts	State Employees	Age Discrimination
4. California	Cal. Labor Code §§1410 to 1433	§1197.5	§1735	Gov. Code of Fair Prac., 7-24-63	Cal. Unemployment Ins. Code §§2070 to 2078
Sex; Age Limits	Yes	Yes	Yes	No	40-64
Agency	FEP Comm'n, 455 Golden Gate Ave. P.O. Box 603 San Francisco 94101 (415)557-2000	Dept. of Industrial Relations Div. of Industrial Welfare 455 Golden Gate Ave. San Francisco 94101	Dept. of Industrial Relations Div. of Labor Law Enforcement 455 Golden Gate Ave. San Francisco 94101 and Contracting Agency	State Agency	Dept. of Human Resources Development (916) 445-8822
Time Limit; Number of Employees	1 year (plus 90 days extension in some circumstances); 5 employees	2 years if no knowledge of discrimination; 180 days if knowledge			6 employees
Process	1, 4	1, 2 or 3, 4	5	5	5

5. Colorado	FEP	Equal Pay	State Contracts	State Employees	Age Discrimination
	Colo. Rev. Stat. §§80-21-1 to 80-21-8	§§80-3-1 to 80-3-5	§§80-18-1 to 80-18-2	none	§§80-11-16 to 80-11-17
Sex; Age Limits	Yes [except for unions and employment agencies; but see §80-4-1(5)]	Yes	No		18-60
Agency	Colo. Civ. Rts. Comm'n. 312 State Serv. Bldg. 1525 Sherman St. Denver 80203 (303)892-2621	Industrial Comm'n. of Colorado 200 E. 9th Ave. Denver	Industrial Comm'n. of Colorado		
Time Limit; Number of Employees	6 months; 6 employees	1 year			
Process	1	1	4		4

	FEP	Equal Pay	State Contracts	State Employees	Age Discrimination
6. Connecticut	Conn. Gen. Stat. Ann. §§31-122 to 31-128	§§31-75 to 31-76	§4-114a	§4-61c	included in FEP, State Contracts, and State Employees laws
Sex; Age Limits	Yes	Yes	No	Yes	40-65
Agency	Comm'n. on Human Rts. & Opportunities 90 Washington St. Hartford 06115 (203) 566-4895	Labor Comm'r. Labor Dept. 200 Folly Brook Blvd. Hartford	Contracting Agency and Comm'n. on Human Rts. & Opportunities	Court of Common Pleas, State Agency	Gov. Code of Fair Prac., 2-28-67
Time Limit; Number of Employees	90 days; 3 employees	1 year			
Process	1	2 or 3, 4	5	2	5

	FEP	Equal Pay	State Contracts	State Employees	Age Discrimination
7. Delaware	Del. Code 10§§710 to 718	none	S.B.266, L.1972	E.O. 9, 7-15-69	included in FEP and State Employees laws
Sex; Age Limits	Yes		Yes	Yes	40-65
Agency	Div. of Industrial Affairs Dept. of Labor 618 North Union St. Wilmington 19805 (302)658-9251		Secretary Dept. of Labor	State Human Relations Comm'n. Old State House Annex Dover 19901 (302)658-5738	
Time Limit; Number of Employees	90 days; 4 employees				
Process	1, 3		5	5	

	FEP	Equal Pay	State Contracts	State Employees	Age Discrimination
8. District of Columbia	Bd. of Commissioners Order #65-768 (Police Regs., Art. 47)		Bd. of Commissioners Order #62-713 (D.C. Regs. §§21-701 to 21-839)	none	none
Sex; Age Limits	Yes		No		
Agency	D.C. Comm'n on Human Relations District Bldg., Rm. 22 14th & E St., NW Washington, D.C. 20004 (202) 629-4723		Contracting Agency		
Time Limit; Number of Employees			90 days		
Process	1, 4		1		

	FEP	Equal Pay	State Contracts	State Employees	Age Discrimination
9. Florida	none	Fla. Stat. Ann. §448.07	none	§§112.041, 112.042	§112.043
Sex; Age Limits		Yes		Yes	
Agency				State Agency	
Time Limit; Number of Employees		6 months after termination of employment			
Process		2		1, 2	5

	FEP	Equal Pay	State Contracts	State Employees	Age Discrimination
10. Georgia*	none	Ga. Code Ann. §§54-1001 to 54-1007	none	none	§54-1102
Sex; Age Limits		Yes			40-65
Agency		Comm'r. of Labor Dept. of Labor State Labor Bldg. 254 Wash. St, Atlanta 30334			
Time Limit; Number of Employees		1 year; 10 employees			
Process		2			4

*Act 581 §§1-9 (3-18-66) prohibits discrimination against the wives of servicemen.

	FEP	Equal Pay	State Contracts	State Employees	Age Discrimination
11. Hawaii	Hawaii Rev. Stat. §§378-1 to 378-10	§387-4	none	none	included in FEP law
Sex; Age Limits	Yes	Yes			
Agency	Dept. of Labor & Industrial Relations 825 Mililani St. Honolulu 96813 (808) 548-3150	Dept. of Labor & Industrial Relations			
Time Limit; Number of Employees	90 days (but 30 days for suspension or discharge); 1 employee				
Process	1, 4	2 or 3, 4			

	FEP	Equal Pay	State Contracts	State Employees	Age Discrimination
12. Idaho	Idaho Code §§67-5901 to 67-5912 / §§18-7301 to 18-7303	§§44-1701 to 44-1704	included in FEP law	none	§§44-1601 to 44-1606
Sex; Age Limits	Yes	Yes			under 60
Agency	*Comm'n. on Human Rts., Dept. of Social Services Statehouse Boise 83702 (208) 384-3550	Comm'r. of Labor Dept. of Labor Indust. Adm. Bldg. 317 Main St, Boise 83702			Comm'r. of Labor
Time Limit; Number of Employees	6 months; 4 employees				
Process	2, 3, 4	2 or 3			1, 2 or 3

*The person must first file a complaint with the Board of County Commissioners where either she or the employer resides; if it appears that an "injunction could be entered," she then goes to the Commission on Human Rights.

	FEP	Equal Pay	State Contracts	State Employees	Age Discrimination
13. Illinois	Ill. Stat. Ann. 48 §§851 to 860	48§§4a, 4b; 48§§1001 to 1015	29§§17 to 24; also included in FEP law; Code of Fair Prac. §4, 7-10-63	Code of Fair Prac. §2, 7-10-63	48§§881 to 887
Sex; Age Limits	Yes	Yes	No	No	over 45
Agency	FEP Comm'n. 160 N. LaSalle St. Chicago 60601 (312)793-2240	Director Dept. of Labor Springfield			
Time Limit; Number of Employees	120 days; 25 employees	6 mos.; 6 employees; 5 employees			1 employee
Process	1	2, 4; 2, 3, 4	5; 2, 4	5	4

	FEP	Equal Pay	State Contracts	State Employees	Age Discrimination
14. Indiana	Ind. Stat. Ann. §§40-2307 to 40-2317a	$40-135	§53-103; also included in FEP law	E.O. 5, 12-15-61	§§40-2318 to 40-2328
Sex; Age Limits	Yes	Yes	No (except for Equal Pay)	No	40-65
Agency	Ind. Civil Rts. Comm'n. 319 State Office Bldg. Indianapolis 46204 (317)663-4855	Wage Adjustment Bd. (317)633-4473	Contracting Agency or State	State Agency	Comm'r. Div. of Labor 1013 State Office Bldg. 101 N. Senate Ave. Indianapolis
Time Limit; Number of Employees	90 days; 6 employees	4 employees			4 months; 1 employee
Process	1	1, 2, 4	5	5	1

	FEP	Equal Pay	State Contracts	State Employees	Age Discrimination
15. Iowa	Iowa Code Ann. §§105A.1-105A.12	none	none	none	none
Sex; Age Limits	Yes				
Agency	Iowa Civil Rts. Comm'n. State Capitol Bldg. Des Moines 50319 (515)281-5129				
Time Limit; Number of Employees	90 days; 4 employees				
Process	1				

16. Kansas	FEP	Equal Pay	State Contracts	State Employees	Age Discrimination
	Kans. Stat. Ann. §§44-1001 to 44-1014	§§44-1101 to 44-1109	S.B. 573, L.1972	Kans. Code of Fair Prac., 11-9-67	none
Sex; Age Limits	Yes	Yes	Yes	No	
Agency	Kans. Comm'n. on Civil Rts. Room 1155 W State Office Bldg. Topeka 66612 (913) 296-3206	Comm'r. Dept. of Labor 41 Topeka Blvd. Topeka 66603	Contracting Agency	State Agency	
Time Limit; Number of Employees	6 months; 4 employees	2 years			
Process	1	2 or 3	5	5	

17. Kentucky	FEP	Equal Pay	State Contracts	State Employees	Age Discrimination
	Ky. Rev. Stat. §§344.010 et seq.	§§337.420 et seq.	none	none	included in FEP law
Sex; Age Limits	Yes	Yes			40-65
Agency	Ky. Comm'n. on Human Rts. 600 W. Walnut St. Louisville 40203 (502) 583-2775	Comm'r. Dept. of Labor State Office Bldg. Annex Frankfort			
Time Limit; Number of Employees	90 days; 8 employees	6 months			
Process	1	2 or 3, 4			

18. Louisiana	FEP	Equal Pay	State Contracts	State Employees	Age Discrimination
	none	none	none	none	La. Stat. Ann. §§23:892 to 23:893
Sex; Age Limits					under 50
Agency					
Time Limit; Number of Employees					25 employees
Process					4

	FEP	Equal Pay	State Contracts	State Employees	Age Discrimination
19. Maine	Maine Rev. Stat. Ann. 5§§4551 to 4631	26§628	none	5§533	included in FEP and State Employees laws
Sex; Age Limits	No	Yes		Yes	
Agency	Maine Human Rts. Comm'n. Statehouse, Rm. 120 Augusta 04330 (207)289-2326			State Personnel Board Statehouse Augusta	
Time Limit; Number of Employees	1 year				
Process	2 or 3	2, 4		4	

	FEP	Equal Pay	State Contracts	State Employees	Age Discrimination
20. Maryland	Md. Code Ann. 49B§§1-30	100§§55A to 55H	78A§7A	E.O., Art. I, 12-9-70	included in FEP law
Sex; Age Limits	Yes	Yes	No	Yes	
Agency	Comm'n. on Human Relations Mt. Vernon Bldg. 701 St. Paul St. Baltimore 21202 (301)383-3689	Comm'r. Div. of Labor & Industry State Office Bldg. 301 W. Preston St. Balt. 21201	Bd. of Public Works State Office Bldg. Room 101 Annapolis 21404	Comm'n. on Human Relations	
Time Limit; Number of Employees	25 employees	1 year			
Process	1	2 or 3, 4	5	5	

	FEP	Equal Pay	State Contracts	State Employees	Age Discrimination
21. Massachusetts	Mass. Gen. Laws Ann. 151B§§1-10	149§§1, 105A-105C	272§98B	E.O. 74, Art. II, 7-20-70	144§24A-24; also included in FEP, State Contracts (E.O.74), and State Employees laws
Sex; Age Limits	Yes	Yes	No	Yes	45-65 (but FEP limits are 40-65)
Agency	Mass. Comm'n. against Discrimination 120 Tremont Ave. Boston 02108 (617)727-3990	Comm'r. Dept. of Labor & Industries 100 Cambridge St. Boston 02202	Mass. Comm'n. against Discrimination	Mass. Comm'n. against Discrimination	Comm'r. Dept. of Labor & Industries
Time Limit; Number of Employees	6 months; 6 employees	1 year			
Process	1, 4	2 or 3, 4	4	1, 4	4

	FEP	Equal Pay		State Contracts	State Employees	Age Discrimination
22. Michigan	Mich. Code §§423.301-423.311	§750.556	§408.397	Mich. State Code of Fair Prac., Art. IX; also included in FEP law	Mich. State Code of Fair Prac., Art. II	included in FEP law
Sex; Age Limits	Yes	Yes	Yes	No	No	35-60 (but Equal Pay limits are 18-65)
Agency	Mich. Civil Rts. Comm'n. 1000 Cadillac Sq. Bldg. Detroit 48226 (313)222-1810	Mich. Dept. of Labor Dept. of Labor Bldg. 300 E. Mich. Ave. Lansing 48933		Contracting Agency	State Agency	
Time Limit; Number of Employees	90-180 days; 8 employees	3 years; 4 employees				
Process	1, 2	4	2 or 3	5	5	

	FEP	Equal Pay	State Contracts	State Employees	Age Discrimination
23. Minnesota	Minn. Stat. Ann. §§363.01 to 363.13	§181.66	§181.59	none	none
Sex; Age Limits	Yes	Yes	No		
Agency	Dept. of Human Rts. 60 State Office Bldg. St. Paul 55155 (612)296-2931		Contracting Agency		
Time Limit; Number of Employees	6 months; 1 employee	1 employee			
Process	1	2, 4	4, 5		

	FEP	Equal Pay	State Contracts	State Employees	Age Discrimination
24. Missouri	Mo. Rev. Stat. §§296.010 to 296.070	§§290.400 to 290. 450	none	none	none
Sex; Age Limits	Yes	Yes			
Agency	Comm'n. on Human Rts. 314 E. High St. Box 1129 Jefferson City 65101 (314)635-7961	Industrial Comm'n. 1904 Missouri Blvd. Jefferson City			
Time Limit; Number of Employees	90 days; 6 employees	6 months			
Process	1, 4	2			

	FEP	Equal Pay	State Contracts	State Employees	Age Discrimination
25. Montana	Mont. Rev. Codes Ann., §§64-301 to 64-303	§§41-1307 to 41-1308	none	none	none
Sex; Age Limits	Yes	Yes			
Agency	Dept. of Labor & Industry 1331 Helena Ave. Helena 59601 (406)449-3472				
Time Limit; Number of Employees					
Process	4	4			

	FEP	Equal Pay	State Contracts	State Employees	Age Discrimination
26. Nebraska	Neb. Rev. Stat. §§48-1101 to 48-1125	§§48-1219 to 48-1227	included in FEP law	none	§§48-1001 to 48-1006
Sex; Age Limits	Yes	Yes			
Agency	Equal Opportunity Comm'n. 233 S. 14th St. Lincoln 68509 (402)471-2024	Equal Oppor. Comm'n.			
Time Limit; Number of Employees	90 days; 25 employees	4 years; 25 employees			1 employee
Process	1, 4	4			4

	FEP	Equal Pay	State Contracts	State Employees	Age Discrimination
27. Nevada	Nev. Rev. Stat. §§613.310 to 613.430	§609.280	§338.125	none	none
Sex; Age Limits	Yes (but a different agency enforces sex discrimination provisions)		Yes		
Agency	Race, Religion, & Natural Origin: Comm'n. on Equal Rts. of Citizens, Nevada State Bldg., 215 E. Bonanza Las Vegas 89101 (702) 385-0104 — Sex: Labor Comm'r.				
Time Limit; Number of Employees	60 days; 15 employees				
Process	2, 3	5	5		

	FEP	Equal Pay	State Contracts	State Employees	Age Discrimination
28. New Hampshire	N.H. Rev. Stat. Ann. §§354-A:1 to 354-A:14	§§275:36-275:41	none	none	included in FEP law
Sex; Age Limits	Yes	Yes			
Agency	Comm'n. for Human Rts. 66 South St. Concord 03301 (603)271-2767	Labor Dept. 1 Pillsbury St. Concord 03301			
Time Limit; Number of Employees	90 days; 6 employees	12 months			
Process	1	4			

	FEP	Equal Pay	State Contracts	State Employees	Age Discrimination
29. New Jersey	N.J. Stat. Ann. §§10:5-1 to 10:5-28	§§34:11-56.1 to 34:11-56.11	§§10:2-1 to 10:2-4, 10:1-10 to 10:1-12 — E.O. 21, Art. II, 6-24-65	§§10:1-10 to 10:1-12 — E.O. 21, Art. I, 6-24-65	included in FEP law
Sex; Age Limits	Yes	Yes	Yes	Yes Yes	
Agency	Div. of Civil Rts. Dept. of Law & Public Safety 1100 Raymond Blvd. Newark 07102 (201)648-2700	Div. of Civil Rts. Dept. of Law & Public Safety	Contracting Agency and Attorney General / Contracting Agency		
Time Limit; Number of Employees	90 days		180 days		
Process	1, 4	2	4, 5 / 5	4, 5 / 5	

	FEP	Equal Pay	State Contracts	State Employees	Age Discrimination
30. New Mexico	N.M. Stat. Ann., §§4-33-1 to 4-33-13	none	included in FEP law	none	none
Sex; Age Limits	Yes				
Agency	Human Rts. Comm'n, Villagra Bldg., Room 120, Santa Fe 87501 (508) 827-2713				
Time Limit; Number of Employees	90 days; 4 employees				
Process	1, 4				

	FEP	Equal Pay	State Contracts	State Employees	Age Discrimination
31. New York	N.Y. Exec. Law §§290-301	N.Y. Labor Law §§199-a, 198	N.Y. Labor Law §220-e	none	included in FEP law
Sex; Age Limits	Yes	Yes	No		40-65
Agency	Div. of Human Rts. 270 Broadway New York City 10007 (212)488-5358	Industrial Comm'n. Dept. of Labor 12, State Office Bldg. Campus Albany 12226	Contracting Agency		
Time Limit; Number of Employees	1 year; 4 employees				
Process	1, 4	3	5		

	FEP	Equal Pay	State Contracts	State Employees	Age Discrimination
32. North Carolina	none	none	none	N. Car. Gen. Stat. §126-16	none
Sex; Age Limits				Yes	
Agency					
Time Limit; Number of Employees					
Process				5	

	FEP	Equal Pay	State Contracts	State Employees	Age Discrimination
33. North Dakota*	none	N.D. Century Code §34-06.1	none	none	§34-01.17
Sex; Age Limits		Yes (state employees only)			40-65
Agency		Comm'r. of Agriculture & Labor State Capitol Bismarck 58501			
Time Limit; Number of Employees		2 years; 1 employee			
Process		2, 3, 4			4

*N.D. Century Code §34-01-18 prohibits discrimination against women jockeys.

	FEP	Equal Pay	State Contracts	State Employees	Age Discrimination
34. Ohio	Ohio Rev. Code Ann. §§4112.01-4112.99	§§4111.17, 4111.19	§§153.581, 153.591, 153.59, 153.60	none	§4101.17
Sex; Age Limits	No	Yes	No		40-65
Agency	Civil Rts. Comm'n. 240 S. Parsons Ave. Room 234 Columbus 43215 (614)469-2785	Dept. of Industrial Relations 220 Parsons Ave. Columbus 43215			Dept. of Industrial Relations
Time Limit; Number of Employees	6 months; 4 employees	12 months; 10 employees			
Process	1	2, 4	5		5

	FEP	Equal Pay	State Contracts	State Employees	Age Discrimination
35. Oklahoma	Okla. Stat. Ann. 74§§951 to 954; 25§§1301 to 1311	40§§198.1-198.2	H.R. 1307; also included in FEP law	none	none
Sex; Age Limits	Yes	Yes	No		
Agency	Human Rts. Comm'n. P.O. 52945 Oklahoma City 73102 (405)521-2360	Labor Dept. State Capitol Oklahoma City			
Time Limit; Number of Employees	90 days; 25 employees				
Process	1	3, 4	5		

	FEP	Equal Pay	State Contracts	State Employees	Age Discrimination
36. Oregon	Ore. Rev. Stat. §§659.010 to 659.115	§§652.220, 652.230	none	none	included in FEP law
Sex; Age Limits	Yes				25-65
Agency	Civil Rts. Div. Bur. of Labor Room 466 State Office Bldg. Portland 97201 (503)229-5741				
Time Limit; Number of Employees	1 employee	1 employee			
Process	1, 2, 4	2			

	FEP	Equal Pay	State Contracts	State Employees	Age Discrimination
37. Pennsylvania	Penn. Stat. Ann. 43§§951 to 963	43§§336.1-336.10	43§153	none	included in FEP law
Sex; Age Limits	Yes	Yes	No		
Agency	Human Relations Comm'n. P.O. Box 3145 Harrisburg 17120 (717)234-8777	Dept. of Labor & Industry 1700 Labor & Industrial Bldg, Harrisburg 17120			
Time Limit; Number of Employees	90 days; 4 employees	2 years			
Process	1, 4	4	5		

	FEP	Equal Pay	State Contracts	State Employees	Age Discrimination
38. Rhode Island	R.I. Gen. Laws §§28-5-1 to 28-5-39	§§28-6-17 to 28-6-21	none	E.O. 8, 6-9-69	§§28-6-1 to 28-6-16
Sex; Age Limits	Yes	Yes		No	45-65
Agency	Comm'n for Human Rts. 244 Broad St. Providence 02903 (401)277-2661	Dept. of Labor 225 Promenade St. Providence		Comm'n for Human Rts.	Dept. of Labor
Time Limit; Number of Employees	4 employees				4 months; 1 employee
Process	1	2, 3, 4		5	1

	FEP	Equal Pay	State Contracts	State Employees	Age Discrimination
39. South Carolina	none	none	none	H.B. 3370, L.1970 (6-23-72)	included in State Employees law
Sex; Age Limits				Yes	
Agency				Comm'n on Human Affairs P.O. Box 11528 Columbia 29211	
Time Limit; Number of Employees				1	
Process					

	FEP	Equal Pay		State Contracts	State Employees	Age Discrimination
40. South Dakota*	S.D. Compiled Laws §§20-13-1 to 20-13-56	$3-6-2	§§60-12-15 to 60-12-21	none	none	none
Sex; Age Limits	Yes	Yes (state employees only)	Yes			
Agency	Comm'n. on Human Relations 5th & Highland Sioux Falls 57103 (605)338-4562	Dir. of Employ., Indust. Comm'n. Pierre 57501	Comm'r. of Labor			
Time Limit; Number of Employees	6 months; 1 employee	2 years				
Process	1	5	2			

*S.D. Compiled Laws §42-7-18.1 prohibits discrimination against women jockeys, and §16-16-4 reaches discrimination against women attorneys.

	FEP	Equal Pay	State Contracts	State Employees	Age Discrimination
41. Tennessee					
Sex; Age Limits			E.O. 17, 1-14-72 Yes	E.O. 17, 1-14-72 Yes	
Agency			Comm'r. of Standards & Purchases, as monitored by: Comm'n. for Human Development* C3 305 Cordell Hull Bldg. Nashville 37219 (615)741-2424	Comm'r. of Personnel, as monitored by: Comm'n. for Human Development*	
Time Limit; Number of Employees			5	5	
Process					

*Agency itself has no power.

42. Texas	FEP	Equal Pay	State Contracts	State Employees	Age Discrimination
	none	Tex. Rev. Civ. Stat., art. 6825	none	art. 6252-16	art. 6252-14
Sex; Age Limits		Yes (state employees only)		Yes	21-65 (state employees only)
Agency				District Attorney and/or County Attorney	
Time Limit; Number of Employees					
Process		5		2, 4	5

	FEP	Equal Pay	State Contracts	State Employees	Age Discrimination
43. Utah	Utah Code Ann. §§34-35-1 to 34-35-8	none	Gov. Code of Fair Prac., E.O., Art. VII, 10-1-65; also included in FEP regulations	Gov. Code of Fair Prac., E.O., Art. I, 10-1-65	none
Sex; Age Limits	Yes		Yes	Yes	
Agency	Anti-Discrimination Div. Industrial Comm'n. State Capitol Bldg. Salt Lake 84114 (801)328-5552				
Time Limit; Number of Employees	1 month; 25 employees				
Process	1		5	5	

44. Vermont	FEP	Equal Pay	State Contracts	State Employees	Age Discrimination
	Vt. Stat. Ann. 21§§495 to 495c	none	included in FEP law	none	none
Sex; Age Limits	Yes				
Agency					
Time Limit; Number of Employees					
Process	4				

45. Washington	FEP	Equal Pay	State Contracts	State Employees	Age Discrimination
	Wash. Rev. Code Ann. §§49.60.010 to 49.60.320	§49.12.175	E.O. 70-01, 1-30-70; E.O., Art. III, 8-2-66	E.O., Art. I, 8-2-66	§49.44.090; also included in FEP law
Sex; Age Limits	Yes	Yes	Yes	Yes	40-65
Agency	Human Rts. Comm'n. 1411 4th Ave. Bldg. Seattle 98101 (206)464-6500		Human Rts. Comm'n.		
Time Limit; Number of Employees	6 months; 8 employees				
Process	1	2, 4	5	5	5

	FEP	Equal Pay	State Contracts		State Employees	Age Discrimination
46. West Virginia	W. Va. Code Ann. §§5-11-1 to 5-11-19	§21-5-6	E.O., 10-16-63	E.O., 12-15-65	E.O., 12-15-65	included in FEP law
Sex; Age Limits	Yes	Yes	No	Yes	Yes	
Agency	Human Rts. Comm'n, P & G Bldg. 2019 E. Wash. St. Charleston 25305 (304)348-2616	Labor Comm'n, Dept. of Labor B-451 Capitol Complex Charleston 25305 (304)348-2195			Human Rts. Comm'n,	
Time Limit; Number of Employees	90 days; 12 employees	1 employee				
Process	1, 4	2, 4	5	5	5	

	FEP	Equal Pay	State Contracts	State Employees	Age Discrimination
47. Wisconsin*	Wisc. Stat. Ann. §§111.31 to 111.37	none	$16.765	none	included in FEP law
Sex; Age Limits	Yes		No		40-65
Agency	Equal Rts. Div. Dept. of Industry, Labor & Human Relations P.O. 2209 201 E. Washington Madison 53701 (608)226-7552		Contracting Agency		
Time Limit; Number of Employees	as soon as possible				
Process	1		5		

*Wisc. Stat. Ann. §256.28 forbids discrimination against women attorneys.

	FEP	Equal Pay	State Contracts	State Employees	Age Discrimination
48. Wyoming	Wyo. Stat. Ann. §§27-257 to 27-264	§§27-210.1 to 27-210.4	included in FEP law	none	none
Sex; Age Limits	Yes	Yes			
Agency	Fair Employment Comm'n. 304 Capitol Bldg. Cheyenne 82001 (307)777-7262	Labor Comm'n. Dept. of Labor & Statistics 304 Capitol Bldg. Cheyenne 82001			
Time Limit; Number of Employees	2 employees				
Process	1	2, 4			

Chart B:
State Laws Forbidding Discrimination in Public Accommodations, Housing, Financing for Housing, and Education

Explanation of chart. This chart gives the legal citation to the pertinent state law so that readers can look up the law themselves. The symbol Ⓢ appearing below the citation means that the statute outlaws sex discrimination as well as discrimination based on race, religion, and national origin. If there is no Ⓢ below the citation, the statute covers only the last three categories. Where two sections are given, one with an Ⓢ and one without it, the latter does not include a prohibition against sex discrimination.

The statutes vary widely in scope and comprehensiveness, and readers will have to do more work to determine how valuable they are. The research for the chart was done in the spring of 1972. Since this is a rapidly changing field, women should double-check to see whether new laws have been passed in their state.

342

In most instances, the citation given is either only to the particular section defining the discriminatory practice or to the first section of a chapter. Readers should therefore look at preceding and following sections to find out about the entire enforcement scheme. They should also check the latest supplement to the cited volume since many of the citations are found in the inserts in the back of the book rather than in the bound volume itself.

To find the agency that enforces the law, try contacting the state employment-discrimination agency (Chart A lists these agencies). In addition, cities often have agencies that enforce laws forbidding discrimination in public accommodations, housing, financing for housing, and education. There has been no attempt to list them here. To locate city or local agencies, try contacting the state employment discrimination agency or write for the *Directory of State and Local Anti-discrimination Agencies,* published by EEOC, which deals primarily with state and local employment-discrimination agencies, many of them enforcing laws covering several kinds of discrimination. To obtain the Directory, write to: Office of State and Community Affairs, EEOC, 1800 G Street, N.W., Washington, D.C. 20506.

CHART B

State	Public Accommodations	Housing	Financing	Education
Alabama				
Alaska	Alas. Stat. §18.80.230	§18.80.240	§18.80.250	§§14.40.050, 14.40.769, 14.40.880 (U. of Alaska only) Ⓢ
Arizona	Ariz. Rev. Stat. Ann. §41-1442			
Arkansas				
California	Cal. Civil Code §51	Cal. Health & Safety Code §35720(1-5); Cal. Civil Code §53	Cal. Health & Safety Code §35720(7)	Cal. Educ. Code §§9001, 9002
Colorado	Colo. Rev. Stat. §25-1-1	§69-7-5(b) Ⓢ	§69-7-5(c) Ⓢ	
Connecticut	Conn. Gen. Stat. Ann. §53-35	§53-35		
Delaware	Dela. Code Ann. 6§4504	6§4603(1-6)	6§4603(7)	
Florida				
Georgia				
Hawaii				
Idaho*	Idaho Code §67-5909(5) Ⓢ	§67-5909(7) Ⓢ	§67-5909(8) Ⓢ	§67-5909(6) Ⓢ
Illinois	Ill. Stat. Ann. 38§13-2			122§10-22.5 Ⓢ ; 122§34-18(7) Ⓢ
Indiana	Indiana Stat. Ann. §40-2309(1) Ⓢ	§40-2309(1) Ⓢ		§40-2309(1) Ⓢ

*The preamble to this law shows that the legislature clearly did not intend to include sex-discrimination coverage; however, the relevant sections of the prohibition itself do cover sex discrimination. Women should attempt to use these provisions.

State	Public Accommodations	Housing	Financing	Education
Iowa	Iowa Code Ann. §105A.6 ⓢ	§105A.13		
Kansas	Kansas Stat. Ann. §44-1009(c)	§44-1016	§44-1017	
Kentucky	Kentucky Rev. Stat. Ann §344.120	§344.360	§344.370	
Louisiana				
Maine	Maine Rev. Stat. Ann. 17§1301	17§1301		
Maryland	Md. Ann. Code 49B§11C (in businesses licensed or regulated by Dept. of Licensing and Regulation) ⓢ ; 49B§11	49B§22	49B§23	
Massachusetts	Mass. Ann. Laws 272§§92A, 98 ⓢ	151B§§4.6, 4.7, 4.9 ⓢ ; (See also 151B§4.11: discrimination because of children)	151B§4.3B ⓢ	76§5 ⓢ ; 151C§2
Michigan	Mich. Stat. Ann. §28.343 ⓢ	§26.1300 (201); §16.114(46)	26.1300(202)	§15.2097 (133)
Minnesota	Minn. Stat.Ann. §363.03, subd. 3; §327.09	§§363.03, subd. 2 (1), (2)	§363.03, subd. 2(3)	§363.03, subd. 5; §§127.07, 127.08
Mississippi				
Missouri	Missouri Rev. Stat. §314.030			
Montana	Mont. Rev. Codes Ann. §64-301			
Nebraska	Neb. Rev. Stat. §18-1724 ⓢ ; §20-122	§20-107	§20-108	

State	Public Accommodations	Housing	Financing	Education
Nevada				
New Hampshire	N. H. Rev. Stat. Ann. §354-A:8 (IV) Ⓢ	§354-A:8 (V) Ⓢ		
New Jersey	N. J. Stat. Ann. §10:5-12(f) Ⓢ ; §10:1-3 Ⓢ	§§10:5-12 (g), (h) Ⓢ	§10:5-12(i) Ⓢ	§§10:5-5(1), 10:5-12(f) Ⓢ
New Mexico	N. M. Stat. Ann. §4-33-7(F)	§4-33-7(G)	§4-33-7(H)	
New York	N. Y. Exec. Law §296.2 Ⓢ ; N. Y. Civ. Rts. Law §40	N. Y. Exec. Law §296.5 Ⓢ ; N. Y. Exec. Law §296.3	N. Y. Exec. Law §296.5(e) Ⓢ	N. Y. Educ. Law §3201-a Ⓢ ; N. Y. Educ. Law §§313, 3201; N. Y. Exec. Law §296.4; N. Y. Civ. Rts. Law §40
North Carolina				
North Dakota	N. D. Century Code §§12-22-30			
Ohio	Ohio Rev. Code Ann. §§2901.35, 4112.02(G)	§4112.02(H)	§4112.02(H)	
Oklahoma	Okla. Stat. Ann. 25§1402			
Oregon	Oregon Rev. Stat. §§30.670, 659.037, 659.045	§§659.033, 659.045		§§345.240, 659.045
Pennsylvania	Penn. Stat. Ann. 43§952 Ⓢ	43§953 Ⓢ	43§955(h)	24§5004
Rhode Island	R. I. Gen. Laws Ann. §11-24-2	§34-37-4(A)	§34-37-4(B)	
South Carolina				
South Dakota	S. D. Compiled Laws §20-13-23 Ⓢ ; §20-12-1	§20-13-20 Ⓢ	§20-13-21 Ⓢ	§20-13-22
Tennessee				
Texas				

State	Public Accommodations	Housing	Financing	Education
Utah	Utah Code Ann. §13-7-3			
Vermont	Vt. Stat. Ann. 13§1451	13§1452(a)		
Virginia				
Washington	Wash. Rev. Code Ann. §§9.91.010, 49.60.215	§§49.60.222, 49.60.224	§49.60.175	§§49.60.040, 49.60.215, 9.91.010
West Virginia	W. Va. Code Ann. §5-11-9(f) ⑤	§5-11-9(g)	§5-11-9(h)	
Wisconsin	Wisc. Stat. Ann. §942.04	§101.60(2)	§101.60(2)	
Wyoming	Wyo. Stat. Ann. §6-83.1			

Chart C:

Name Change

Explanation of Chart. The first column, headed "Name Change Court and Statute," gives the legal citation to the state law setting forth the court procedures for changing one's name. It also lists the name of the court that handles the procedure in each state. States where married women may not use the procedure are noted (see code below). States where the statutory procedure is exclusive or where criminal penalties may be imposed for changing one's name unlawfully are also marked; in these states, women should not change their name by mere usage but should use the statutory procedure, unless they have competent legal advice that the latter is not necessary.

The second column, "Reregistration and Notification Laws and Penalties," lists those states requiring reregistration or notification of state authorities when a person's name changes. The laws generally require reregistration for voting and notification of authorities as to one's driver's license, motor-vehicle registration, certificate of title for a motor vehicle, and being a notary public (see code below). In a few states, a penalty for failing to comply with these requirements is set forth. In addition, the voting reregistration statutes sometimes specifically require reregistration of a person whose name changes, although this is not noted on the chart. Most state laws do not formally set forth any penalty for failure to comply with the law. (See generally the discussion at pages 242–247.)

The third column, "Divorce Laws and Limits," shows states with laws affirmatively stating that women who have divorced may change their name back to their maiden name, a former husband's name, or another name. States that limit this right to women with no children, to women with no minor children in their custody, or to women who have not been declared the guilty party are also noted (see code below).

The last column is headed "Interpretation: Name Change by Law or Custom." It indicates states where judicial decisions, state statutes, or attorney-general opinions strongly suggest that the state will take one of two positions: (1) a woman's name automatically changes when she marries; (2) she has an option and can decide whether or not to change her name (see code below). If the former position is indicated, women should seriously consider using the statutory name-change procedure. (See discussion at pages 246–247.) An example of how to read the last column can be taken from Alabama, which has "J/L/DL (1972)." This means that a 1972 *judicial* decision, involving a person's *driver's license,* found that under Alabama law a woman's name changes automatically upon marriage as a matter of *law.* Thus, married women in Alabama will have to use the name-change procedure in order to retain their father's name or change to a third name other than their husband's if they want to avoid state penalties (here, loss of one's driver's license). This column does not indicate very old decisions (anything prior to 1930 is not listed), nor is it the final word;

skillful lawyers will often be able to argue successfully against the implications of these precedents. Finally, the research on attorney-generals' opinions is incomplete; and in any case, such opinions do not carry a great deal of legal weight.

Code

First Column

No-MW—married women may not use the statutory name-change procedure

(exclusive)—a person may not change his or her name by usage but must use the statutory name-change procedure

H—husband

W—wife

Second Column

R—a person whose name changes must *reregister*

N—a person whose name changes must *notify* the proper authorities

DL—required as to *driver's license*

V—required as to *vote*

MVR—required as to *motor vehicle registration*

CT—required as to *certificate of title* of motor vehicle

NP—required as to being a *notary public*

Third Column

X—the state has a law allowing a divorced woman to change her name

NC—a divorced woman must have *no children* in order to change her name

NG—a divorced woman must *not* be the *guilty* party in order to change her name

Fourth Column

    L—the woman's name changes automatically when she marries, as a matter of *law*

    C—a woman has an option of changing her name when she marries since a change is only a matter of *custom*

    J—a *judge's* decision indicates whether change is by law or custom

    S—a *statute* indicates whether change is by law or custom

    AG—an *attorney general's* opinion indicates whether change is by law or custom

    DL—relates to the *driver's license*

    MVR—relates to *motor vehicle registration*

    NP—relates to *notary public*

    V—relates to being able to *vote*

    NCS—relates to *name-change statute*

CHART C

State	Name Change Court and Statute	Reregistration and Notification Laws and Penalties	Divorce Laws and Limits	Interpretation: Name Change By Law or Custom
Alabama	Probate Court Ala. Code 13§278 (exclusive)	DL(N) (unwritten regulation)		J/L/DL (1972)
Alaska	Superior Court Alas. Stat. §9.55.010	MVR(N), DL(N), V(R)	X	
Arizona	Superior Court Ariz. Rev. Stat. Ann. §12-601	V(R) (optional)	X	
Arkansas	Chancery or Circuit Court Ark. Stat. §34-801	V(R) (constitution)	X-NC	
California	Superior Court Cal. Civ. Pro. Code §1275	V (woman must sign in both pre- and post-marriage or pre- and post-divorce names when she votes), DL(N)	X (annulments only)	
Colorado	District or County Court Colo. Rev. Stat. §20-1-1	V(R) (optional), DL(N)		
Connecticut	Superior Court Conn. Gen. Stat. Ann. §52-11	V (ambiguous)	X	AG/C (1941) AG/L/MVR (1934)
Delaware	Superior Court Dela. Code Ann. 10§5901	V(R)	X	
District of Columbia	Superior Court D.C. Code §16-2501		X	
Florida	Chancery or Circuit Court Fla. Stat. Ann. §§62.031, 69.02	DL(N), V(N), NP		S/C/NP

State	Name Change Court and Statute	Reregistration and Notification Laws and Penalties	Divorce Laws and Limits	Interpretation: Name Change By Law or Custom
Georgia	Superior Court Ga. Code Ann. §79-501		X	
Hawaii	Lieutenant Governor Hawaii Rev. Stat. §574-5 (exclusive)		X	S/L (law requires that wife use husband's surname)
Idaho	District Court Idaho Code Ann. §7-801	V(N&R)		
Illinois	Circuit Court Ill. Stat. Ann. 96§1	V(R), DL(N)	X	J/L/V (1945)
Indiana	Circuit Court Ind. Stat. Ann. §3-801	V(N) (woman may vote in professional name)	X	
Iowa	District Court Iowa Code Ann. §674.1 No-MW	MVR(N), V(R)		S/L/NCS
Kansas	District Court Kansas Stat. Ann. §60-1401	DL(N), V(R)	X	
Kentucky	County Court Kentucky Rev. Stat. Ann. §401.010 No-MW	V(R), DL(N)	X-NG	S/L/NCS
Louisiana	District Court La. Rev. Stat. Ann. § 13:4751 (exclusive)	V(N)		J/C/Marriage License (1931)
Maine	Probate Court Maine Rev. Stat. Ann. 19§781	V(N), DL(N)	X	AG/L/Marriage License (1951-1954)
Maryland	Court of Equity Md. Ann. Code 16§123; Md. Rules BH70-75	DL(N), MVR(N), CT(N), V(R)		J/C/V (1972)
Massachusetts	Probate Court Mass. Ann. Laws 210§12	MVR(N), DL(N), NP	X	

State	Name Change Court and Statute	Reregistration and Notification Laws and Penalties	Divorce Laws and Limits	Interpretation: Name Change By Law or Custom
Michigan	Probate Court Mich. Stat. Ann. §27.3178(561) (when H changes name, that of W changes automatically)	NP (must continue to use original name until commission expires)	X-NC	S/L/NCS
Minnesota	District Court Minn. Stat. Ann. §259.10	DL(N)	X	
Mississippi	Chancery Court or Chancellor In Vacation Miss. Code Ann. §1269-01			
Missouri	Circuit Court Mo. Rev. Stat. §527.270		X	
Montana	District Court Mont. Rev. Codes Ann. §93-100-1	DL(N)		
Nebraska	District Court Neb. Rev. Stat. §61-101	V(R)		
Nevada	District Court Nev. Rev. Stat. §41.270	DL(N)—$1 penalty; V(R)	X	AG/L (1944) AG/L/Candidacy (1966)
New Hampshire	Probate Court N. H. Rev. Stat. Ann. §547.7	MVR(N), DL(N)	X (only when woman initiates proceedings)	
New Jersey	County or Superior Court N. J. Stat. Ann. §2A:52-1	V(R), NP (must use both maiden and married name, hyphenated)	X	

State	Name Change Court and Statute	Reregistration and Notification Laws and Penalties	Divorce Laws and Limits	Interpretation: Name Change By Law or Custom
New Mexico	District Court N. M. Stat. Ann. §22-5-1	MVR(N), CT(N) (a crime to use a false name to obtain MVR or CT fraudulently), V(N) (optional)		
New York	County, Supreme or, in New York City, Civil Court N. Y. Civ. Rts. Law §60	V (married woman may vote in either maiden or married name)		S/C/V
North Carolina	Superior Court N. Car. Gen. Stat. §101-2	MVR(N), CT(N)	X	
North Dakota	District Court N. D. Century Code §32-28-01	DL(N)		
Ohio	Probate Court Ohio Rev. Code Ann. §2717.01	V(R)	X	J/C/Election Law (1961)
Oklahoma	District Court Okla. Stat. Ann. 12§1631 (exclusive)	DL(N)	X-NG	
Oregon	Probate Court Ore. Rev. Stat. §33.410	V(R)	X	AG/L (1950-1952)
Pennsylvania	Court of Common Pleas Penn. Stat. Ann. 54§1	MVR(N)	X	
Rhode Island	Probate Court R. I. Gen. Laws Ann. §8-9-9	V(N) (optional)	X	
South Dakota	Circuit Court S. D. Compiled Laws §21-37-1		X-NC (minor in mother's custody)	
Tennessee	Circuit, Probate, or County Court Tenn. Code Ann. §23-801	V(R)		

State	Name Change Court and Statute	Reregistration and Notification Laws and Penalties	Divorce Laws and Limits	Interpretation: Name Change By Law or Custom
Texas	District Court Tex. Rev. Civ. Stat., art. 5928	DL(N)	X	
Utah	District Court Utah Code Ann. §42-1-1	MVR(N), CT(N)		
Vermont	Probate Court Vt. Stat. Ann. 15§811 (married person needs spouse's consent, but when H changes name that of W changes automatically)	DL(N), MVR(N)— $10 penalty for both	X	S/L/NCS
Virginia	Circuit Court Va. Code. Ann. §8-577.1 (person who changes name "unlawfully" subject to fine of $10-$100 and up to 60 days in jail)	V(N) (optional)	X	
Washington	Superior Court Wash. Rev. Code Ann. §4.24.130	DL(N), V(R)	X	
West Virginia	Circuit Court W. Va. Code Ann. §48-5-1 (person who changes name "unlawfully" subject to fine of up to $100 and up to 60 days in jail)	MVR(N), CT(N), V(R)	X-NC	
Wisconsin	Circuit or County Court Wisc. Stat. Ann. §296.36	V(R), DL(N) —penalty of up to $100 fine and/or up to 6 months in jail for failure to comply	X-NC	
Wyoming	District Court Wyo. Stat. Ann. §1-739			AG/C/DL (1972)

Chart D:

Sources of Legal Help and Women's Organizations

Explanation of chart. The following chart is necessarily incomplete but includes all groups the author knows about. It should help the woman who needs to find a lawyer to take a case or a counseling group to give her advice, who wants to join a woman's organization to work on legal problems, or who wants to do legal research on women's problems. Readers should also check the chapters themselves for additional materials and organizations. Women looking for lawyers should be aware that some women have begun forming feminist or all-woman law firms; this is an additional source that should be checked out in any local community.

One caveat is in order. Lawyers active in the woman's movement report that many women who could afford to pay something often expect legal help for free. Even when women's organizations have lawyers willing to take cases on a volunteer basis, there are still office and court costs to be covered. Women in private practice must charge money to survive. Women with some income should be prepared to pay fees, if necessary, or make contributions to voluntary organizations in order to support the work of other women.

CHART D

A. FEMINIST LEGAL HELP

1. Baltimore Women's Law Center
   525 St. Paul Place
   Baltimore, Maryland 21202
       (301) 752-3656, ext. 20
       (Office hours: Mon.-Fri., 11-5)

(A volunteer group of women lawyers, law students, and other women interested in furthering women's rights through law, the center represents women in sex-discrimination cases, works on legislative reform, does educational work, maintains a referral system for non-sex-discrimination legal problems, and offers counseling on various legal problems.)

2. Bellamy, Blank, Goodman, Kelly, Ross and Stanley
   36 West 44th Street, Suite 1201
   New York, New York 10036
       (212) 869-0020

(A feminist law firm, which has received foundation funding to undertake major sex-discrimination test cases. It opened in March 1973 and also does general practice work.)

3. Boston Women's Legal Collective
   698 Massachusetts Avenue
   Cambridge, Massachusetts 02139
       (617) 492-5200
(A collective of seven women—both lawyers and nonlawyers—who do educational work on women's legal rights
and take some sex discrimination cases as well as divorce
cases.)
4. Center for Women Policy Studies
   2000 P Street, N.W., Suite 508
   Washington, D.C. 20036
       (202) 872-1770
(A nonprofit corporation of two women lawyers and a
woman economist interested in furthering women's rights
through law and in conducting studies in sex discrimination
in a few selected areas. In those areas, the lawyers will
occasionally file *amicus curiae* briefs or handle test litigation.)
5. Clinical Course on Women and the Law
   N.Y.U. Law School
   Washington Square South
   New York, New York
       (212) 598-1212
(A law-school clinical course, in which students supervised
by the professor handle sex-discrimination cases.)
6. Clinical Course on Women and the Law
   Rutgers Law School
   180 University Avenue
   Newark, New Jersey 07102
       (201) 648-5561
(A law-school clinical course, in which students supervised
by the professor handle sex-discrimination cases.)

7. Clinical Program in Employment Discrimination
   c/o Prof. Otto Hetzel
   Wayne State University School of Law
   Detroit, Michigan
       (313) 577-3930

(A law-school clinical course, in which students supervised by the professor handle employment-discrimination cases.)

8. Clinical Program on Sex Discrimination in Employment
   c/o Prof. Jane Picker
   Cleveland State Law School
   Cleveland, Ohio
       (216) 687-2528

(A law-school clinical course, in which students supervised by the professor handle sex-discrimination-in-employment cases.)

9. Employment Rights Project
   Columbia University Law School
   435 West 116th Street
   New York, New York 10027
       (212) 280-4291

(A law-school clinical course, in which students supervised by the directors handle employment-discrimination cases.)

10. Human Rights for Women
    1128 National Press Building
    Washington, D. C. 20004
       (202) 737-1059

(A small, nonprofit corporation of women lawyers and other women interested in furthering women's rights through law and in conducting studies in sex discrimination. The lawyers, who work on a volunteer basis, occasionally file *amicus curiae* briefs or handle test cases at the appellate level in selected sex-discrimination cases. HRW publishes a periodic newsletter, which is available free to contributors, and a series of articles on "Law and Women." Its "Job Discrimination Handbook" is available for $.50.)

11. Law School "Women and the Law" Courses
(Many law schools now offer courses on "Women and the Law." Teachers or students in these courses might be able to direct women to lawyers sympathetic to sex-discrimination issues. Call the law school for the name and phone number of the teacher. The following is a partial list of law schools offering such courses: American; Boalt Hall [Berkeley]; Boston; Case Western Reserve; Catholic; Cleveland State; Columbia; DePaul; Duke; Georgetown; George Washington; Golden Gate; Harvard; Hastings; Howard; Indiana; New York University; Northwestern; Ohio State; Rutgers—Newark; Stanford; State University of New York at Buffalo; Suffolk; Temple; University of Alabama; University of California at Davis; University of California at Los Angeles; University of Chicago; University of Colorado; University of Connecticut; University of Kansas; University of Maryland—Baltimore; University of Michigan; University of New Mexico; University of Pennsylvania; University of San Francisco; University of Santa Clara; University of Washington; University of Wisconsin; Vanderbilt; Villanova; Yale.)

12. Law School Women's Groups
(In many law schools, women law students have formed feminist groups, which would probably be willing to work with other women's organizations, and could show women how to do legal research and help develop paralegal projects. The students might also be able to direct women to sympathetic lawyers. Call local law schools for the name of the women's group and a contact person, or write to the National Law Women's newspaper, which maintains a list of law school contacts. Its name and

address are: *Pro Se*, National Law Women's Newsletter, 79 Dartmouth Street, No. 2, Boston, Massachusetts 02116; tel. [617] 262-6720.)

13. Los Angeles Women's Center Legal Program
    1027 Crenshaw Boulevard
    Los Angeles, California
        (213) 937-3964

(A group of volunteer women lawyers and law students who provide legal counseling on family-law problems, education, and training, and who do some test-case litigation and work for legislative reform. Law students in the program from the University of Southern California receive academic credit for work on women's legal problems.)

14. Michigan Feminist Lawyers
(The Women's Advocate Office has a list of such lawyers. Contact: The Women's Advocate Office, Ann Arbor, Michigan; tel. [313] 763-4186.)

15. New Women Lawyers
    New York, New York
        (212) 242-8455

(A volunteer group of women lawyers who file *amicus curiae* briefs in selected sex-discrimination cases and serve as a clearinghouse trying to get more women lawyers involved in women's rights suits. For information, contact Carol Libow at the telephone number listed.)

16. NOW Legal Defense and Education Fund, Inc.
    c/o Sylvia Roberts, President
    P.O. Box 3081
    Baton Rouge, Louisiana 70821
        (504) 342-4527

(The fund is the legal arm of the National Organization for Women, although it is a separate organization. It will represent women in a few, selected test cases and it occasionally files *amicus curiae* briefs in important cases.)

17. WEAL Educational and Legal Defense Fund, Inc.
    621 National Press Building
    Washington, D.C. 20004
        (202) 638-4560

(The fund is the legal arm of the Women's Equity Action League, although it is a separate organization. It will represent women in a few, selected test cases; it has been most active in the field of discrimination in education.)

18. Women's Law Fund
    17210 Parkland Drive
    Shaker Heights, Ohio 44120
        (216) 621-3443

(A foundation-funded group that does sex-discrimination litigation in all fields.)

19. Women's Law Project
    Washington, D.C. and Philadelphia, Pennsylvania

(A small group of women lawyers, which is seeking foundation funding in order to do sex-discrimination litigation. It hopes to begin operating in November 1973. Check the telephone directories for a listing or call the Philadelphia Women's Center, tel. [215] SA4-9511.)

20. Women's Legal Defense Fund
    Washington Area Women's Center
    1736 R Street, N.W.
    Washington, D.C. 20009
        (202) 232-5293

(A large volunteer group of women lawyers, law students, and other women interested in furthering women's rights through law. The fund represents women in sex-discrimination cases involving important discrimination issues or affecting a large number of women. It also gives general legal advice to various women's organizations, provides counseling in the fields of employment rights, domestic relations, and unfair credit practices, and does legislative reform and educational work.)

21. Women's Rights Project
    American Civil Liberties Union
    22 East 40th Street
    New York, New York 10016
        (212) 725-1222

(A national ACLU project devoted solely to sex-discrimination litigation and reform. The project also advises local ACLU chapters on sex-discrimination cases and issues.)

22. Berlin, Roisman and Kessler
    1712 N Street, N.W.
    Washington, D.C. 20036
        (202) 833-9070

(A public-interest law firm, some of whose members handle sex-discrimination cases as well.)

23. Equal Rights Advocates
    Davis, Dunlop and Williams
    433 Turk Street
    San Francisco, California 94102
        (415) 441-2618

(A feminist law firm which handles both sex-discrimination test cases and a general practice.)

B. OTHER SOURCES OF LEGAL HELP

1. American Civil Liberties Union
   22 East 40th Street
   New York, New York 10016
      (212) 725-1222
(Consult the local chapter in your state or city; it will be listed in the telephone directory under either ACLU or the state or city name, e.g., New York Civil Liberties Union. ACLU chapters often have staff lawyers, and they call on many volunteer lawyers to take civil-liberties cases.)
2. Center for Constitutional Rights
   853 Broadway
   New York, New York 10003
      (212) 674-3303
(A foundation-funded group with a staff of lawyers who provide legal help in a variety of civil liberties and civil-rights cases. The center has been very active in the sex-discrimination area.)
3. Center for Law and Social Policy
   1600 20th St., N.W.
   Washington, D.C.
      (202) 387-4222
(A foundation-funded public-interest law group with a staff of lawyers who provide legal help in a variety of cases. The center has two women lawyers who work exclusively on sex-discrimination studies and litigation.)

4. Equal Employment Opportunity Commission
   Title VII Lawyers Panels
(Local commission offices maintain lists of lawyers willing
to take Title VII employment-discrimination cases. Women
generally work out fee arrangements with the lawyer. For
the local EEOC office, consult the phone directory under
United States Government, or write the national office:
Office of Public Information, EEOC, 1800 G Street, N.W.,
Washington, D.C. 20506.)

5. International Union of Electrical, Radio and Machine
   Workers
   Ruth Weyand, Associate General Counsel
   1126 16th Street, N.W.
   Washington, D.C. 20036
        (202) 296-1200
(IUE has a staff of seven full-time lawyers, who provide
advice and free representation for all employees whom
the union represents. IUE lawyers have been very active
in fighting sex discrimination and have brought nationwide
lawsuits on important issues. They also hold women's conferences for rank-and-file employees and have established
Women's Representatives in many locals.)

6. Lawyers' Committee for Civil Rights Under Law
   733 15th Street, N.W.
   Washington, D.C. 20005
        (202) 628-6700
(This address is the national office. The Lawyers' Com-
mittee has offices in other cities: Atlanta, Boston, Chicago,
Jackson, Kansas City, New York, Philadelphia, San
Francisco, and Beverly Hills. In these cities, the telephone
number will be listed in the directory under Lawyers'
Committee For Civil Rights Under Law or under Lawyers'
Committee for Urban Affairs. In Beverly Hills, check the
Beverly Hills Bar Foundation. Volunteer lawyers and a

few paid staff lawyers handle a variety of civil-rights and civil-liberties cases for the Lawyers' Committee. A large percentage of their employment-discrimination cases are brought on behalf of women. In Washington, D.C., Philadelphia, and San Francisco, the Lawyers' Committee has special programs that help women and minorities find lawyers for employment-discrimination cases.)

7. Legal Aid Programs

(In many communities, there are Legal Aid Societies, whose staff and volunteer lawyers provide free legal help for the poor. The office number should be located in the phone book, or officials at a local law school might be able to direct women to the nearest Legal Aid office.)

8. Mexican-American Legal Defense and Educational Fund (MALDEF)
   145 Ninth Street
   San Francisco, California 94103
       (415) 626-6196

(The fund also has branch offices in Denver and San Antonio, which are listed in the phone directory. It has a paid staff of 20 lawyers, plus 250 volunteer lawyers, who handle a gamut of civil-rights cases. The fund is interested in sex-discrimination cases in which the issues affect minority women. It also has a special program to refer women and minorities to lawyers in employment-discrimination cases.)

9. NAACP Legal Defense and Educational Fund
   10 Columbus Circle
   New York, New York 10019
       (212) 586-8397

(This group specializes in racial discrimination and civil-rights cases but might do some sex-discrimination work for minority women.)

10. National Lawyers' Guild
    23 Cornelia Street
    New York, New York 10014
        (212) 255-8028
(The national office is located at the above address. The guild also has offices in Atlanta, Boston, Chicago, Cleveland, Denver, Detroit, Los Angeles, Milwaukee, Philadelphia, Pittsburgh, Portland [Oregon], San Francisco, San Jose, Seattle, and Washington, D.C., which can be located through the telephone directory. Most guild help comes from volunteer lawyers, although a few offices maintain a small paid staff. Current projects include the areas of prison law, military and the draft, police brutality, computer data-banks, and civilian surveillance; a few offices may do some work in sex discrimination. One guild office has prepared a list of women lawyers, although the list may be limited to California. To obtain it, write to: National Lawyers' Guild, P.O. Box 673, Berkeley, California 94701.)

11. National Education Association—DuShane Emergency
    Fund
    1201 16th Street, N.W.
    Washington, D.C. 20036
        (202) 833-4111
(The DuShane Fund funds litigation to protect teachers' constitutional rights in general. It has spearheaded the litigation against mandatory maternity leaves, commonly imposed on teachers in towns across the nation.)

12. Neighborhood Legal Services Programs
    Office of Legal Services
    Office of Economic Opportunity (OEO)
    1200 19th Street, N.W., L509
    Washington, D.C. 20506
        (202) 254-5218

(OEO funds neighborhood legal-services programs throughout the nation to provide free legal help for the poor. This is an option for any woman who does not have much money. Call the local office to find out what the eligibility levels are (the programs will not help people who make more than a specified amount of money). If you cannot locate a program in the telephone directory, OEO maintains a directory of all programs ("Legal Services Projects and Legal Services Project Directors," OEO Pamphlet 6140-2, May 1972), which can be obtained by writing to the national office.

OEO also funds special centers that do concentrated work in particular fields, such as housing, economic development, health, social welfare, youth, or family law. Women with problems in particular areas might find these centers willing to help them. Generally the names of such groups are descriptive, and a center can be located through the OEO pamphlet.)

13. Southern Legal Action Movement
   P.O. Box 54472
   Atlanta, Georgia 30308
       (404) 876-5257

(This group puts out a monthly paper, holds conferences, and has contacts with sympathetic attorney law students, and legal workers throughout the South. It might be a good source of information on how to find an attorney interested in sex-discrimination work in the South.)

C. WOMEN'S PARALEGAL COUNSELING GROUPS

(Note: Women should also check with the listed feminist groups—both legal and nonlegal—to see whether they offer or know of comparable services. The following list represents only those groups that the author knows offer counseling.)

Divorce.

1. Chicago Divorce Project
   Chicago Women's Liberation Union
   852 West Belmont Street, Room 2
   Chicago, Illinois 60657
       (312) 348-2011

(The group does counseling and lawyer referrals, and helps women negotiate their own divorces in certain situations.)

2. New Haven Women's Center
   3438 Yale Station
   New Haven, Connecticut 06520

3. Seattle Divorce Co-op
   For information, write to:
       Beth Becker
       Pandora
       4224 University Way, N.E.
       Seattle, Washington

(The co-op helps women handle their own uncontested divorces.)

4. Women In Transition
   Philadelphia Women's Center
   4634 Chester Avenue
   Philadelphia, Pennsylvania 19143
     (215) SA4-9511

(This project provides counseling, crisis housing, lawyer referrals, and helps women handle their own divorces in certain situations.)

5. Women's Legal Defense Fund Legal Project
   Domestic Relations Counseling
   1736 R Street, N.W.
   Washington, D.C. 20009
     (202) 232-5293

6. Los Angeles Women's Center Legal Program
   1027 Crenshaw Boulevard
   Los Angeles, California
     (213) 937-3964

(The center counsels women who wish to handle their own divorce, from filing the first forms to gaining the final judgment. Contact G. Franklin at the above address.)

7. The author understands that there are divorce groups in San Diego, and Rochester, New York, but has been unable to locate their addresses or phone numbers. Another source of information is "Do It Yourself Divorce," which explains procedures for handling your own divorce in California, thus reducing costs to the $40.50 court filing fee. It is available from *Goodbye To All That* (June 21, 1971 issue), Box 3092, San Diego, California 92103.

Employment Rights.

1. Insurance Employees for Equal Rights
   c/o Joan Peterson
   Box 26384
   San Francisco, California 94126
     (415) 347-5696 (after 6:00 P.M.)

(This organization will send material to other insurance employees filing sex-discrimination complaints against their employers.)

2. Michigan FOCUS on Equal Employment for Women
   Contact: Jean King
          (616) 761-2398
3. Women In City Government United (WICGU)
   225 Broadway, 22nd floor, Room 12B
   New York, New York 10007
          (212) 566-1422

(WICGU runs a "hot line" for information on sex discrimination in city-government employment. It will help women file EEOC charges, and attorneys will give legal advice where necessary.)

4. Women's Job Rights Project
   620 Sutter Street, No. 318
   San Francisco, California 94102
          (415) 771-1092 (office); (415) 771-8212 (messages)

(There are two clinics, one in Berkeley and one in San Francisco.)

5. Women's Legal Defense Fund Legal Project and
   National Capitol Area NOW—
   Employment Rights Counseling
   Washington Area Women's Center
   1736 R Street, N.W.
   Washington, D.C. 20009
          (202) 232-5293

Credit.

1. Baltimore Women's Law Center
   525 St. Paul Place
   Baltimore, Maryland 21202
          (301) 752-3656, ext. 20
                (office hours: Mon.-Fri., 11:00 A.M.-5:00 P.M.)
                             or

Zatella Giles
1303 North Kenwood Avenue
Baltimore, Maryland 21213
    (301) 327-4718

2. Center for Women Policy Studies
2000 P Street, N.W., Suite 508
Washington, D.C. 20036
    (202) 872-1770

(The center has a foundation grant to study credit discrimination and has published *Women and Credit*, listing all groups around the country that are working on credit problems and what they are doing. The report is available from the center.)

3. Women's Legal Defense Fund Legal Project
Credit Counseling
Washington Area Women's Center
1736 R Street, N.W.
Washington, D.C. 20009
    (202) 232-5293

4. Sharyn Campbell, National Coordinator
NOW Task Force on Credit and Finance
1518 Corcoran Street, N.W.
Washington, D.C. 20009
    (202) 667-9060

(The task force has produced a manual giving instructions and sample letters for self-help, individual action, and a group credit project. It is available for $3.00 from: NOW, 1957 East 73rd Street, Chicago, Illinois 60649.)

Rape.

1. Los Angeles Anti-Rape Squad
Los Angeles Women's Center
1027 Crenshaw Boulevard
Los Angeles, California 90019

(This group is starting a "hot line" to help women who have been raped.)

2. Rape Crisis Center
   Washington, D.C.
        (202) 333-RAPE
3. Rape Crisis Line
   Chicago, Illinois
        (312) 728-1920

(Hours: Wednesday through Saturday, 6:00 P.M. to midnight. Women will accompany rape victims to the police, hospitals and courts, and will refer people to counselors. They plan to start groups with rape victims and educate the public on rape.)

4. Seattle Anti-Rape Squad
   c/o University YWCA
   4224 University Way N.E.
   Seattle, Washington
5. Women's Crisis Center
   Ann Arbor, Michigan
        (616) 761-WISE
6. Groups in Boston and Philadelphia have also established hot lines. Women in other cities are attempting to start Rape Crisis Centers; among the cities are Baltimore, Cleveland, New York, San Francisco, and Tampa (Florida). If the group has been started, its phone number might be available from Directory Assistance under Rape Crisis Center.

For information on *How To Start A Rape Crisis Center,* write to:

Rape Crisis Center
P.O. Box 21005—Kalorama Street Station
Washington, D.C. 20009

The center asks for a donation (not a charge) of $1.25. It also publishes a bimonthly newsletter.

Another pamphlet, *Stop Rape,* by Women Against Rape, is available from:

Women's Liberation of Michigan
Room 516
2230 Witherell
Detroit, Michigan 48201

D. NATIONAL WOMEN'S ORGANIZATIONS

(Note: These groups are generally concerned with women's rights, with a wider focus than legal work, and are not composed primarily of lawyers or law students. There is no attempt to list every women's group. The list names only those groups that have many local chapters and are active on a national level. To contact the local branch, check the local phone directory or write the national office.)
Organizations.
1. Federally Employed Women (FEW)
   621 National Press Building
   Washington, D.C. 20004
   (202) 638-4404
2. National Committee on Household Employment
   (NCHE)
   1625 Eye Street, N.W., Suite 323
   Washington, D.C. 20006
   (202) 872-1056

(A private, nonprofit service that helps household workers to organize locally. It publishes a free newsletter.)
3. National Organization for Women (NOW)
   1957 East 73rd Street
   Chicago, Illinois 60649
   (312) 922-4536
4. National Welfare Rights Organization (NWRO)
   1424 16th Street, N.W. (3rd floor)

Washington, D.C. 20036
(202) 483-1531
5. National Women's Political Caucus
1302 18th Street, N.W., No. 603
Washington, D.C. 20036
(202) 785-2911
6. Women's Equity Action League (WEAL)
621 National Press Building
Washington, D.C. 20004
(202) 638-4560
7. Women's Action Alliance
370 Lexington Avenue, Room 601
New York, New York 10017
(212) 685-0800

Directories.

1. *Handbook on Women Workers* (1969)
Women's Bureau
U.S. Department of Labor
14th and Constitution Avenue, N.W.
Washington, D.C.

(An extremely valuable resource book, it provides detailed statistics and information on women workers. Pages 302-331 list a variety of organizations of interest to women: civil, religious, and social organizations; professional and business organizations; general service organizations of business and professional women; educational organizations; political and legislative organizations; patriotic organizations; farm and rural organizations; and labor organizations.)

2. *Mushroom Effect, A Directory of Women's Liberation*
P.O. Box 6024
Albany, California 94704

(This directory was published in 1970; it may or may not be updated or even still available. However, it is inexpensive and lists nationwide feminist contacts and groups. Cost: $.50 each; $.45 for 25 or more copies.)

3. *The Whole Woman Catalog*
   P.O. Box 1171
   Portsmouth, New Hampshire 03801

(This directory, published in the fall of 1971, again may or may not be updated and currently available. Like *Mushroom Effect,* it lists feminist groups and contacts in towns and states throughout the country. Cost: $1.00.)

4. *Women's Organizations and Leaders—1973 Directory*
   Today Publications
   621 National Press Building
   Washington, D.C. 20004
        (202) 628-6663

(The most current of the directories, but extremely expensive at $20 per copy.)

E. WOMEN'S LOBBY ORGANIZATIONS AND NEWSLETTERS

(Note: Many of the national women's organizations have actively lobbied at both the Federal and state level for important women's-rights legislation, including—most notably—the Equal Rights Amendment. Those interested in lobbying should contact those groups and, in addition, the following groups, most of which are devoted solely to lobbying on women's issues.)

1. National Federation of Business and Professional Women's Clubs, Inc.
   2012 Massachusetts Avenue, N.W.
   Washington, D.C. 20036
      (202) 293-1100

(The primary purpose of this group is not lobbying, but it is one of the leaders in the nationwide lobbying effort for the Equal Rights Amendment. In addition, it publishes a "Legislative Newsletter," which can be obtained from the above address.)

2. *WEAL Washington Report*
   WEAL
   621 National Press Building
   Washington, D.C. 20004
      (202) 638-4560

(An excellent newsletter giving concise reports on the status of legislation affecting women. Cost: $5 for a subscription.)

3. *The Woman Activist*
   2310 Barbour Road
   Falls Church, Virginia 22043

(Another excellent legislative and lobbying newsletter. Cost: $5 for individuals; $10 for institutions.)

4. Women United
   c/o Margaret Laurence
   Box 300
   Washington, D.C.

(This group's major activity has been lobbying for the Equal Rights Amendment.)

5. Women's Lobby, Inc.
   1345 G Street, S.E.
   Washington, D.C. 20003
        (202) 547-0082

(The group formed recently to lobby on behalf of women's rights. It has regional correspondents; names and phone numbers are available from Carol Burris, President, at the above address. The group also puts out a newsletter, *Women's Lobby Alerts*.)

F. PUBLICATIONS AND OTHER SOURCES OF INFORMATION ON LEGAL DEVELOPMENTS

1. *Employment Practices Guide*
   Commerce Clearing House, Publications Department
   4025 West Peterson Avenue
   Chicago, Illinois 60646
   (312) 267-9010

(This law reporter publishes in full new cases and laws in the field of employment discrimination. A must for any lawyer handling employment-discrimination cases, it is generally available in law libraries. Cost: $100 for a one-year subscription, which includes the bound volumes to date.)

2. *Fair Employment Practice Cases*
   Bureau of National Affairs
   1231 25th Street, N.W.
   Washington, D.C. 20037
   (202) 223-3500

(This reporter also publishes in full new cases and laws in the field of employment discrimination. Again, it is a must for any lawyer handling employment-discrimination cases and is generally available in law libraries. Cost: $110 for a one year subscription, plus $12 per volume for prior bound volumes.)

3. National Conference of Law Women

(A group of women law students, lawyers, and legal workers, which holds a national conference once a year and regional conferences more frequently. Its principal focus is on using members' legal talents to help women in general. The conference for 1973 was held in Columbia, South Carolina. For up-to-date information, contact *Pro Se* [see item 4]. The conference would be a good place to get information about nationwide legal efforts on behalf of women, as well as to make contact with various local groups.)

4. *Pro Se*
   National Law Women's Newsletter
   79 Dartmouth Street, No. 2
   Boston, Massachusetts 02116
       (617) 262-6720

(A newsletter on legal developments and women's legal groups. Cost: $5 for individuals, $2 for women law students, $15 for women's groups. The sponsor of *Pro Se* is compiling a list of feminist groups at law schools. Women's groups who need help in legal research and counseling might write for this list.)

5. Project on the Status and Education of Women
   Association of American Colleges
   1818 R Street, N.W.
   Washington, D.C. 20009
       (202) 265-3137

(The project educates administrators, teachers, and students on the status of women in education and on legal requirements for ending sex discrimination. Write for information on these subjects and on affirmative action to eradicate sex discrimination. The project will provide technical assistance to women who want to promote affirmative action on campus.)

6. *Sex Discrimination and the Law: Causes and Remedies,* Babcock, Freedman, Norton & Ross (Little, Brown & Co. 1974)

(A legal casebook on sex discrimination and the law, covering a variety of fields: constitutional law, family law, criminal law, employment discrimination, media, education, abortion, and public accommodations. It will be available in 1974.)

7. *Sex-Based Discrimination and the Law,*

Davidson, Ginsburg & Kay (West Publishing Co. 1974) (A legal casebook on sex discrimination and the law, covering a variety of fields: constitutional law, family law, criminal law, employment discrimination, education, abortion, and public accommodations. It will be available in 1974.)

8. Undergraduate "Women and the Law" courses

(College women interested in learning more about women's legal rights can now take a course on "Women and the Law" at many schools, or lobby to establish such a course. A partial list of colleges and free schools offering the course includes: Antioch College; Beaver College; Bethlehem, Pennsylvania, Adult Education; Brandeis University; Hampshire College; People's Law Institute, Washington, D.C.; People's Law School, Berkeley; People's Law School, Portland, Oregon; Prince George's County Community College; State University of New York at Buffalo; University of Alaska; University of California at Irvine; University of Pennsylvania; Wellesley College; Wells College; Yale College.)

9. *Spokeswoman*

5464 South Shore Drive

Chicago, Illinois 60615

(312) 667-3745

(An excellent monthly newsletter, which supplies current information on nationwide developments—both legal and nonlegal—by feminists and women's organizations. It also lists new publications and articles. Cost: $7 for individuals, $12 for institutions.)

10. Women's Bureau
     U.S. Department of Labor
     Washington, D.C. 20210
          (202) 961-2188

(The Women's Bureau is a branch of the Labor Department; it publishes a wide variety of very useful information about women and women's legal status. Write and ask for their materials, listed in the Bureau's leaflet, *Publications of the Women's Bureau,* and also for studies on women's legal status by the Citizens' Advisory Council on the Status of Women.)

11. *Women's Rights Law Reporter*
     Rutgers Law School
     180 University Avenue
     Newark, New Jersey 07102

(A law reporter that summarizes new cases and laws affecting women's rights. It is published biannually and costs $15 for individuals [6 issues], $28 for libraries, and $3 for any single issue. A must for anyone who wants to keep abreast of current developments in all legal areas affecting women's rights.)

Susan C. Ross is currently a partner in Bellamy, Blank, Goodman, Kelly, Ross & Stanley—a law firm specializing in feminist litigation. She has served on the General Counsel's staff of the Equal Employment Opportunity Commission and on the Board of Directors of the Women's Legal Defense Fund. In addition to *The Rights of Women*, Ms. Ross has co-authored a casebook entitled *Sex Discrimination and the Law*. She has also taught law school courses on women and the law.